D0505048

INTERMEDIATE
BUSINESS

HAVERING SIXTH FORM
COLLEGE LIBRARY

WITHDRAWN FROM HAVERING COLLEGES
SIXTH FORM LIBRARY

Michael Fardon

Glynis Frater

John Prokopiw

OSBORNE

© Michael Fardon, Glynis Frater, John Prokopiw, 2000

All rights reserved. No part of this publication may be reproduced, stored in a retrieval system, or transmitted in any form or by any means, electronic, mechanical, photo-copying, recording or otherwise, without the prior consent of the copyright owners, or in accordance with the provisions of the Copyright, Designs and Patents Act 1988, or under the terms of any licence permitting limited copying issued by the Copyright Licensing Agency, 90 Tottenham Court Road, London W1P 9HE.

Published by Osborne Books Limited
Unit 1B Everoak Estate
Bromyard Road
Worcester WR2 5HN
Tel 01905 748071
Email books@osbornebooks.co.uk
Website www.osbornebooks.co.uk

Cover design by Hedgehog
Page design by Richard Holt

Printed by the Bath Press, Bath

British Library Cataloguing in Publication Data
A catalogue record for this book is available from the British Library

ISBN 1 872962 09 2

contents

acknowledgements

The authors would like to thank the following people who have been instrumental in the preparation of this book: Frank Adcock, Mike Gilbert, Rosemarie Griffiths, Hedgehog Design, Richard Holt, Barbara Jones, Jon Moore, Roger Petheram and Jim Taylor.

Osborne Books is grateful to the following organisations for their assistance and for giving permission, where appropriate, to use original material: Abbey National, Barclays Bank Plc, Biz/ed, The Body Shop International Plc, British Broadcasting Corporation, British Franchise Association, Cadburys, Co-operative Bank Plc, Co-operative Retail Services Limited, Co-operative Wholesale Services, The Controller of Her Majesty's Stationery Office, Department of Trade and Industry, Harrison Clark Solicitors, Malvern Hills Science Park, Marks & Spencer Plc, McDonald's, Nissan Sunderland, Office for National Statistics, One-on-One Fitness Centre, The Post Office, Prontaprint Plc, Robert Hitchins Properties, Severn Trent Water, Start-rite Shoes Limited, Tesco Direct, Tesco Plc, The Mail on Sunday, Transport for London, Vauxhall Motors Limited, W H Smith, Worcestershire County Council.

Lastly Osborne Books would like to thank QCA and the Awarding Bodies for their invaluable help and advice during the preparation of this text.

authors

Michael Fardon has worked in international banking and lectured in banking and finance before becoming Managing Editor at Osborne Books. He has written and co-authored a number of financial, business education and Key Skills books and resource packs. He has also been involved in the drafting and editing of GNVQ qualifications for QCA and Edexcel.

Glynis Frater is a writer and consultant in vocational education. She has been involved in the development of resource material for use in the delivery of GNVQ programmes and has contributed to a number of publications, policy debates and journals. She has extensive experience of the management and delivery of GNVQ Business Studies courses.

John Prokopiw has had many years teaching experience in the areas of Business Studies and Personnel Management. He is co-author of texts written for Osborne Books and the Institute of Personnel Development. He is currently Course Director of ICS courses at Worcester College of Technology.

the text

Intermediate Business has been written to cover the three compulsory Units of the Intermediate Business Award:

Unit 1   Investigating how businesses work

Unit 2   How businesses develop

Unit 3   Business finance

The text follows closely the Curriculum 2000 specifications and so is suitable both for the revised vocational award and also the revised Part One.

Individual chapters follow in most cases the topic headings set out in the Unit specifications. These are clearly identified on the first page of each chapter in the box under the chapter title.

This book also includes support material for a Human Resources option unit which many centres will be adopting as a 'compulsory' externally assessed option.

tutor pack

A teacher's Tutor Pack has been compiled to accompany this book. It contains assessment guidance (including answers to a number of the Activities), sample external test papers and photocopiable material. If you would like to find out more about this Pack, please contact the Osborne Books Sales Office on 01905 748071.

running order

Intermediate Business starts with Unit 2 – business ownership, business activities and influences on business – for a number of reasons. First, the authors considered that this approach painted the business world with a 'broader brush' and would enable students to gain a sense of perspective before they concentrated on the internal workings of business required by Unit 1. Secondly, the assessment requirement for Unit 2 is for a comparison of two businesses; this again will enable the student to gain a 'macro' view before concentrating on the workings of a single business in Unit 1 which provides a 'micro' view.

There is no reason, of course, why the two Units should not be run in tandem, as suggested in the published specifications. This would help with the research the students have to carry out; it may well be that the large business chosen for Unit 1 could be the same as the larger business chosen for Unit 2. The text of this book recognises this possibility – there is no suggestion that one Unit has to follow the other.

The Business Finance unit is placed as the third section in the book because it is more of a discrete entity. Tutors should note, however, the links between the Finance function explained in Chapter 8 and the practicalities of business finance set out in Chapters 11 to 16. It is important that students can link the Finance function with the other business functions. It is all too easy to get lost under a pile of financial documents and forget that they relate to other functions such as sales, production, administration and customer care.

internal assessment and student activities

Intermediate Business recommends that students should compile a Portfolio for all Units, including those that are externally assessed.

The Activities in **Intermediate Business** (highlighted by the pencil icon) collectively cover all the assessment requirements of the compulsory units. The Activities are designed as learning activities to be used inside and outside the classroom. Some Activities are designated 'Portfolio Activities' – they have an 'open book' icon and are printed in a different colour. It is vital that students tackle these because they provide the essential evidence required for the Portfolio.

The planning of the chapters and Activities in this book has been based very much around the 'assessment grid' published by the Awarding Bodies. It is important that students understand the grading structure and what they have to do to achieve a Pass, a Merit and a Distinction. The Activities give them this flexibility.

Students should read the Assessment Guide set out at the beginning of each compulsory unit (pages 12, 76 and 228) and understand what they have to do for each unit.

external testing and revision

At the time of writing, external tests were the means of assessment for the Business Finance Unit and Human Resources Optional Units (main award) and for all three compulsory units (Part One).

In order to help students prepare for these external tests and to revise the subject matter, each chapter concludes with a summary, key terms and half-a-dozen multiple-choice questions.

Although at the time of writing there was no 'question bank' of past papers, the type of questions provisionally suggested by the Awarding Bodies have been reproduced in this text – and this should prove helpful to students.

The Tutor Pack which accompanies this book contains practice tests and gives further guidance on preparation for external testing.

Key Skills 2000

One of the changes in Curriculum 2000 has been to 'decouple' Key Skills from the mainstream vocational units which constitute the Business Awards. The Key Skills are no longer compulsory, but they do form the basis of the Key Skills Qualification which centres may be offering.

Osborne Books has responded to this by publishing a series of photocopiable packs at all three levels – **Business Key Skills**. These sets of assignments, presented in business scenarios, are ideal for the Key Skills qualification. For further details please access www.osbornebooks.co.uk or contact the Osborne Books Sales Office on 01905 748071.

resources for courses

The need for access to a wide range of resources is mentioned in the 'Student Notes' section on pages 9 and 10. As more and more information becomes available on-line, students should be encouraged to access real businesses and also to make use of the excellent facilities offered by educational websites such as www.bized.ac.uk

feedback

Osborne Books welcomes your feedback on this book. We appreciate both positive and negative comments which originate from teachers and from students. Please let us know by mail, e-mail (books@osbornebooks.co.uk) and telephone (01905 748071) and we will take note of everything you have to say, and will respond.

Michael Fardon, Glynis Frater, John Prokopiw

Spring 2000

what is a GNVQ?

GNVQ stands for **G**eneral **N**ational **V**ocational **Q**ualification. What is it? A GNVQ is a broadly-based ('General') qualification which is recognised throughout the country – it is 'National'. It can lead to further qualifications or a job. The word 'Vocational' means that it relates to an area of work – in your case the business world. With a Business GNVQ you will be given the knowledge and skills you will need in a business job. A GNVQ means being able to 'do' a job as well as 'knowing' about it. A GNVQ qualification provides skills that employers like; it also enables you to progress to a further qualification.

what is a Unit?

Units are areas of study which make up the course. For the Intermediate Award in Business you have to complete and pass six Units:

- **three Compulsory Units** – in which you learn about the different types of business, how they work and how they deal with Finance

- **three Optional Units** – which cover areas such as retailing, individuals and the organisation, consumer protection and personal finance

If you are doing the 'Part One' in Business you only have to do the three compulsory units. All the compulsory units are in this book.

Unit portfolios

Two of the Compulsory Units and two of the Optional Units are assessed through your coursework which is presented in a **Portfolio** – this is a word for the folder containing your work which is known as **Assessment Evidence**. Do not be put off by all the jargon – Assessment Evidence just means the work you have collected together so that you can be graded by your Assessor. The grades you can get are Pass, Merit and Distinction. The type of work you have to complete successfully for these grades is shown on pages 13, 77 and 229.

Unit external tests

Four of the six Units are assessed by Portfolio (unles you are doing the Part One) and the remaining two – one Compulsory Unit (Business Finance) and one Optional Unit – are assessed by an **External Test** set by your Awarding Body. These tests are likely to contain simple short answer questions. If you study the chapters in this book and get plenty of practice answering short questions, like the ones at the end of each chapter, you should have no problem passing!

how the chapters can help you

All the chapters in this book begin with an introduction which tells you what the chapter is about and what you will learn.

The chapters finish with a summary and key terms telling you what you should have learnt. Do not skip these sections – they are there to help you.

The chapters also contain Activities for classwork and for investigation. Some of the activities are shown as 'Portfolio Activities' with a symbol of an open book like this . . .

These are Activities whch will provide Assessment Evidence for your Portfolio.

Other Actvities are for classwork and fieldwork investigation . . .

The chapters also contain Case Studies; when you read these through, try to relate them to situations that you have encountered in businesses that you have investigated, visited on work experience or worked for.

unit assessment guides

At the beginning of each compulsory Unit in this book are Unit Assessment Guides (pages 12, 76, 228) These explain the Evidence you need to collect for your Portfolio. Read these through carefully. Notice that they explain exactly what is required for the Pass, Merit and Distinction grades.

the internet and other resources

In your Intermediate Business course you will do a lot of investigation. You will have to find out about a small business and a large business and see how they deal with other businesses and with the public. You will also investigate a larger business in more detail to see how all the different jobs are carried out and how the business manages its finances.

Sometimes it will not always be possible to investigate a business at first hand. You may need to read newspaper articles, magazine articles or textbooks. The best source of information is undoubtedly the internet. You can access business websites direct, you can also look at media sites or educational websites.

Try these sites for examples of companies and a charity:

www.virgin.com   www.cadburyschweppes.com

www.gner.co.uk   www.tesco.co.uk

www.manutd.com   www.halifaxplc.com

www.toysrus.co.uk   www.nspcc.org.uk

Try these sites for examples of Government bodies which affect businesses:

www.oft.gov.uk   www.dti.gov.uk

Try these sites for statistics and business news:

www.ons.gov.uk   www.bbc.co.uk/news

Lastly, for a useful and informative site which contains a wealth of information about a wide range of businesses, try Biz/ed, the educational website:

www.bized.ac.uk

The internet is constantly developing and changing so try browsing around sites, download and print off financial documents from our own website:

www.osbornebooks.co.uk

Surf creatively!

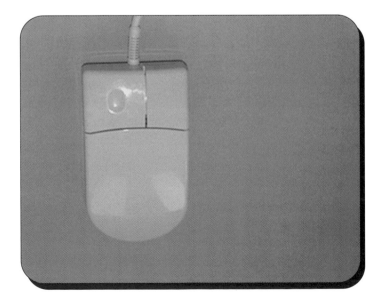

section one

HOW BUSINESSES DEVELOP

introduction

In this unit you will investigate and learn about:

*   the different types of business ownership

*   how businesses vary in size

*   what businesses do – what they produce

*   how businesses can be classified according to what they do

*   how businesses fit into the wider business world

*   how businesses are affected by external influences such as competing businesses and changes in customers' buying habits

*   how businesses respond to these influences

*   how businesses decide where to locate their operations

*   how businesses react to the demands of all the people who have an interest in the business – the owners, the customers, public opinion – people known as 'stakeholders'

chapters in this section

assessment guide

Unit 2: How businesses develop

what you will need for your Portfolio

For this Unit you will investigate two different businesses and compile Case Studies on both of them. The businesses will be:

• a small business such as a one person business or a partnership

• a larger business such as a limited company, a co-operative or a franchise

The Portfolio Activities in the chapters will enable you to compile these Case Studies as you go along.

The evidence you produce will show that you understand how different types of business operate and what the owner takes on when he or she starts the business. You will also see to what extent each business is affected by external influences and how the owners respond to those influences.

The tasks you undertake will include the following:

1   a description of the different types of business ownership and how this affects the position of the owner

2   a description of the different types of product, the ways they can be classified by 'industrial sector' and whether the sectors are growing or declining in the UK

3   a description of the activities of your chosen businesses and whether those activities are growing or declining in the UK

4   an explanation of why each business has located where it has

5   a description of the range of people and organisations which have an influence on the two businesses (the stakeholders)

Now study the next page and appreciate how you can achieve a Pass, a Merit or a Distinction in this Unit.

evidence you will need to produce . . .

to achieve a Pass in this Unit

1 a description of the type of ownership of the two businesses and what that ownership involves for the owners of the businesses in terms of legal status and liability for what the business does and owes; you should also explain how the type of business ownership suits the business activity

2 a brief description of the industrial sector to which the businesses belong and evidence of the trends (growth or decline) in that sector over the last ten years – tables and graphs would be useful evidence

3 a full description of the main activities of each business and evidence of the trends (growth or decline) in those activities over the last ten years – again, tables and graphs would be useful evidence

4 an explanation of why each business is located where it is and the influences on location which are most significant for the businesses – particularly the influence of their competitors and local employment trends – a map of the area with suitable notes would be useful evidence

5 a description of the internal and external stakeholders of the two businesses, what their interests are, how they are changing, the ways in which they influence the activities of the businesses, and how the businesses are responding to those influences; you should be able to show that smaller businesses tend to have fewer stakeholders

to achieve a Merit in this Unit you must also provide . . .

6 an explanation of how the trends in the growth or decline of a UK business sector are affecting one of the businesses you are investigating – is the business in line with current trends? if not, why not?

7 an explanation of why the influence of stakeholders on one business is different from their influence on the other business – here you should look at the difference in size, ownership and range of activities of the two businesses

8 a well researched and logically organised couple of Case Studies – the emphasis should be on quality rather than quantity, on independent work, effective collection and use of statistical data for analysing trends, correct use of business terminology

to achieve a Distinction in this Unit you must also provide . . .

9 a sound understanding of how external influences are affecting the businesses and the decisions they make – these should include UK trends, location factors and stakeholder influences

10 an effective comparison of the two businesses – this should cover the significant differences and could take the form of a table or an appropriate section in the conclusion of the Case Studies

11 an explanation of how there might be conflicts of interest between different stakeholders in any one business – for example between shareholders and employees when a business reduces staffing or between customers and the local community when a big new development is planned

1 Ownership of business

Unit 2: How businesses develop
Ownership

what this chapter is about

This chapter looks at the different types of business ownership and what that ownership involves for the people who run businesses. For your portfolio work you will have to investigate *two* types of business ownership:

• a small business
• a larger business

This chapter will give you the background knowledge for you to make your choice. It will describe and contrast the different responsibilities and benefits involved in business ownership.

what you will learn from this chapter

● Small businesses include:

• the sole trader – the 'one-person' business
• the partnership – two or more people in business together

The owners of these two types of business stand the greatest risk when putting their money into the business, but they often get greater job satisfaction and reward.

● Larger businesses include:

• private and public limited companies – owned by shareholders
• publicly owned businesses – owned by Central Government (eg the Post Office, the BBC) and Local Authorities (eg Fire Service)
• co-operatives – owned by members who 'club' together to run a business
• franchises – buying the right to trade under a well-known trading name such as Prontaprint or Burger King

People who have an ownership share in larger businesses may have limited risk and involvement in those businesses.

sole traders

definition

A sole trader is a person trading in his or her name, or under a trading name.

If you set up in business, you may do so for a number of reasons: you may be fed up with your present job, you might develop a hobby or interest into a business, you may have been made redundant. Most people setting up in this way do so on their own. They become *sole traders.* Over 2 million of of the 3.6 million businesses in the UK are formed as sole traders.

By definition these businesses will be *small* businesses. Sometimes a sole trader might employ people, but more frequently a sole trader is one person working on their own.

a trading name?

If you are a sole trader you can use your own name, or make up a trading name. You do not have to register a trading name, but you may find yourself in court if you use someone else's name. You cannot, for instance, get away with opening a shop and calling it 'Marks & Spencer' or 'Next'! If you look through the adverts in Yellow Pages you will get a good idea of the names used in different trades. Take mobile disco operation or plumbing, for example. The following names are all in current use:

phase 2	**REACT FAST**
Party Time	**Pronto!**
Total Entertainment	*City Plumbing Services*

A catchy business name is important because that is what the business will be remembered by.

what is the risk?

In law a sole trader is liable for all the debts of the business. He or she has what is known as *unlimited liability.* This means that if the business fails the sole trader will have to repay personally *all* the business debts, and may have to sell his or her personal belongings to pay off those debts. The debts might include borrowing from the bank, money owed to suppliers, the wages of employees. The sole trader may be taken to Court and be made bankrupt if these debts are not repaid.

If someone is setting up in business as a sole trader this unlimited liability is a responsibility which has to be thought about very carefully, particularly if that person is married and has children.

the documentation

Starting as a sole trader is very simple as there is little paperwork to be done. You do not have to draw up any rulebooks or business agreements as you are the only person involved. Once you have decided on a name you will need to get business cards and stationery such as letterheads and invoices printed. The only registration that may be required is if the business is likely to receive a large sales income, in which case registration for VAT will be necessary. For more explanation of VAT see page 302.

what are the advantages?

There are a number of advantages of becoming a sole trader:

control   you are your own boss and control the business yourself

it is simple   there is little 'red tape' (form filling) for starting to trade

reward   you are entitled to all the profit

and the disadvantages?

risk   it is risky– you are on your own, with no-one to share the responsibilities of running the business – as we have seen, you have unlimited liability – if the business 'goes bust' (bankrupt) then you 'go bust' too

time pressure   you will need to work long hours to meet tight deadlines

inexperience   you may only have skills in certain areas: you may be a good salesperson but not know so much about finance or marketing

illness   if you are ill, you may have no cover to enable the business to carry on

financing   it is more difficult as a sole trader to raise money to expand the business

It is clear that setting up in business as a sole trader involves total commitment in terms of money invested, time, and the risk involved.

Activity 1.1

Sole traders

Look at the adverts below and answer the questions at the bottom of the page.

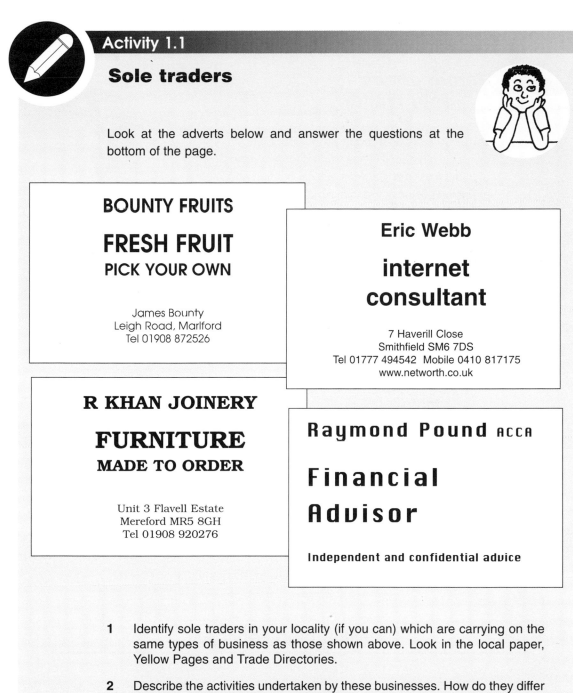

BOUNTY FRUITS

FRESH FRUIT
PICK YOUR OWN

James Bounty
Leigh Road, Marlford
Tel 01908 872526

Eric Webb

internet
consultant

7 Haverill Close
Smithfield SM6 7DS
Tel 01777 494542 Mobile 0410 817175
www.networth.co.uk

R KHAN JOINERY

FURNITURE
MADE TO ORDER

Unit 3 Flavell Estate
Mereford MR5 8GH
Tel 01908 920276

Raymond Pound ACCA

Financial
Advisor

Independent and confidential advice

1   Identify sole traders in your locality (if you can) which are carrying on the same types of business as those shown above. Look in the local paper, Yellow Pages and Trade Directories.

2   Describe the activities undertaken by these businesses. How do they differ in what they produce for the customer?

3   Do you think these types of businesses are increasing or decreasing in number in your area, or staying about the same? Ask your tutor, your family and people you know who work in business.

Case Study

Jamie Jones
sole trader

Jamie Jones wants to set up business on his own as a plumber. He has worked for a number of years for Pipex Services, a local heating and plumbing business. He thinks that he can make more money working on his own and he wants the freedom of being his own boss. He also has a number of customers whom he knows will give him business.

He has saved £5,000 and has recently won £10,000 on a lottery. He plans to invest this money in a second-hand van costing £7,000 and on tools and equipment costing £1,500. The remaining money he will use to finance his advertising and other running expenses and to keep him going until the business starts bringing the money in and starts to make a profit.

Jamie is married, with two children, and lives in a house worth £85,000. He has a mortgage of £25,000.

He has been advised to get a business card printed and a letterhead designed:

J J Plumbing Services

J Jones
15 Hawksworth Villas
Mereford MR3 9H
Tel 01908 653194 Mobile 07710 718617

business card

J J Plumbing Services

J Jones
15 Hawksworth Villas
Mereford MR3 9H
Tel 01908 653194 Mobile 07710 718617

letterhead

Activity 1.2

Jamie Jones
sole trader

Jamie Jones   realises that you know a thing or two about business. He asks you a number of questions. Write down your answers.

1   "I am calling myself J J Plumbing Services. Is this OK, or do I have to register the name anywhere?"

2   "I have had my business card and business stationery printed. Is there any other paperwork I have to do? It doesn't seem very much to me."

3   "What financial risks do I run in setting up as a sole trader? I wouldn't want to put my family at risk."

4   "Is there any limit on the hours I can work? My previous employer didn't like me working overtime."

5   "What happens if I am ill? I used to get sick pay from my previous employer?"

6   "I have always enjoyed my work. Do you think that there are any big benefits of working as a sole trader?."

Portfolio Activity

Part of your portfolio assessment is based on the choice of a small business – either a sole trader or a partnership (see the next page).

As preparation for this assessment you should be identifying sole trader and partnership businesses which you could use for gathering evidence. The businesses could be:

• a business for which you have done work experience at some time

• a business which you are visiting as part of your course

• a business for which you have done a part-time job

• a business run by someone you or your family knows

• a business which is in the form of a published Case Study

It is important that you talk to your tutor before approaching the businesses.

Keep the answer to the Jamie Jones and King & Maisie activities (on this page and page 22). They will be useful when you come to compile your Portfolio evidence.

partnership

definition

A partnership is a group of people working together in business in order to make a profit.

A partnership is straightforward to set up – it involves two or more people running a business together. They share control of the business, and own it between them. Examples of partnerships include groups of builders, doctors, dentists, accountants, and solicitors.

A partnership is the next step up from a sole trader business: it is no more than a group of sole traders working together in a more organised framework.

A partnership is also a suitable structure for a small business. At the time of writing there were approximately 700,000 partnership businesses in the UK (compared with over 2 million sole traders).

a trading name

A partnership – often known as a 'firm' – can either trade in the name of the partners, or under a suitable trading name. For example if M Smith & T Ahmed set up a glazing business, they could call themselves 'Smith and Ahmed & Co.' or adopt a more catchy name such as 'Classy Glass Merchants'. You should note that the '& Co.' does not mean that the partnership is a company. The photograph below shows a sign displayed outside the premises of a firm of solicitors.

the risk element – partners and unlimited liability

In law each partner is liable for *all* the debts of the partnership. Like the sole trader a partner has *unlimited liability*. This means that if one partner runs up a big debt, each or all of the other partners could be asked to pay all of it off. You clearly have to be careful when you take on a partner.

documentation – Partnership Agreements

Most partnerships have a Partnership Agreement, a document normally drawn up by a solicitor. This sets out matters such as the amount of capital (money investment) contributed by each partner, the sharing out of profit (and losses) by the partners, and what to do if there is a dispute. It is a good idea to have a Partnership Agreement because if something does go wrong – if there is a dispute – it will set out how the matter can be settled.

A Partnership Agreement is not essential, but it does contribute towards the smooth running of a business. Extracts from a typical Partnership Agreement are shown in the Case Study which starts on the next page. As far as stationery is concerned, partnerships need all documents – such as letters and invoices – to show the names of all the partners.

the advantages of being a partner

There are a number of advantages in forming a partnership business:

finance	you can raise more capital (money) – there are more people to contribute
expertise	there are likely to be more skills available – one partner may be a technical expert, another a good salesperson, another a financial expert, and so on
free time	there is cover for holidays and sickness
documentation	there is less 'red tape' than in the formation and running of a limited company (see page 26)

disadvantages of being a partner

There are also drawbacks:

debt	you may be asked to pay off all the debts of the partnership if the business fails
partners	you are liable for the business deals of the other partners (this could be a problem if a deal went badly wrong); also, partners may fall out with each other

Case Study

King & Maisey & Co
partners in law

Solomon King and John Maisey are both solicitors working in commercial law firms in Liverpool city centre.

They both earn over £40,000 a year but are tired of the pressures of working in large organisations. They wish to leave their salaried positions and join forces to create a new legal partnership which they will call King & Maisey & Co. This will be set up in Ormskirk, outside Liverpool.

They have some savings to provide start-up costs. They also arrange a bank loan to provide the extra finance that they will need.

As lawyers they know the need for a Partnership Agreement and correctly presented stationery.

They have agreed the following:

*   they will contribute £50,000 capital each
*   they will share profits equally
*   if there is any dispute, an official Arbitrator can be appointed to sort things out

Set out below are extracts from the letterhead and Partnership Agreement. Note that the Partnership Agreement will be a great deal longer than the extracts shown here; it will deal with issues such as the bank they use and what happens when they want to stop working as partners.

King & Maisey & Co, Solicitors

Equity House
191, High Street
Ormskirk
L39 4OA
Tel 01703 129845 Fax 01703 129444
email KM@goblin.com

Partners:
Solomon King, LLB
John Maisey, LLB

letterhead

PARTNERSHIP AGREEMENT

MADE on 30 June 2000

BETWEEN Solomon King of 45 Park Gardens, Ormskirk

AND John Maisey of Flat 7, Parkway Mansions, Maghull

IT IS HEREBY AGREED AS FOLLOWS

extracts now follow . . .

1. Solomon King and John Maisey will become and remain partners for a period of five years from the date of this Agreement.

2. The Partners shall practise in partnership in the firm name of King & Maisey & Co at the address Equity House, 191, High Street, Ormskirk.

3. The initial capital of the partnership shall be in the sum of £100,000, to be contributed by the partners equally.

4. The partners shall be entitled to the net profits arising from the business in equal shares, or such other shares as may from time to time be agreed by the partners.

5. Each partner shall be entitled to five weeks holiday in each year.

6. Should any dispute arise at any time between the partners with regard to this agreement or in respect of the rights, duties and liabilities of the partners in the conduct of partnership business, then an independent Arbitrator shall be appointed. The ruling of the independent Arbitrator shall be accepted by both Partners.

Signed by
Solomon King of 45 Park Gardens, Ormskirk

Solomon King

in the presence of Henry Purcell, 45 Melody Gardens, Birkenhead

Henry Purcell

Signed by
John Maisey of Flat 7, Parkway Mansions, Maghull

John Maisey

in the presence of Henry Purcell, 45 Melody Gardens, Birkenhead

Henry Purcell

Activity 1.3

King & Maisey & Co
partners in law

Answer the questions below. The answers can be found in the Case Study and in the text before the Case Study.

1   What is the investment made by each partner in the new business?

2   How will the partners share the profits?

3   What is the liability of Solomon for partnership debts run up by John?

4   What is the liability of John for partnership deals – for example an agreement to rent some computer equipment – set up by Solomon?

5   What could happen if there was a dispute between the two which they could not sort out?

6   Do the partners' names have to appear on any partnership stationery?

7   What advantages does a partnership have over a sole trader business when it comes to taking time off?

Portfolio Activity

Your portfolio assessment is based on the choice of a small business – either or a sole trader or a partnership – and also a larger business such as a limited company, a franchise, co-operative or a public sector business.

As preparation for this assessment you should also identify the larger business which you will use for evidence. Again you could draw on work experience, personal contact or a business for which you work part-time – a Saturday job, for example. It is important that you talk to your tutor before approaching the businesses.

You should set out in writing:

1   A definition of both types of business.

2   An explanation of the legal status of the owners (are they separate from the business? what is their liability for the business?).

3   A description of the ownership documents (if there are any) and their purpose.

4   Comments on how the type of business ownership (eg sole trader, partnership) relates to the size of each business.

limited company

limited company – reducing the risk to the owners

A limited company is a business
- *owned by shareholders*
- *run by directors*
- *set up as a body which is separate from its owners (the shareholders)*

A limited company is very different from a sole trader or partnership business. The sole trader or partner *is* the business; if the business goes 'bust' then so does the owner. The shareholder owner of a limited company *stands apart* from the business, which is a body in its own right. If the company goes 'bust' the shareholder is protected by *limited liability and* does not lose all his or her money – just the money invested in the shares of the company.

To remind you of the terminology:

sole trader or partner . . . *unlimited liability* . . . the owner goes bust (bankrupt) if the business goes 'bust'

limited company . . . *limited liability* . . . the shareholder does not go bust if the company goes 'bust'

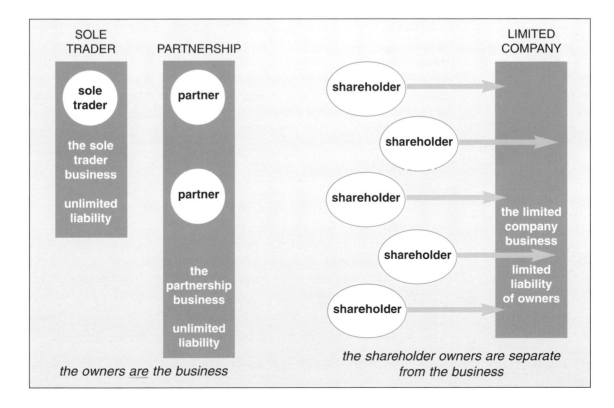

private and public limited companies

A limited company will either be:

- a *private limited company* (abbreviated to Ltd), or
- a *public limited company* (abbreviated to Plc)

Most small or medium-sized businesses which decide to incorporate (become a company) become private limited companies; they are often family businesses with the shares held by the members of the family. Private companies cannot offer their shares for sale to the public at large, and so they may find it difficult to raise money.

Public limited companies are larger than private companies, and a number of them are household names. They can offer their shares for sale on the Stock Market in order to raise money, but not all public limited companies do this.

To remind you of the difference between the two types:

- private limited company . . . with 'Limited' or 'Ltd' in the name . . . shares are not sold to the public . . . small in size . . . often local family businesses
- public limited company . . . with 'Plc' in the name . . . . . . shares are often sold to the public . . . large in size . . . nationally known names

who controls limited companies?

Shareholders own a limited company and appoint directors to control the management of the company and plan for its future. In the case of a private limited company, the shareholders often *are* the directors, and so the shareholders can be said to control the company.   The chief director is the *managing director.* In the case of a public limited company the shareholders can only speak and vote at company meetings (often only once a year) and it is the directors who control the company.

documentation

Small businesses such as sole traders and partnerships require relatively little in the way of paperwork. Setting up a limited company, on the other hand, requires a fair amount of 'red tape'. Companies are regulated by Companies House, a government-owned agency. All companies have to register with Companies House and are issued with the company equivalent of a birth certificate – the Certificate of Incorporation. In addition, a company will also need two further documents:

- the Memorandum of Association – which states what the company can do
- the Articles of Association – the internal 'rulebook' for the directors

All this paperwork is normally organised for the directors by a solicitor or accountant – and this can cost a lot in fees.

limited company documentation

advantages of limited companies

limited liability   if you are a shareholder you have limited liability for the company's debts; you are protected if the company goes 'bust'

financing   public limited companies can raise large amounts of capital (money) on the Stock Exchange in order to expand

disadvantages of limited companies

cost   a limited company is expensive to set up – you will need to pay solicitors' and accountants' fees for the necessary paperwork

paperwork   'red tape' – you need to send an annual return form and financial accounts to Companies House (the central register for companies) every year

Case Study

Progress Computing Limited
a new company

Seven people in the computing business are setting up a new manufacturing company to be called Progress Computing Limited. They will all become directors.

The company will be a private limited company to start with, but if it grows according to plan, the directors hope it will convert into a public limited company within five years so that it can raise further finance on the Stock Markets.

The directors will also be shareholders as they are each contributing £50,000 which will become the share capital of the new business. The directors have also negotiated a £30,000 business loan from the bank.

They have placed all the paperwork of starting the business in the hands of their Accountants.

Activity 1.4

Progress Computing Limited
a new company

Answer the questions below. The answers can be found in the Case Study and in the text before the Case Study.

1 What type of company will Progress Computing Limited be?

2 What type of company will Progress Computing Limited possibly convert to in five year's time? Why should it do this?

3 What is the share capital of the new company?

4 What type of liability will each shareholder director have, and what amount of money can each director stand to lose?

5 What are the documents that their Accountants will have to arrange, and what is the function of those documents?

6 Why do you think Progress Computing Limited is not being set up as a sole trader or partnership business?

co-operatives

The term 'co-operative' refers to two types of business:
- a retail Co-operative Society – which sell goods and services to the public
- co-operative – a group of people 'clubbing' together to produce goods or to provide a service

We will deal with each of these in turn.

retail Co-operative Societies – the background

Retail co-operative Societies date back to 1844 when a group of twenty eight Rochdale weavers, suffering from the effects of high food prices and low pay, set up a society to buy food wholesale, ie at the same price as it was sold to the shops. This food was then sold to the members at prices lower than the shop prices, and the profits distributed to the members in what was known as a dividend, the level of which depended on the amount of food they had bought. These self-help co-operatives grew in number during the nineteenth century, but declined in the later twentieth century, largely because of competition from the 'big name' retailers such as Tescos, Sainsbury and Asda.

the Co-op today

A well-known example of a retail co-operative is the Co-operative Wholesale Society (CWS), which took over the operations of Co-operative Retail Services in April 2000. This group of companies is generally known as 'the Co-op'. It operates a wide range of businesses, including 1100 food stores, the UK's largest funeral business, car dealerships, travel services and opticians. It also incorporates the insurance company CIS and the Co-operative Bank.

The Co-operative Wholesale Society operates a number of on-line services, including on-line banking.

Visit www.co-op.co.uk for full details of this group of companies.

who owns the Co-op?

A retail Co-operative Society is owned by its members. You can become a member by filling in a form obtainable from your local Co-op store and buying a share, normally for £1. As a member you have voting rights (one vote per member) and can often obtain discounts at the Society's retail shops and the use of other facilities such as funeral services.

other co-operative ventures

The term 'co-operative' also applies more loosely to co-operative ventures. At the time of writing there are around two thousand co-operatives which carry out a number of different functions:

trading co-operatives

Groups of individuals, such as farmers, who do not have the resources in terms of capital and time to carry out their own promotion, selling and distribution, may 'club' together to store and distribute their produce. They may also set up co-operative ventures to purchase machinery and equipment.

workers co-operatives

A workers co-operative may often be found where the management of a business is not succeeding and a shut-down is proposed. The 'workers' step in, with the consent of the management, and take over the ownership and running of the business with the aim of 'making a go of it' and at the same time safeguarding their jobs.

co-operatives on the internet

For an up-to-date view of co-operative ventures carry out a UK search on the internet through www.yahoo.co.uk using the word 'co-operative'.

franchises

what is a franchise?

The franchise system was first established in the USA and is now a rapidly growing business sector in the UK. A franchise is an established business name – eg Burger King or Prontaprint– which is 'sold' to someone setting up in business.

The two people involved in the deal are:

- the *franchisor*, the person who has developed a certain line of business, such as clothes retailing, hamburgers, drain clearing, and has made the trading name well-known
- the *franchisee*, the person who buys the right to trade under the well-known trading name

In return for a substantial initial fee the person setting up (the franchisee) receives full advice and in some cases the necessary equipment. As the business trades, a 'royalty' percentage of takings is paid to the franchisor.

The illustration below shows the way Prontaprint, a well-known name in the 'quick print' business, promotes its business idea to people interested in taking up a franchise – becoming a franchisee.

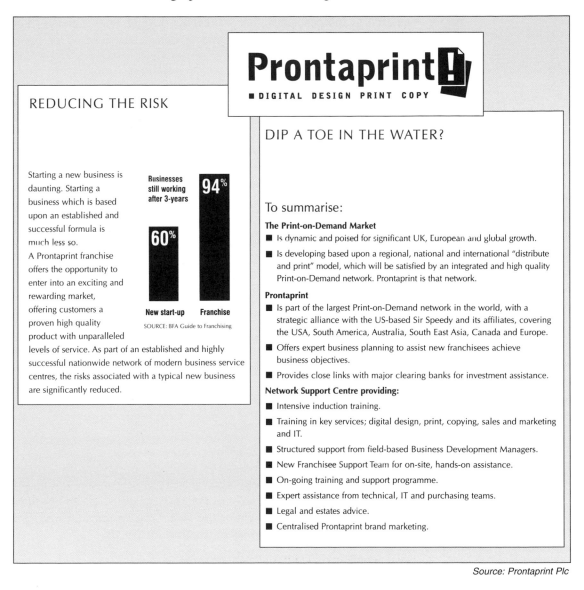

Prontaprint!

■ DIGITAL DESIGN PRINT COPY

REDUCING THE RISK

Starting a new business is daunting. Starting a business which is based upon an established and successful formula is much less so.

A Prontaprint franchise offers the opportunity to enter into an exciting and rewarding market, offering customers a proven high quality product with unparalleled levels of service. As part of an established and highly successful nationwide network of modern business service centres, the risks associated with a typical new business are significantly reduced.

Businesses still working after 3-years

94%

60%

New start-up   **Franchise**

SOURCE: BFA Guide to Franchising

DIP A TOE IN THE WATER?

To summarise:

The Print-on-Demand Market
■ Is dynamic and poised for significant UK, European and global growth.
■ Is developing based upon a regional, national and international "distribute and print" model, which will be satisfied by an integrated and high quality Print-on-Demand network. Prontaprint is that network.

Prontaprint
■ Is part of the largest Print-on-Demand network in the world, with a strategic alliance with the US-based Sir Speedy and its affiliates, covering the USA, South America, Australia, South East Asia, Canada and Europe.
■ Offers expert business planning to assist new franchisees achieve business objectives.
■ Provides close links with major clearing banks for investment assistance.

Network Support Centre providing:
■ Intensive induction training.
■ Training in key services; digital design, print, copying, sales and marketing and IT.
■ Structured support from field-based Business Development Managers.
■ New Franchisee Support Team for on-site, hands-on assistance.
■ On-going training and support programme.
■ Expert assistance from technical, IT and purchasing teams.
■ Legal and estates advice.
■ Centralised Prontaprint brand marketing.

Source: Prontaprint Plc

advantages of a franchise

- you are entering into a business which has been tried and tested in the market
- your business may well have a household name such as Burger King
- you are more likely to be able to raise finance from a bank for a franchise
- you should receive training, and in some cases, be provided with tried and tested equipment

disadvantages of a franchise

- the initial cost of going into the franchise – the payment to the franchisor
- a proportion of your takings also go to the franchisor
- you are less independent in that you cannot develop the business as you wish – you cannot change the name or change the method of doing business

Franchises – UK facts and figures

total franchisors	568
total franchisees	29,100
total annual sales from franchises	£7 billion

who does what? – some examples

business	franchisees
Building services	1080
Catering and hotels	3675
Cleaning services	1775
Direct selling	3995
Parcels and taxis	1520
Quick Printing	600
Retailing	4785
Vehicle services	2035

where are the franchises? – percentage distribution in the UK

London	15	South East	17
West Midlands	11	East Midlands	7
East Anglia	5	South West	9
North West	9	Yorkshire	7
North & North East	7	Wales	3
Scotland	7	N Ireland	2

Source: British Franchise Association

Activity 1.5

Franchising

1   A friend of yours is thinking of setting up in business when she leaves college. She says "I reckon a franchise is a good idea – it takes a lot of the hard work away from starting up in business."

   (a)   Write down the reasons why buying into a franchise takes away the hard work of starting up in business.

   (b)   Now write down some of the disadvantages of taking on a franchise.

   (c)   Find out some names of franchises in which you think your friend may be interested.

2   Look at the facts and figures table on the opposite page.

   (a)   What types of businesses are franchises, on the whole? Are they in manufacturing or services? Why do you think this is the case?

   (b)   In which three geographical areas are franchises most common? Why do you think this is?

publicly owned businesses

private and public sectors

Businesses are either:

• private sector businesses or

• public sector businesses

The *private sector* includes businesses which are directly or indirectly owned by private individuals. Most businesses in the UK are in the private sector. They include all the businesses covered so far in this chapter, from one person businesses to large companies.

Public sector organisations, on the other hand, are directly or indirectly controlled by the government. They include:

• Public Corporations

• Local Authority enterprises

public corporations

Public corporations are bodies established by Act of Parliament, and owned and financed by the State, for example the Post Office, the Bank of England and the BBC. Public corporations are run by a Board of Management headed by a chairperson appointed by the Government. There used to be more public corporations, but in the 1980s and 1990s a number of them were *privatised*. In other words they were sold off to the public by the government, which turned them into public limited companies, enabling the public to buy their shares. British Gas, BT and British Airways are examples of privatisations.

public corporations

local authority enterprise

'Local Authority' is a term applied to local governing councils which operate both in the county areas and also in city areas. Local Authorities have a wide range of services to administer. These include education, environmental health, planning, refuse collection, social services, transport, fire services, libraries and leisure facilities. They finance these from three main sources:

- Central Government Grants
- local taxation (currently the Council Tax)
- income from local authority enterprise

Local authority enterprises include a wide variety of commercial activities, including, for example:

- leisure – swimming pools, sports centres, golf courses
- transport – local bus services
- car parks
- local lotteries

a local authority sports centre

Activity 1.6

Publicly-owned businesses

One type of local authority enterprise is a facility (such as a leisure centre) owned by the local authority and run by outside contractors.

Identify one of your local authority facilities and find out:

(a) who the outside contractors are

(b) the range of services provided within the facilities

business size

When you investigate the range of businesses in your area you will see that they range from the small one-person business to the national and international names seen in the High Street. How do you classify businesses by size? The most common methods of classification are by the number of employees and by the money amount of annual sales – by 'turnover'.

classification of size by employee

The government divides businesses into three classifications:

small business	1 to 49 employees
medium-sized businesses	50 to 249 employees
large businesses	250 or more employees

classification of size by annual sales

Another way of looking at the size of a business is to compare it with other businesses in terms of its annual sales figure, often known as the sales turnover.

Activity 1.7

The size of the business

THE NUMBER OF UK BUSINESSES – BY EMPLOYEE

size (employees)	type	number of businesses
0-49	(small business)	3,626,620
50-249	(medium-sized business)	24,610
250 and over	(large business)	6,660
TOTAL		3,657,890

1   Which is the most common size of business? Why do you think this type is the most common? What percentage of the total is this type of business? What type of business ownership is represented here?

2   Which is the least common size of business? What percentage of the total is this type of business? What type of business ownership is represented here?

3   Write down two advantages of working in a small business and two advantages of working in a large business.

4   Draw up a pie chart showing the three categories in the table shown above. If you can, draw up the figures on a spreadsheet and use the computer to generate the pie chart. Make sure all your labelling is clear.

Activity 1.8

Comparing business size

Read through the two business profiles and answer the questions that follow.

business 1 – sole trader

TARIQ'S SPICYBURGERS

Tariq is a local businessman who has set up a fast food burger outlet in the town. He has called his business 'Tariq's SpicyBurgers'. After his first year of trading he is able to provide the following figures:

TARIQ'S SPICYBURGERS

Sales outlets	1
Total employees (including Tariq)	6
Male employees	4
Female employees	2
Employees working 35 or fewer hours per week	5
Employees aged under 20	2
Sales for the year	£156,500
Profit for the year	£23,500

business 2 – multinational company

McDONALD's

McDonald's also has a burger bar in the town. McDonald's is a 'multinational' business, operating over 23,000 restaurants (some as franchises) in over 100 countries worldwide.

McDonald's UK figures are as follows:

Sales outlets	836
Total employees	43,000
Male employees	54%
Female employees	46%
Employees working 35 or fewer hours per week	90%
Employees aged under 20	71%
Sales for the year	£1,088,448,000
Profit for the year	£100,154,000

Source: Biz/ed

1 Draw up a table comparing the two businesses. The table should show:
   • the number of outlets for each business
   • the number of employees per restaurant
   • the mix of male/female employees (make sure you use either percentages or numbers – you will have to do some converting here)
   • the sales figure for the year
   • the profit figure
   • the profit figure as a percentage of sales (ie profit x 100 ÷ sales)

2 Using the data in the table, write short notes on the differences (ie in sex, hours and age) between the people that Tariq employs and the staff at McDonald's. Comment on the profit percentage of the two businesses. Is this what you would expect?

CHAPTER SUMMARY

- A sole trader is an individual in business; a partnership is a group of individuals in business. Together they are the most common forms of small business.

- Sole traders and partnerships are owned wholly by the individuals who run them. The owners have unlimited liability.

- Larger businesses include limited companies, which can be:

  – private limited companies – often small family businesses, or

  – public limited companies – larger companies which include household names

- Limited companies are owned by shareholders and run by appointed directors (who can also be shareholders). Shareholders only have limited liability for their company's debts.

- A co-operative is a business which is developed by individual members 'clubbing' together to run an enterprise.

- Other larger businesses include publicly owned corporations (such as the BBC) and local authority enterprises; 'publicly owned' means that they are owned or controlled by the government

- A franchise is an arrangement where the person running the business buys the right to trade under a well-known name. Franchises can be small or large.

KEY TERMS

sole trader	an individual trading in business.
partnership	a group of individuals trading together in business
limited company	an organisation owned by shareholders who are separate from the business
unlimited liability	the liability for paying off all the debts of a business
limited liability	where the business owner (eg a company shareholder) can only lose the money he or she has invested
co-operative	a business set up and owned by its members and operating for their benefit
franchise	an arrangement where a franchisee sets up in business using the trading name of the franchisor
private sector business	businesses which are owned by individuals, and not the government
public sector business	a business which is owned or controlled by the government (or local authority)

MULTIPLE CHOICE QUESTIONS

1   A sole trader business has unlimited liability. This means that the owner
   A   is not limited to the type of business he/she can carry out
   B   does not have to register for Value Added Tax
   C   is liable for all the debts of the business
   D   is not liable for all the debts of the business

2   A firm of solicitors is most likely to be set up as a
   A   sole trader business
   B   partnership
   C   co-operative
   D   franchise

3   A well-known high street bank is most likely to be set up as a
   A   partnership
   B   private limited company
   C   public limited company
   D   franchise

4   A shareholder of a limited company has limited liability. This means that he/she:
   A   does not have to be a company director
   B   is fully liable for limited company debts
   C   is only liable for the amount of money invested
   D   does not have to attend company meetings

5   If a business is a public sector business, this means that the business
   A   provides a service to the general public
   B   is a public limited company
   C   is owned by individual members of the public
   D   is owned or controlled by the government

6   A business setting up as a partnership is likely to have a partnership agreement regulating the running of the business. This is likely to cover:
   A   shareholders' investment, profit share, disputes
   B   partners' investment, profit share, disputes
   C   certificate of incorporation, profit share, disputes
   D   memorandum of association, profit share, disputes

2 What businesses do

what this chapter is about

This chapter looks at the wide range of activities which businesses carry out and examines trends to see which types of business are growing in number and which are in decline.

what you will learn from this chapter

- different businesses carry out a wide range of activities including:

  - retailing – small shops, supermarkets, internet stores
  - service businesses – banks, health clubs, hairdressers
  - manufacturing of goods – cars, stereos, biscuits, drinks
  - transport – rail companies, airlines, car hire firms
  - communications – mobile phone companies
  - natural resources businesses – farming, fishing, mining

- you will understand how these types of business have traditionally been grouped in three separate classifications known as 'industrial sectors':

  - *primary sector* businesses which extract and make use of natural resources such as farms, fisheries and mines

  - *secondary sector* businesses which manufacture products

  - *tertiary sector* businesses which provide the services we use, eg banks, insurance companies, health clubs, holiday companies

- there are trends in the way these different types of business are developing in the UK; for example manufacturing is declining, service businesses are increasing in number

how businesses are different

a definition?

When studying businesses you need to have a clear idea in your mind of what a 'business' is. It could be defined as follows:

A business is an organisation which makes a product or provides a service.

If you think about businesses that you deal with on a daily basis, you will see that they vary a great deal.

Activity 2.1

The range of business activities

Look at the pictures below and on the next page and answer the questions at the bottom of the next page.

1   Identify the pictures shown here with the following areas of business activity:

   retailing   manufacturing   transport   financial services

   communications   leisure   using natural resources

Picture 1 is best described as   ....

Picture 2 is best described as   ....

Picture 3 is best described as   ....

Picture 4 is best described as   ....

Picture 5 is best described as   ....

Picture 6 is best described as   ....

Picture 7 is best described as   ....

2   Write a brief description of each of the business activities.

3   Write down ways in which you think the businesses shown rely on each other.

trends in types of business

If you look at the businesses that people deal with in the UK you will see that some types of business activity are in decline while other types are expanding rapidly in number. Examples of businesses that are in decline are those that deal with natural resources, such as mining. Examples of businesses that are growing in number are retailers and mobile phone and internet providers.

Read through the following press reports and carry out the activity which follows.

Coal Industry faces extinction

The coal industry continues to shrink as Ellington Colliery, the last deep mine in Northumberland is due to close. In 1947 there were 1,000 deep mines in operation, employing 1 million workers and producing 186 million tonnes of coal a year. In 1999 there were just 17 pits employing 12,000 miners and producing 36.7 million tonnes. Cheap imports of coal is put down as the main cause of the crisis in the coal industry

Amazon.co.uk breaks all records

Amazon.co.uk, the UK arm of the highly successful US internet bookshop Amazon.com has now become the third biggest book retailer in the UK, behind W H Smith and Waterstones, after a period of very rapid growth. Amazon.co.uk despatches its on-line orders from its 500,000 sq feet Milton Keynes distribution centre. Its customers normally receive delivery within 48 hours, sometimes with a substantial discount.

US boss Jeff Bezos says 'Our customers tell us what we want to do next'. This now involves sales of CDs and other merchandise.

Activity 2.2

Investigating businesses

1 What types of business activity are carried out by the businesses described in the press cuttings. What are the reasons for the growth of the one and the decline of the other?

2 Divide into groups within the class. Each group is to investigate one of the following eight types of business activity in your local area: retailing (shops), financial services, communications, manufacturing, leisure services, transport businesses, any business which uses natural resources, eg farms, fisheries.

Each group will make a list of as many examples of each type of business as it can find, eg 'Marks & Spencer' for retailing, the local bus company for transport.

Each group should also try and find out if the type of business is growing or becoming less common, and why this might be so.

The groups should then report back in a general discussion and decide:

• what types of business are growing in number, and why

• what types of business are declining in number, and why

industrial sectors

As we have just seen, businesses can be classified according to what they do. Another way of classifying businesses is into three 'industrial sectors' ...

primary sector - extracting raw materials

This involves the extracting of natural resources, ie raw materials for use in the manufacturing process. Examples of primary production are mining, farming, market gardening, fishing and forestry.

secondary sector – manufacturing products

This is the next stage of production; it involves the processing of raw materials into the manufactured product: fruit into pies or juice, wood into chipboard, metal into cars, and so on.

tertiary sector – providing services

This third classification involves a business providing a service rather than a manufactured item; examples include catering, shops, insurance, travel, and advertising.

Activity 2.3

industrial sectors

Into which industrial sector would you classify the following businesses? What links can you identify between any of them which make them depend on each other?

1 a salmon farm	2 a supermarket	3 a car manufacturer
4 a market garden	5 a tyre manufacturer	6 a travel agent
7 an airline	8 a restaurant	9 a catering firm

Portfolio activity

1   Describe the areas of activity carried out by the two businesses you have chosen for your investigation. State whether their products are manufactured items or services, or both.

2   Identify the likely customers and suppliers of the two businesses.

3   State the industrial sector to which the two businesses belong and list some other businesses which make up those sectors.

the chain of production

Businesses depend on each other. From the last Activity you will have seen that . . .

> providers of raw materials and natural resources (primary sector)
>
> supply manufacturers (secondary sector) who produce goods
>
> for service providers such as shops (tertiary sector)

This chain of production can be clearly illustrated in the car industry:

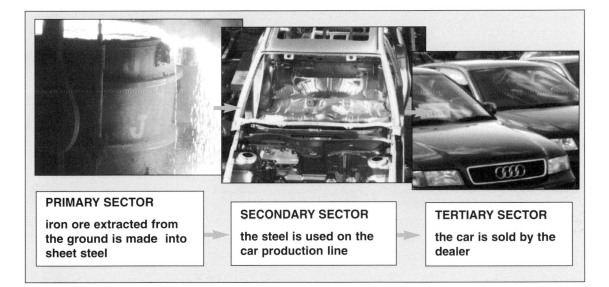

PRIMARY SECTOR

iron ore extracted from the ground is made into sheet steel

SECONDARY SECTOR

the steel is used on the car production line

TERTIARY SECTOR

the car is sold by the dealer

Activity 2.4

chains of production

Identify the two chains of production which are likely to be set up between the following businesses:

home furnishing store   **fishery**   **supermarket chain**

timber company   **food processing company**   **furniture manufacturer**

Draw two flow diagrams with boxes and arrows (like the one shown above) illustrating your answers. Include on your diagrams a description of the activity of each business and the industrial sector to which the business belongs. Use the wording on the diagram on this page as a guide.

from producer to consumer

You can see from the varied enterprises shown on the previous pages that businesses depend on each other for their survival. At the end of the line in each case is the consumer of the goods. If the customer does not buy the goods or services in question, the businesses cannot survive.

distribution of goods – wholesalers and retailers

It is important to realise how the consumer in each case obtains the goods or services. If we look at the supply of goods – the distribution of goods – the traditional process is for the goods to be sold by the manufacturer to a wholesaler or distributor who then sells them to a retailer (shop). The consumer then buys the goods from the shop. The 'line of distribution' looks like this (note the reference to industrial sectors in the diagram):

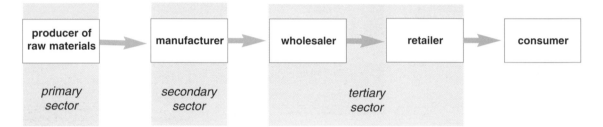

Some retailers – supermarkets for example – buy direct from the manufacturer. The line of distribution will then miss out the wholesaler, but will still span all three industrial sectors, as you can see from the diagram.

from local business to multinational

Your investigations into types of business will also show that geographical spread can vary greatly. Businesses are divided into the three main types described below. Find examples of these in your area:

local business
A business which operates in one locality, eg the local plumber, taxi service, firm of solicitors.

national business
A business which operates throughout the country, eg a well-known chain of shops, a bank, the Royal Mail.

multinational business
A business which is based in one country but which operates in a number of different countries. For example, The Ford Motor Company, based in the USA, makes Fords, Jaguars and Volvos in different European states.

trends in business sectors

In this chapter we have seen that the main classifications of businesses are:

- by *geography* – local, national and multinational
- by *industrial sector* – using natural resources (primary sector), manufacturing (secondary sector) and service businesses (tertiary sector) – in other words they are classified by what the businesses *do*

Because of the way the economy works the 'mix' of businesses never stands still. Some types of business will do well and expand and others will struggle and decline. In general recent trends have been

- an increase in the number of services businesses (tertiary sector)
- a decline in the manufacturing industries (secondary sector)
- a decline in agriculture, forestry and fishing (primary sector)

Now read the Case Studies and answer the questions.

Activity 2.5

trends in business

The Good Life
organic food on the Net

The 'Good Life' is an on-line store which has recently opened. Run by a husband and wife team from their Suffolk farmhouse premises, 'Good Life' offers a wide range of organic foods: fruit, vegetables, cheeses, meat – all sourced from approved local suppliers and importers. The business is basically a mail order operation: orders are taken on the website and over the telephone and despatched within 48 hours by carrier.

The owners recently commented 'We have been delighted by the way the business has taken off – we have customers in the UK and abroad. Orders are increasing day-by-day.'

questions

1 What industrial sector does this business belong to?

2 Is 'Good Life' expanding or contracting?

3 Do you think the business sector to which 'Good Life' belongs is growing or declining?

4 What do you think are the advantages to the business of trading on the internet?

5 Can you find examples of this type of business in your area?

Grantley Switchgear
parts for the car industry

Grantley Switchgear, based in the West Midlands has recently announced a new round of redundancies and lay-offs.

Managing Director John Grantley has said 'We have had to take these measures because of falling demand for our products. More and more car manufacturers are sourcing their switchgear from the Far East where prices are lower because of the cheap labour over there. We still have some loyal customers, but the way forward is far from easy. Our main hope is to specialise in new technology such as traffic navigation systems which are now being fitted in some cars as standard equipment.'

questions

1 What industrial sector does this business belong to?

2 Is the business expanding or contracting?

3 Why is the business expanding or contracting?

4 What is the business planning to do in order to survive?

questions

1 What industrial sector does this business belong to?

2 What problems is the owner having?

3 How can the farmer survive if he has these problems?

4 What do you think the business could do in order to increase income and survive?

Ivor Davies – sheep farmer
is it worth it?

Welsh sheep farmer Ivor Davies recently reported that he had sold his sheep at auction and made less than £3 per animal.

He sold 180 ewes for just £720, but after deduction of auction house commission, VAT and other taxes he received only £486 for the animals, an average of £2.70 each.

'I don't know why I bother' commented Mr Davies. 'I have had to rear the sheep and then pay £150 to transport them to auction. There is no money in this business for me. I own my farm and my family help out but I haven't had a holiday for five years and my children have no new clothes. It's a dead end business.'

sources of statistics

Statistics for trends in different types of business are available nationally and locally. National trends are set out in the publications of the Stationery Office and statistics about small and medium-sized businesses are produced in the Department of Trade and Industry's *SME Statistical Bulletin* . Summaries of these figures are illustrated below and on the next two pages.

Local trends are available from local authorities, often produced in the form of an annual report.

national data – small and medium-sized businesses

type of business	1997		1998	
	businesses	*employed*	*businesses*	*employed*
Agriculture, forestry, fishing	220,865	532,000	192,840	499,000
Manufacturing	322,210	4,466,000	332,135	4,451,000
Retail, wholesale, repairs	526,395	4,269,000	553,715	4,423,000
Financial services	51,540	981,000	65,935	1,026,000

Source: DTI

local data

'Worcestershire has experienced trends in employment that are common to Great Britain as a whole . . . greater growth in service sector employment compared to primary and secondary sectors.'

'Growth Sectors' include Electronics, Instruments, Wholesales, Hotels, Tourism, Financial Services, Computer Services, Education, Health, Telecommunications, Media and Leisure.

'Horticultural crops account for 4,100 hectares and have experienced a gradual decline over the past decade. The national trend of falling dairy herd numbers has been experienced in Worcestershire, and looks set to continue in the future.'

Source: Worcestershire County Council

Activity 2.6

National and local trends

Read the national and local data set out on this page. See what trends you can identify and then answer the following questions:

1 What evidence can you find from the data that the primary sector – eg agriculture and horticulture – is in decline?

2 What evidence can you find from the data that some areas of manufacturing are in decline and others are expanding?

3 What conclusions can you draw about the services sector?

examples of national statistics

The figures here have been summarised from a variety of sources including two publications published by The Stationery Office:

- *Social Trends*, an annual publication which contains a wealth of information about the earnings and spending patterns of the UK population
- *Labour Force Survey*, a quarterly publication which sets out employment statistics

You should be able to find these publications in good reference libraries. The tables and Activities set out here are designed to help you with your Portfolio work. They show the trends in the industrial sectors over a ten year period. You should be able to relate these trends to the types of businesses that you are investigating.

Activity 2.7

Trends in industrial sectors – 1

Portfolio activity

The table below shows the value of goods and services produced in the UK by the three industrial sectors from 1979 to 1998.

1 Using a computer spreadsheet or graphing package draw a line graph or a multiple bar chart showing the trend over the time period.

2 Write down your comments on the trends shown by the graph.

3 Write down an explanation of how these trends are affecting the two businesses you are investigating.

industrial sectors:
the value of goods and services produced in the UK (as a percentage)

	1979	1990	1998
	%	%	%
Primary Sector	7	4	3
Secondary Sector	37	32	20
Tertiary Sector	56	64	77

Trends in industrial sectors – 2

Portfolio activity

The table below is different from the previous one because it shows the percentage of the workforce employed by different types of business in the UK from 1981 to 1998.

1   Sort out the types of business shown below into the three industrial sectors.

2   Add up, where appropriate, the percentage of each industrial sector. You will only need to do this in one case!

3   Draw up a new table – preferably on a computer spreadsheet– with the dates in the columns and a row for each of the three industrial sectors.

4   Draw a line graph or multiple bar chart to show the trends. How do they compare with the previous graph? Why do you think the data you have used might make the graphs different?

5   Draw up a pie chart to show the 1998 results. How does this compare with what you have found out about the trends in the types of business in your area? If there are differences, try and find out why.

people employed in different types of business in the UK (as a percentage)			
	1981 %	1991 %	1998 %
Agriculture	2	2	2
Manufacturing	25	19	17
Distribution, hotels, catering, repairs	20	22	23
Financial services	11	15	17
Transport & communications	6	6	6
Construction	5	4	4
Energy and water supply	3	2	1
Other services	28	30	40
	100	100	100

CHAPTER SUMMARY

- Businesses are involved in a wide range of different activities: retailing, services, manufacturing, transport, communications, and businesses such as fishing which make use of natural resources.

- These types of business are grouped in three separate classifications known as 'industrial sectors':
  - *primary sector* businesses which extract and make use of natural resources
  - *secondary sector* businesses which manufacture products
  - *tertiary sector* businesses which provide services such as retailing, financial services, leisure services

- National and local statistics show that:
  - primary industries, such as agriculture, are declining
  - some traditional secondary (manufacturing) businesses are declining and newer technology businesses are expanding
  - the tertiary (services) sector is expanding

KEY TERMS

business	an organisation which makes a product or provides a service.
primary sector	the industrial sector which makes use of natural resources
secondary sector	the industrial sector which manufactures products
tertiary sector	the industrial sector which provides services
wholesaler	a business which buys from a manufacturer and sells to a retailer
retailer	the shop that sells to the consumer – the end-user of the product
local business	a business which operates in one locality
national business	a business which operates throughout the country
multinational business	a business which operates in a number of different countries but is based in one country

MULTIPLE CHOICE QUESTIONS

1   Which of the following represents businesses from the primary sector?
   A   farms, fisheries, mines
   B   farms, fisheries, manufacturers
   C   farms, fisheries, multinationals
   D   farms, fisheries, media services

2   Which of the following represents businesses from the secondary sector?
   A   banks, builders, building societies
   B   car manufacturers, component manufacturers, car garages
   C   mines, media services, medical services
   D   clockmakers, car manufacturers, chemical manufacturers

3   Which of the following represents businesses from the tertiary sector?
   A   farms, fish and chip shops, frozen food stores
   B   banks, building societies, bookmakers
   C   fitness centres, fish and chip shops, silicon chip manufacturers
   D   taxi firms, train companies, car manufacturers

4   A wholesaler
   A   sells direct to the general public
   B   sells direct to factory shops
   C   sells direct to retailers
   D   sells direct to distributors

5   A multinational is a business which:
   A   is a local business
   B   operates in a number of different countries
   C   is given grants for employing people from different countries
   D   operates in only one country

6   A reduction in the number of farmers and an increase in the number of fast food outlets would mean:
   A   a decline in the primary sector and an expansion in the tertiary sector
   B   an expansion in the primary sector and an expansion in the tertiary sector
   C   a decline in the secondary sector and an expansion in the tertiary sector
   D   a decline in the primary sector and an decline in the tertiary sector

3

Influences on business – location and stakeholders

Unit 2: How businesses develop
Location and stakeholders

what this chapter is about

The last two chapters have looked at businesses from the inside. They have looked at different types of business activity and different forms of ownership. This chapter looks at the outside influences on business which affect the decisions businesses make and the way they operate. The first set of influences is what makes a business decide where to locate. The second involves the influence of the stakeholders of the business. Stakeholders are people who have an interest in and influence over the business, for example customers, employees and the local community.

what you will learn from this chapter

● The decision of a business to locate in a particular place is affected by a number of different factors, for example:
  – suitable transport links with suppliers and being near the sources of supply
  – competition with other similar businesses in the area
  – being near its customers
  – the availability of suitably-skilled people to work in the business
  – the availability of premises and financial help from the government and the European Union
  – historically it is where that type of business has located in the past
● Businesses are influenced by their stakeholders. These are people and organisations whose views they have to consider when making decisions. They include, for example, their customers (who need good service) employees (who need rewarding), shareholders (who need good profits), the local community (which needs looking after) and the government (which makes laws and regulations that have to be respected).

the location of business

choosing a location

What makes a business decide to set up in a certain location? Some of the most important influences are personal factors. In the first place, many businesses are already based in a particular location; history and tradition says that is where they should be. Any expansion or relocation may well be in the same area, because that is where the workforce lives and the commercial contacts have been established. Secondly, the owner of a business may well want to set up in a certain location because he or she happens to like it!

Personal considerations apart, a business will need to ask a number of questions when deciding to set up in a particular location.

do we need to be near to natural resources?

If a business is dependent on natural resources, it is likely to be sited near to the source of the materials it needs. Brick manufacturers, for example, concentrate in areas where suitable clay is to be found. Scotch whisky is highly dependent on the peaty quality of Scottish water and is therefore distilled on site in Scotland. Businesses that bottle mineral water will clearly want to be near the springs.

locating near the source of natural resources

Activity 3.1

Location of business

– being near natural resources

An activity for discussion or for individual work.

Make a list of examples of businesses which are located in a certain area because of the natural resources which are available there.

transport links with customers and suppliers

Some businesses need access to the transport system – major motorways, airports, railway stations; this is particularly important if the business has a large and active salesforce travelling in the UK and overseas.

The transport system is also needed to transport raw materials and finished goods. This may be a critical factor for siting the business. If a manufacturer relies on the use of heavy and bulky raw materials which are expensive to transport, and the finished product is less bulky and cheaper to transport, the factory will locate nearer to the source of raw materials. If, on the other hand, the finished product is bulkier than the raw materials, the production plant will be located nearer to the purchaser in order to save transport costs. The Millennium Eye big wheel in London is an extreme example of this – it was actually built on site.

Activity 3.2

Location of business

– being near transport links

On the opposite page are extracts from publicity material for a business park in Tewkesbury, Gloucestershire. You want to start a garden tool manufacturing business which needs to distribute its products throughout the UK.

1 Write down what you think are the transport advantages of locating at the Tewkesbury Business Park?

2 Can you think of any other advantages of locating in a rural area such as Tewkesbury rather than in an urban area like Bristol or Cardiff?

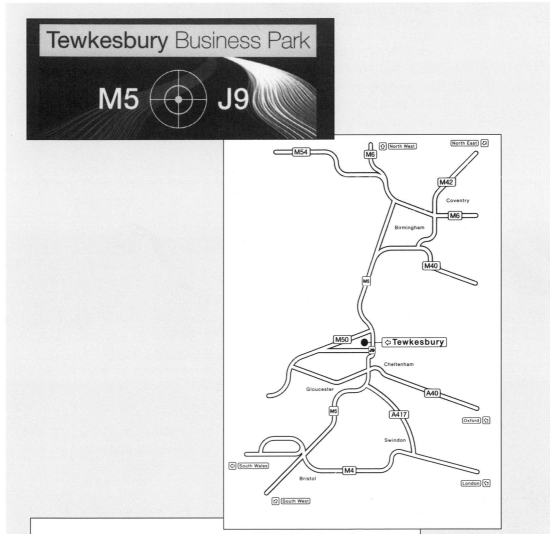

Tewkesbury Business Park is an established business location, strategically located alongside the M5 at Junction 9 giving immediate access to the national motorway network, with both Birmingham and Bristol within an hour's drive. The historic town of Tewkesbury is located immediately to the west and provides excellent amenities and services. In addition, the regional shopping centre of Cheltenham is 9 miles to the South.

Rail links are provided from Ashchurch Parkway (1 mile) Inter-City services are available from both Cheltenham and Gloucester.

reproduced by kind permission of Robert Hitchins Properties

being near the customers?

Some businesses do not need to be 'near' their markets, because their markets do not have a definite geographical location. Car manufacturers, for example, distribute to dealers throughout the UK and abroad. Their decision of where to locate rests on factors such as the cost of land, the availability of skilled labour and government assistance. Mail order companies, too, sell to a nationwide market, and can locate anywhere within easy reach of the transport system.

Some markets, however, have a very precise geographical location – this is particularly true of service industries. A small businesses such as a kiosk that sells sandwiches and drinks must be in the area that it serves.

Activity 3.3

Location of business
being near the customer

1   Look at the two pictures of businesses shown below.

Why are they located where they are. How important is it that they are near to their customers? Write down the reasons for your answer in both cases.

2   Chose six local businesses and find out why they have chosen their particular location.

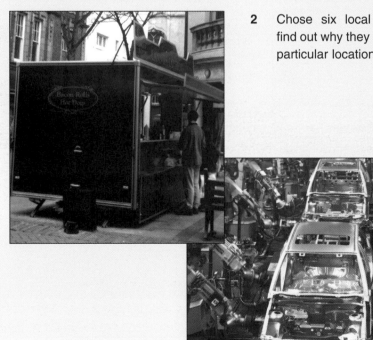

what is the competition doing?

The decision of where to locate a business will also depend on the extent of the competition in the area. If the business is a service business it will need to be seen in the same sort of location as its competitors, for example:

- supermarkets in out-of-town locations
- travel agents and banks in town centres

The reason for this is that people expect to see similar businesses in the same neighbourhood. If a business sets up in an unusual location it may not get as many customers as businesses in the areas in which you expect to see them.

If the business is a manufacturing business the location of its competitors will not be so important – it does not normally deal direct with the public. The over-riding factor will be the manufacturer's ability to deliver its products as quickly and cheaply as possible to its customers. Many manufacturers operate from premises on industrial estates.

Coping with competition is very important to a business; it is dealt with in more detail in the next chapter, on page 80.

Activity 3.4

Location of business
dealing with competition

This picture shows three car dealerships in a row. They are situated along a main road on the outskirts of a town.

1   What factors have caused them to choose this type of location?

2   Why should they choose to be next to their competitors?

3   Find examples of groupings of businesses in your area. Try to find out how long each business has been there and why the newer businesses decided to locate where they did.

the labour factor

It is easier to recruit employees in some parts of the country than in others. This may affect the choice of where to set up business. Generally speaking, wages are higher in urban areas and in the South East, reflecting the higher costs of living in those areas. If a business is labour intensive (in other words it employs many people), some businesses may be attracted to areas where labour is cheaper. Of course this choice may not always exist – a business may have to set up in a particular part of the country because that is where the owners live, or where there are natural resources, or customers.

Activity 3.5

Location of business
the cost of labour

Average weekly full-time earnings in the UK regions		
	male £	*female* £
North East	352	265
North West	365	274
Yorkshire & Humberside	376	277
East Midlands	397	279
West Midlands	367	266
East of England	443	309
London	514	383
South East	458	315
South West	378	267
Wales	334	269
Scotland	382	282
Northern Ireland	307	246

Source: Labour Force Survey

This table shows how much on average male and female full-time employees earn (before tax) in the different regions of the UK.

1   Take five different regions, including your own region and the highest and lowest figures, and draw up a bar chart showing the average weekly earnings. Include both the male and the female earnings on your chart. How does your region compare?

2   Given a free choice, where would you set up a factory employing 1,000 people. Give reasons for your choice.

3   Why do you think the average wage for males and females is so different?

unemployment trends

When investigating the businesses for your assignment you are required to look at the employment trends in your area. You will find that wage rates will be higher in areas which have fuller employment. This is a factor (apart from Government Assistance – see page 64) which may persuade a new start-up business to move to an area with higher unemployment.

The table below shows the employment and unemployment figures for the regions. The figures (shown in 000s) have been extracted from the *Labour Force Survey*, published by The Stationery Office.

regional employment and unemployment

	1996 000s total employed	1996 000s total unemployed	1999 000s total employed	1999 000s total unemployed
North East	968	92	1071	111
North West	2084	297	3074	204
Yorkshire/Humberside	1938	267	2311	146
East Midlands	1710	228	2009	117
West Midlands	2085	271	2472	171
East	2178	341	2646	103
London	2634	445	3326	263
South East	3228	547	3970	158
South West	1851	365	2370	105
Wales	1038	164	1228	103
Scotland	2032	228	2298	176
N Ireland	548	80	687	56

Activity 3.6

employment and unemployment

– the trends in your area

Find the figures for your area in the table shown above. Using those figures and the figures for three other areas . . .

1   Work out the unemployment percentage* for 1996 and 1999 for the four areas. Present your results in the form of a bar chart.

2   Comment on the trends. How might they affect businesses which are employing staff in the four areas. (Look at the Earnings Table on page 58).

* To do this, multiply the unemployed total by 100 and then divide this result by the employed and unemployment totals added together.

the skills factor

The skills of the labour force is another important factor. Certain areas are well-known for particular skills: for example the Cambridge area and the M4 'corridor' for computer technology. Businesses are therefore attracted to certain areas because of the skills that exist there.

In the Case Study below you will see how the technological skills available in Malvern in the West Midlands are used to attract new businesses to the area. Read the Case Study and then answer the questions on the next page.

Case Study

Locating where the skills are
Malvern Hills Science Park

The Malvern Hills Science Park is a purpose-built complex suitable for office and laboratory use.

The skills available locally are those developed in the government-run DERA (Defence Evaluation and Research Agency).

DERA has had a hand in innovations such as radar, liquid crystal flat panel displays and the technology used in thermal imaging cameras.

Some of the world's most technically adventurous people are making their way to Malvern. Amongst them are companies, large and small, from Japan and America, from Taiwan and from Continental Europe. Some are existing sector leaders and some are small ambitious newcomers. Many are companies working in leading edge research and others are seeking solutions to everyday technical problems. All believe that the key to their future prosperity is to be found there. *Why?*

An amazing range of technologies has been developed over many years within the Defence Evaluation and Research Agency (DERA) for military use. The British Government is keen that this expertise should, where strategically acceptable, be made accessible to companies able to develop productive relationships with DERA. They want to enhance Great Britain's technological strengths and to develop centres of excellence that will be the envy of the world.

You and your staff can now interact creatively with free thinking specialists in your own field. They will bring fresh minds and access to undreamed of technologies to address your problems.

mhsp
**malvern hills
science park**

The Malvern Hills Science Park is located immediately adjacent to the DERA site in Malvern. Situated in an area of outstanding natural beauty at the foot of the Malvern Hills, the Science Park is at the heart of a region of emerging technology-based companies.

It has excellent road and rail links to the Midlands, London, Wales and the North and is conveniently situated for Birmingham International and London Heathrow airports.

By Road:

M5 and M50	20 minutes
London Heathrow	2 hours
Birmingham International Airport	1 hour 15 minutes
Oxford	1 hour 20 minutes

By Rail:

Great Malvern – London (direct)	2 hours 15 minutes
Great Malvern – Birmingham New Street	1 hour

Source: Malvern Hills Science Park

Activity 3.7

Locating where the skills are
Malvern Hills Science Park

1   What is the source of the scientific skills in the Malvern area?

2   What type of technology has been developed in Malvern?

3   Where are the new businesses coming from?

4   How can the Science Park benefit Malvern?

5   What other attractions might draw businesses to the Malvern area?

6   How accessible is Malvern from the rest of the UK?

help from the Government

Businesses are helped by the UK Government and the European Union (EU). Businesses receive assistance from both in the form of grants and incentives. The areas of the UK that qualify for assistance were revised in 2000 to bring them in line with European Union guidelines for aid.

Any business starting up or relocating will obviously find it advantageous to set up in an assisted area. Car manufacturers have been greatly helped in this way.

UK Government assistance

The UK Government provides financial help – Regional Selective Assistance – to businesses setting up in areas which have traditionally had higher levels of low earnings and unemployment. This assistance – grants, cheap rents, free and subsidised advice – is administered through the Department of Trade and Industry, normally referred to as the DTI.

Details can be obtained from your local office of the Department of Trade and Industry (or the Welsh Office in Cardiff and the Scottish Office in Glasgow.) The areas given assistance are known as the Assisted Areas. They are shown as shaded areas on the map on the next page. They are divided into three 'tiers':

Tier 1 (dark shading)

These are the areas of greatest need and include Cornwall, Merseyside, South Yorkshire, West Wales and the Welsh Valleys, all of Northern Ireland (not shown on the map).

Tier 2 (light shading)

These are local areas of need. They do not qualify for grants as high as those in Tier 1.

Tier 3 (not shown on the map)

This applies to businesses employing up to 250 people in certain areas of the UK.

You will be able to find out about the status of your own locality by contacting your nearest DTI office or Business Link.

European Union assistance

Financial assistance is also available from the EU in the form of the European Structural Fund. This fund works on a similar tier system to the one shown above, and the areas covered are more or less the same.

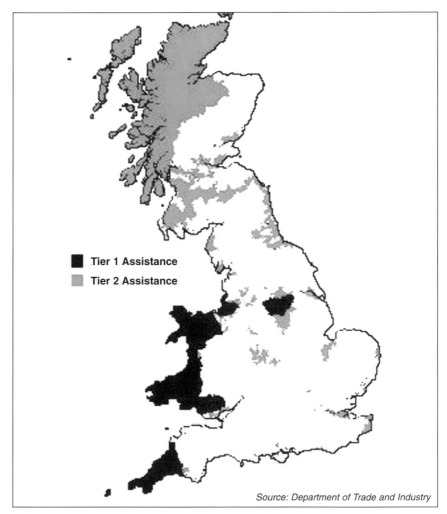

Source: Department of Trade and Industry

Tier 1 Assistance
Tier 2 Assistance

The proposed Assisted Areas.
(note: at the time of going to press these areas were awaiting EU approval)

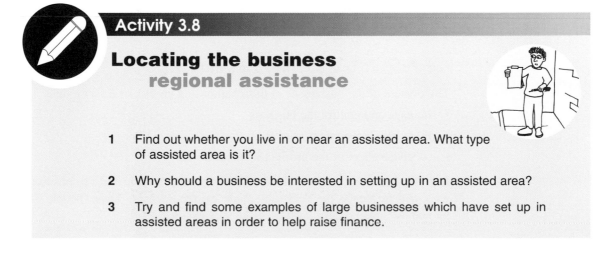

Activity 3.8

Locating the business
regional assistance

1 Find out whether you live in or near an assisted area. What type of assisted area is it?

2 Why should a business be interested in setting up in an assisted area?

3 Try and find some examples of large businesses which have set up in assisted areas in order to help raise finance.

Activity 3.9

Locating the business

Portfolio activity

1   Explain why the two businesses you have chosen are located where they are. Involve factors such as availability of natural resources, costs, transport links, being near to customers, being near to the competition, the availability of labour and skills, Government assistance.

2   In each business which are the most important factors affecting location, for example the availability of labour, Government grants?

3   Have there been any changes in the competitors in the area recently – may this have affected the location of the businesses?

4   Explain how employment trends in the area may have affected the choice of location.

5   Reproduce a map showing the local area and the location of the two businesses. Mark on the map any significant factors, for example where the competitors are, important transport links, where the workforce live. Make sure that there are explanatory notes with the map relating it to the factors you have mentioned.

business stakeholders

the role of the business owners

The owners of the businesses in this chapter to a greater or lesser extent

- manage and control the business
- make the decisions
- receive a share of the profits (or losses)

But they do not operate in isolation. There are other people and organisations who will influence the decisions made by the owners. These people are known as 'stakeholders'.

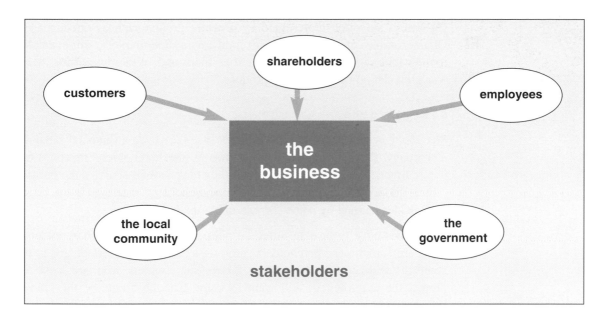

stakeholders

Stakeholders are people who have an interest – a 'stake' – in the business. It matters to them what the business does. These people may have a direct investment, or they may be affected by the activities of the business. Whatever the situation they can act to influence the way a business is run. They include:

- customers
- shareholders
- employees
- the local community
- the government

customers

Many businesses are customer-focused - in other words they aim to keep their customers happy by looking after them, listening to their views and meeting their needs. With businesses in such keen competition, a customer ignored is a customer that is lost.

If customers' views are not taken into account, the results can be serious: the environment-conscious public, for example, were persuaded by the environmental pressure group Greenpeace to stay away from Shell petrol stations when the oil company planned to sink an old oil platform, which would have polluted the sea. Shell may well have lost valuable income over this decision.

Customers are often represented by pressure groups such as Greenpeace. Other examples of pressure being exerted are on supermarkets – for example in the withdrawal of genetically modified foods and, at the time of the 'beef war', the ban on certain French produce.

shareholders

Shareholders are clearly stakeholders because they have a financial stake in a company. Their wishes are made known in the shareholders' meetings of public limited companies. One interest they have is their share of the profits – their dividend. A frequent criticism in shareholders' meetings is the large pay package earned by some 'fat cat' directors.

Companies have to bear in mind the political views of their shareholders: there are sometimes shareholders' protests against the export of goods to countries with oppressive regimes. Other shareholders who are keen to protect the environment will want to know that the company they have invested in has a sound environmental policy.

employees

Employees are stakeholders in a business because a contented and motivated workforce will help a business to succeed. If the owners of a business neglect employee training, welfare and pay levels in the interests of profits, it is likely to lose them money in the long run. Businesses are also involving employees more and more in decision-making; some have set up 'workers councils' which are common in Europe.

The Trade Unions, although declining in influence, still do a valuable job in representing the views of employees.

the local community

The local community has an interest in local business for a number of reasons. The local community needs full employment, a clean environment and support for local events and charities. Local pressure groups can often have significant influence on business decisions – blocking planning for new business projects, for example.

Businesses need to take account of these needs and pressures by offering employment locally, and not 'bussing in' cheap labour from other areas. They may also sponsor local sporting and charitable events and help the environment by planting trees.

Some supermarkets are now offering crêches for children, bottlebanks for recycling glass and clothes banks for local charity collections. Businesses are now often seen to be socially responsible as a result of pressure from local communities.

the government

The government has an interest in and influence over business. Laws cover areas such as planning, Health & Safety regulations, environmental hazards and the ways employees are treated The government also taxes businesses through the Inland Revenue, using the money raised to invest in areas such as transport and the Health Service.

Activity 3.10

Social responsibility to stakeholders
the Co-operative movement

In recent years Co-operative Retail Services Limited (now part of the Co-operative Wholesale Society) has published a 'Social Report' setting out the ways in which the organisation mees the needs of its various stakeholders. Study the extracts below and answer the questions.

SOCIAL OBJECTIVES

social objectives for the customer

"Offer high quality goods and services to customers at the lowest possible prices."

social objectives for the members (shareholders)

"To provide a fair return . . . on members' investment."

social objectives for the employees

"Provide broad facilities for training and continued education . . . Maintain the best possible working conditions."

social objectives for society

"Give support to self-help and voluntary organisations . . . Do everything in its power to protect the environment and ensure efficient use and protection of natural resources."

Source: Co-operative Retail Services Limited

1   What stakeholders can you identify? Is this a complete list of business stakeholders?

2   Do you see any conflicts which might arise between any of the social objectives listed?

stakeholders and the size of the business

It is important to appreciate that the size of the business you are investigating will affect the number of stakeholders involved in that business. Generally speaking, the larger the business, the more stakeholders will have an interest in it.

A sole trader, for example, will not have to worry about

- shareholders – there are none – the sole trader takes the profit

- employees – if it is a 'one person' business there may be none

- the local community – the sole trader is unlikely to make much impact here

The one type of stakeholder the sole trader will depend upon is the customer. The customer is ignored at the sole trader's peril!

If on the other hand the business is larger, a company for example, the whole range of stakeholders is likely to influence what it does.

stakeholders and conflicts of interest

Sometimes, as suggested in Activity 3.10 on page 69, there will be a conflict between the demands of stakeholders which the business will have to deal with. For example:

- customers may want low prices for a company's products and this may reduce shareholders' profits

- customers of a shop may want longer opening hours which may cause problems with the workforce having to work unsociable hours

- customers of a shop may want Sunday opening hours which may run into trouble with the government's Sunday trading laws

- a business decides to give donations to charitable causes in the local community – this will reduce profit to shareholders

- a business decides to give donations to a charitable cause which is sponsored by a company that makes alcoholic drinks – this upsets members of the community who are opposed to alcoholic drinks

- the government's clean air legislation requires that a factory installs an expensive air filtration unit on its production line

Activity 3.11

Stakeholders in business
– influences and conflicts

The following situations involve:

• stakeholders having an influence over decisions that businesses make

• conflicts of interest between different stakeholders

Write down the influences and conflicts you can identify in these situations.

1 What different types of stakeholders might have an influence on a small family-run general stores 'corner shop'? What would the stakeholders be interested in?

2 What different types of stakeholders might have an influence on a large public limited company which manufactures cars? What would the stakeholders be interested in?

3 From your answers to 1 and 2, what difference does the size of a business make on its range of stakeholders and the influence they have?

stakeholder issues for class discussion

1 Customers of a private limited company which runs a store in the town want prices to be cut substantially. What stakeholder interests would this
   (a) benefit?
   (b) harm?

2 How would stakeholder interests be affected if a large supermarket chain decided that it wanted to build a new superstore on a greenfield site on the outskirts of a town or city near you?

3 A local company has started to 'bus in' production line workers every day from a new town 25 miles away. The company says that it cannot get the employees locally.

   A friend of yours says that the company is paying such low wages that nobody locally wants to work there.

   What stakeholder influences are affected in this situation?

4 Try and find an example from the TV or in the press where a business has changed its activities (eg changed the products that it sells) because of public pressure. What benefits has it gained from this change?

Activity 3.12

Stakeholders in business
– comparing two businesses

Portfolio activity

Produce a report on the influence of stakeholders on the two businesses you are investigating. The report can include the following tasks:

1 Identify the stakeholders of the two businesses that you have investigated and explain what their interests are.

2 Describe any current issues (if any) which interest the stakeholders in decisions that the businesses are taking – for example changing prices, developing new sites, affecting the environment.

  How are the businesses responding to these issues – how they changing their policy?

3 How do the stakeholders differ between the two businesses. Does one business have more stakeholders than the other? Why should this be?

4 Is the influence of stakeholders on one business as strong as on the other? Does the size of the business make any difference?

5 Explain why there might be conflicts of interest between the stakeholders of one of the businesses. This is most likely to occur in the larger business. How will the business deal with these conflicts?

6 Write a summary explaining how and why external influences – and these include factors such as economic trends, the location of the business as well as stakeholders' influence – interact and affect the decisions made by the businesses.

CHAPTER SUMMARY

- The location of a business will depend on a number of very different factors:
  - the need to be near the source of raw materials
  - the cost of getting in materials and goods from suppliers
  - the need to be near good transport links
  - being near the customers
  - the pressure to be near where the competitors are
  - the cost of labour – local wage rates
  - the availability of suitably-skilled people to work in the business
  - the availability of financial help from the government and the EU
- Businesses are influenced by stakeholders.
- Stakeholders are people and organisations whose views businesses have to consider when making decisions.
- Stakeholders include:
  - customers (who need good service)
  - employees (who need looking after and rewarding)
  - shareholders (who need a good return on their investments)
  - the local community (support of charities, care of the environment)
  - the government (laws and regulations that have to be respected).

KEY TERMS

natural resources	resources from the earth which are used or extracted by business
labour	the supply of people who work in business
labour intensive	a business which uses many people in making its product
DTI	Department of Trade and Industry – the government department which is responsible for managing financial and other assistance to business
Assisted Areas	the areas in the UK which are eligible for financial and other assistance
stakeholder	people and organisations whose views businesses have to consider when making decisions
social responsibity	the responsibility a business has to society at large – to help charities and conserve the environment

MULTIPLE CHOICE QUESTIONS

1   The need to locate a business near the supply of natural resources is likely to be most important for
    A   an organic food shop
    B   a holiday company
    C   a mineral water bottling plant
    D   a wine merchant

2   The need to locate a business near the UK motorway network is likely to be most important for
    A   a company that manufactures cars
    B   a company that sells holidays
    C   a manufacturer that distributes its own products
    D   a farming co-operative

3   The need to locate a business near its customers is likely to be most important for
    A   a shoe shop
    B   a manufacturer
    C   a mail order company
    D   a farmer

4   To which type of stakeholder is business profit most likely to be of the greatest interest?
    A   a customer
    B   a shareholder
    C   the local community
    D   the government

5   To which type of stakeholder is caring for the environment most likely to be of the greatest interest?
    A   a customer
    B   a shareholder
    C   the local community
    D   an employee

6   To which type of stakeholder is a cut in prices most likely to be of the greatest interest?
    A   a customer
    B   a shareholder
    C   an employee
    D   the government

section two

HOW BUSINESSES WORK

introduction

In this unit you will investigate and learn about:

- how businesses have aims – for example making a profit, helping the community

- the ways in which businesses measure their success in achieving their aims

- the way in which businesses divide up their areas of activity called 'functions' – for example marketing and sales, finance, customer service

- the different ways in which businesses organise their functions into a 'structure' with the management at the top

- the different methods of communication and the importance of communication in an organisation

- the ways in which the structure of an organisation can affect the success of its communications

chapters in this section

assessment guide

Unit 1: Investigating how businesses work

what you will need for your Portfolio

For this Unit you will produce a Case Study of a large or medium-sized business that you have investigated. The business may also be the larger business that you are studying for Unit 2.

The Portfolio Activities in the chapters will enable you to compile this Case Study as you go along.

The evidence you produce will show that you understand how the business 'works' – what it sets out to do, how it is organised and how it looks after its customers.

The tasks you undertake will include the following:

1. a description of what the business does, what its aims and objectives are

2. a description of the purposes and activities of four areas of the business, including human resources (but not customer services, which is covered in Task 5)

3. a description of how the different areas of the business communicate with each other and with people outside the business

4. a description of the organisational structure of the business and a comparison with a contrasting structure

5. an oral presentation covering the customer service of the business you have investigated

6. a record of your sources of information

Now study the next page and appreciate how you can achieve a Pass, a Merit or a Distinction in this Unit.

evidence you will need to produce . . .

to achieve a Pass in this Unit

1   a description of what the business does, what its aims and objectives are

2   a description of the purposes and activities of four functional areas of the business, including human resources (but not customer services, which is covered by an oral presentation – see 6 below); you should include examples of job roles from each of the four areas

3   a description of how the law protects employees by ensuring the employer allows equal opportunities in the workplace – the description should include the purpose of the four main Acts related to employment law covered in Chapter 10

4   an explanation, using at least six examples, of how different functional areas in the business communicate with each other and with people and organisations outside the business

5   a comparison of the organisational structure of your chosen business with another and different organisational structure, explaining the communication flows in both structures

6   an illustrated oral presentation of how the customer service of your chosen business compares with best practice – including (but only if necessary) suggestions for how it could be improved; your notes and visual aids should be included in the Portfolio, together with the Tutor's comment

7   a list of the sources of evidence used in your research, for example: written sources, interviews, visits, talks, work experience – details should include names of people and organisations and dates

to achieve a Merit in this Unit you must also provide . . .

8   a clear explanation of how the functional areas of your chosen business work together to achieve the aims and objectives of the business (this is an expansion of 1 and 2 above)

9   an explanation of how employment law protects employees, using a situation which might arise under each of the four main Acts covered in the text

10   an explanation of how effective communications are helping the business to meet its aims and objectives and how aspects of communication – eg speed or confidentiality are appropriate in different situations

to achieve a Distinction in this Unit you must also provide . . .

11   an evaluation of strengths and weaknesses in the organisational structure and communication flows of your chosen business, explaining how these may affect its success in achieving its aims and objective – in other words, show how it is helped or hindered by its structure and channels of communication

12   a demonstration of a coherent understanding of how your chosen business works – showing that you have used accurately researched material in a logical way and have drawn appropriate conclusions

4 The aims of business

what this chapter is about

The last three chapters – covering Unit 2 – have looked at businesses in general and seen what they do, how they are owned and how outside influences affect the decisions they make. In your investigations you will have compared two different businesses.

The assessment of Unit 1, on the other hand, looks at the internal workings of a single business. In this chapter we look at what businesses aim to do and see how those aims can differ.

what you will learn from this chapter

- One set of aims of a business involves being successful:
  - making a profit
  - increasing sales
  - beating the competition
  - expanding the business

- Another set of aims of business involves maintaining levels of quality:
  - providing good customer service
  - ensuring quality in the running of the business
  - making sure the product is always of the highest quality

- Another set of aims of business involves meeting some of the needs of the stakeholders described in the last chapter:
  - helping charities and voluntary organisations
  - preserving the environment

- Businesses set targets – objectives – for these aims. They need to see from time-to-time how successful they are in meeting their aims so that they can take action if there is a problem.

aims and objectives

what does this mean?

You will often hear people refer to 'aims and objectives' in one phrase. What is the difference between the two? In basic terms:

an aim is what you set out to do

an objective is a target you want to achieve

For example, a business *aim* is to make a profit. A business *objective* is to make a profit of over £100,000 next year.

In this chapter you will look at the different aims of businesses and the objectives they set so that they can measure how successful they are.

different types of aims and objectives

the financial success story

For many businesses making money is an important aim. Success in this area can be measured in a number of ways:

- making sure that sales of its products are as high as possible, ie maximising sales
- achieving a good level of profit
- expanding sales outlets or increasing the number of services provided

Activity 4.1

Tariq Mehta
Taxiworld

Tariq Mehta has set up a minicab business 'Taxiworld' in Southwold. Initially the business is just Tariq himself, driving his own car. He works long hours, including weekends and nightshifts. His hard work is rewarded and in his first six months he has taken £25,000 in fares. His profit is good because he lives at home and owns his car.

After the first six months in business he wants to expand. He decides to bring in his cousin Babu as a second driver. He says to Babu "Now we have your car too we can earn £50,000 in the next six months and much of that will be profit."

discussion point
What are Tariq's main aims and objectives in running the business?

beating the competition

For some businesses, beating the competition is one of the main aims of running the business. One way to beat the competition is to cut prices. You will probably be aware of 'price wars' between food supermarkets and also between airlines. The problem here, of course, is that if you cut prices you may attract extra customers, but you may also cut profits.

Activity 4.2

Tara Smith
Videostar

Tara Smith runs a video hire business from a shop 'Videostar' on the outskirts of Lincoln. She has a reasonable number of local customers, but has her eye on areas which are further away, but which are served by video hire stores in those areas. She wants to expand her sales and possibly put her competitors out of business. She has enough capital to open up and run two further hire shops.

discussion points
How could Tara expand her sales into those areas? What problems and dangers does she face in doing this?

Can you think of any other types of businesses for which beating the competition is a major aim? Can you think of any leaders of business who are very competitive?

providing quality in business

For some businesses maintaining levels of quality is an important aim. This can be achieved in a number of ways:

- providing a high level of customer service
- ensuring quality standards in the running of the business
- making sure that the product is always of the highest quality

Many businesses run customer care schemes (see page 132) and invest heavily in staff training. They appreciate that a high level of customer service means that customers will come back again.

Quality applies not only to the product (whether it is a manufactured item or a service) but also to the way the business itself is run. This is known as 'Quality Assurance' for which a government 'kitemark' can be awarded.

All these applications of quality in the business involve a cost, and so may reduce profit. The business owner will soon point out, however, that if the business is run in line with quality standards, it will attract more customers – and more customers mean more income.

Activity 4.3

McDonald's
Quality control

A dedicated Quality Assurance team in the UK is responsible for monitoring the quality of McDonald's food products, both in the restaurants and at the suppliers at all stages of production. This involves a continuous round of visits and inspections at McDonald's production facilities, distribution centres and restaurants. It even extends to the farms which sow the seeds and provide the food in the first place.

In the restaurants no delivery is accepted until a series of quality and safety checks are completed. All restaurant staff receive training in food safety and hygiene and food preparation procedures. All restaurants complete a Daily Product Safety Checklist to ensure that the food served is of the highest quality. *(Source: Biz/ed).*

1   What areas of production does the Quality Assurance team cover?

2   How does the aim to maintain Quality extend to the restaurant staff?

3   Someone points out to you that "McDonald's would save a lot of time and money if they didn't bother with all this checking business." What would be your reply in defence of the aim to maintain quality?

helping society

Nationally-known charities – such as Mencap and NSPCC – are themselves businesses which are wholly devoted to their main charitable cause. Like any other business they have business aims:

* to cover their costs
* to compete for donations from business and the public
* to become well-known household names
* to look after their staff and to maintain quality standards

Local charities also aim to cover their costs and to become well-known names in the neighbourhood.

Many other businesses actively help society by giving to national and local charities, sponsoring local events, helping with community projects and providing resources for education. You may have heard of the 'computers for schools' tokens given out by the supermarket chains.

Why do businesses do this? A business that is seen to be helping society will retain the respect of customers. A business that advertises its good work is likely to gain new customers.

Activity 4.4

Helping run-down areas
a Tesco partnership

The supermarket chain Tesco has announced its involvement in a 'Charter for Regeneration' which sets out its intention to help regenerate inner-city and industrial sites in some of the most deprived areas in the UK.

Tesco is working in partnership with bodies including The Employment Service, Local Authorities and local training providers. The first two projects are in Seacroft, Leeds, and in Leyland, Lancashire.

How is Tesco doing this? By opening foods stores in deprived areas and creating approximately 2,000 new jobs. The aim of the Tesco 'Social Plan' is to

- get unemployed people back to work
- to sponsor basic skills and employability training
- to help provide transport and childcare to enable people to work

Jobs offered by Tesco will:

- include vacancies with flexible working patterns and part-time positions
- provide good pay and benefits
- provide training (free courses) and career progression

(Source Tesco Plc)

questions for discussion and answering in writing

1   What is Tesco doing to help inner-city and industrial sites?

2   What type of organisations are Tesco's partners?

3   What are the main aims of the Tesco 'Social Plan'?

4   What are the attractions of the new jobs that Tesco will create?

5   Why is Tesco keen to be involved in this project?

being environmentally friendly

There is increasing evidence that the earth's resources are being depleted and damaged by business on a worldwide scale. Not only are resources running out, but pollution is damaging the balance of gases in the atmosphere, leading to global warming. These trends directly result from worldwide industrial processes. Businesses are under increasing pressure from governments and pressure groups such as Greenpeace to carry out a policy of *sustainability*. This means adopting objectives such as:

• cutting down on pollution

• not wasting natural resources

• using recycled materials wherever possible

• using energy efficiently

what are the advantages?

Businesses like to be seen to be helping to save the environment. If they are thought to be socially responsible, consumers are more likely to think the better of them and therefore more likely to buy their products. Also, savings on the use of resources such energy use can also mean savings on cost; this directly helps to boost profits.

Activity 4.5

Ecological sustainability
Co-op Bank objectives

The Co-operative Bank has reported success in meeting targets for cutting down on pollution and waste of natural resources. The annual targets successfully met include:

• recycling of at least 15% of steel and aluminium cans purchased

• recycling of at least 15% of plastic cups purchased

• recycling of 100% of flourescent tubes

• reduction in the use of paper by 10%

• recycling of 30% of paper used

questions for discussion and answering in writing

1   How has the Co-op Bank's success in meeting its targets helped to sustain the environment?

2   In what other ways can these savings help the Co-op Bank?

3   Can you think of any other ways a business like the Co-op Bank can help towards environmental 'sustainability'?

mission statements

A business such as a public limited company will often set out its main aims in a 'mission statement'. It may also set out its view of how it sees itself in a 'vision statement'. Here are two examples – a vision statement from Boots the Chemists and a mission statement from BT:

> Our vision is to be the world's leading retailer of products and services that help make our customers look good and feel good.

> BT's mission, our central purpose, is to provide world-class telecommunications and information products and services, and to develop and exploit our networks, at home and overseas, so that we can:
> - meet the requirements of our customers
> - sustain growth in the earnings of the group on behalf of our shareholders, and
> - make a fitting contribution to the community in which we conduct our business

You will see that the Boots vision statement is 'customer-focused'. It does not mention the company's other aims such as profitability and social responsibility, although those will be very important to it. BT's mission statement, on the other hand, is more comprehensive: it covers the needs of the main stakeholders – customers, shareholders and the community.

Activity 4.6

Mission Statements
The Body Shop and McDonald's

Set out on the next page are the Mission Statements of The Body Shop and McDonalds. Read them through and answer the questions set out below. You could discuss the Mission Statements in small groups in class and then write your answers individually.

1 Which Mission Statement belongs to which company?

2 What business aims can you identify in the two Mission Statements?

3 How and why are the two Mission Statements so different?

(a)

> *To be the family restaurant that people enjoy more. This will be achieved through five strategies: Development, Our People, Restaurant Excellence, Operating Structure, and The Brand*
>
> **Development**
> Lead the Quick Service Restaurant market by a programme of site development and profitable restaurant openings.
>
> **Our People**
> Achieve a competitive advantage through people who are high calibre, effective, well motivated and feel part of the McDonalds team in delivering the company's goals.
>
> **Restaurant Excellence**
> Focus on consistent delivery of quality, service and cleanliness through excellence in our restaurants.
>
> **Operating Structure**
> Optimise restaurant performance through the selection of the most appropriate operating, management and ownership structures.
>
> **The Brand**
> Continue to build the relationship between McDonald's and our customers in order to be a genuine part of the fabric of British society.
>
> *Source: Biz/ed*

(b)

> ### Our Reason for Being
>
> *to dedicate our business to the pursuit of social and environmental change*
>
> To creatively balance the financial and human needs of our stakeholders: employees, customers, franchisees, suppliers and shareholders.
>
> To courageously ensure that our business is ecologically sustainable, meeting the needs of the present without compromising the future.
>
> To meaningfully contribute to local, national and international communities in which we trade, by adopting a code of conduct which ensures care, honesty, fairness and respect.
>
> To passionately campaign for the protection of the environment and human and civil rights, and against animal testing within the cosmetics and toiletries industry.
>
> To tirelessly work to narrow the gap between principle and practice, while making fun, passion and care part of our daily lives.
>
> *Source: Biz/ed*

Portfolio activity

1 Describe the main aims and objectives of the business you are investigating for your Portfolio. How do they relate to the main activities and products of the business?

2 Are the aims and objectives of the business set out in a Mission Statement? If they are, copy it out and explain how it reflects the aims and objectives of the business. If they are not, draft one out, show it to your tutor, and, if you have the opportunity, discuss it with the management of the business.

meeting business objectives

the planning and monitoring process

The management of a business not only sets objectives in areas such as sales, profit, customer service and environmental sustainability, it has to measure how successful it has been in meeting those objectives. If it has not been successful, it will have to ask why it has fallen short of its target and it should take action, either by changing the objective or by taking other action within the business.

We will now look at some of the business objectives we have already discussed and see how the management of a business sets targets and then measures its success.

sales and profit targets

A business normally looks ahead – often over a twelve month period – and forecasts the amount of sales it will achieve by means of a sales budget. When you go out for the evening you will need to budget for (estimate) the amount you are going to spend (eg club entrance, drinks, taxi home). In the same way a business will budget for expenses and income. A budget is simply an estimate of money a business will receive or spend over a given time period. Alternatively a budget can project the number of items produced or sold. Businesses budget for sales and for profit (which is sales less costs). Look at the example of a six month sales budget shown below.

SALES BUDGET	January	February	March	April	May	June	Total
	£	£	£	£	£	£	£
Product A	1,000	1,000	1,000	1,000	1,000	1,000	6,000
Product B	1,500	1,500	1,500	1,500	1,500	1,500	9,000
Product C	2,500	2,500	2,500	2,500	2,500	2,500	15,000
Total	5,000	5,000	5,000	5,000	5,000	5,000	30,000

As time goes by, the management of the business can see how sales are performing. If the sales are off target, decisions will have to be made, for example:

- sales are lower than they should be – should prices be cut to encourage sales? should the sales targets be reduced and made more realistic?

- sales are higher than target – the business can now afford to expand

The management of the business has to make realistic decisions. If the management sits back and ignores the situation, the business will be in trouble!

environmental targets

As businesses and stakeholders become more aware of the need for sustainability – preserving the environment – so the setting of environmental targets has become more common. As we saw earlier in the chapter, the Co–operative Bank has set a number of environmental targets and has published its success rate . . .

> recycling of at least 15% of steel and aluminium cans purchased
> recycling of at least 15% of plastic cups purchased
> recycling of 100% of flourescent tubes
> reduction in the use of paper by 10%
> recycling of 30% of paper used

quality targets – customer services

Most businesses set quality targets, often as part of their 'Quality Assurance'. Many public services, railway operating companies for example, set targets for reliability and punctuality as part of their 'Customer Charter'. Performance against these targets is monitored carefully and regularly published. An extract from the London Underground Charter is shown below.

Improving Service

UNDERGROUND

Our commitment
London Underground aims to deliver the best possible service for all its customers. You want a quick, frequent and reliable train service, a safe, clean and welcoming station environment with up-to-date information and helpful, courteous staff. This means a continuous, demanding programme of improvements to meet rising expectations.

Our targets
To drive and measure these improvements, performance targets covering many aspects of our service have been agreed with Government as part of the Citizen's Charter programme. If you would like to know more, please contact our Customer Service Centre.

Activity 4.7

Performance targets

As part of your investigation of businesses in your area, collect examples of the setting of targets for business objectives, for example:

- sales performance (eg selling 1,000 holidays, £250,000 annual sales)

- expansion targets (eg opening 5 new shops a year)

- environmental targets (eg a 10% reduction in power used)

- quality and customer service targets (eg 95% punctuality of buses)

CHAPTER SUMMARY

- Businesses have 'aims' – in basic terms these are things that they set out to do. Sometimes business aims can conflict with each other.
- Most businesses set out to make a financial success of what they are doing, for example:
  - making as large a profit as possible
  - increasing sales each year
  - making the business expand
- Another aim of business is to beat the competition. One way of doing this is by cutting prices. One problem here is that cutting prices can reduce profits.
- Another set of aims of business involves providing quality. This can include: providing good customer service, ensuring quality in the running of the business and making sure the product is always of the highest quality.
- Another set of aims of business involves meeting the needs of the community, for example helping charities and voluntary organisations and helping to preserve the environment. These help to increase customer respect and loyalty.
- Business managers set targets – objectives – for areas such as sales and profit, environmental sustainability and customer satisfaction. They need to see how successful they are in meeting these aims so that they can take action if there is a problem and adjust their objectives if they need to.

KEY TERMS

aim	what a business sets out to do
objective	a specific target which the business intends to achieve
customer service	ensuring that customers are treated in line with set 'quality' guidelines
Quality Assurance	'quality' guidelines laid down by a business for carrying out all aspects of its operations
quality control	procedures for checking that the product of a business – whether it is a manufactured product or a service – meets established quality standards
sustainability	cutting on down on wastage of natural resources and energy, recycling and reducing pollution
mission statement	a statement setting out the aims – the mission (or vision) – of a business

MULTIPLE CHOICE QUESTIONS

1   A business which sponsors a school expedition overseas is helping to achieve which main business aim?
    A   profitability
    B   sustainability
    C   social responsibility
    D   quality assurance

2   A business which cuts down on energy waste is helping to achieve which main business aim?
    A   business expansion
    B   sustainability
    C   social responsibility
    D   quality assurance

3   A business which increases its turnover by 20% each year is achieving which main business aim?
    A   sales maximisation
    B   sustainability
    C   quality control
    D   social responsibility

4   A business which brings in improved standards for checking its products as they come in from the suppliers is achieving which main business aim?
    A   profitability
    B   business growth
    C   quality control
    D   social responsibility

5   'Sustainability' is best described as:
    A   keeping profits as high as possible
    B   beating the competition on a national basis
    C   cutting down on employees pay and perks
    D   cutting down on wastage of natural resources

6   A 'mission statement' is best described as:
    A   a statement of business profit or loss
    B   a statement of business aims
    C   a salesperson's travel plan for the week
    D   a Quality Assurance plan

Business functions and business structures

5

what this chapter is about

All businesses have to organise themselves into different areas of activity – sales or production, for example. These are known as functional areas. These functional areas help the business achieve the aims described in the last chapter. The Sales function will help it provide customer care and increase sales, Production will ensure a quality product. This chapter provides an introduction to the different function areas; later chapters will explain each function in more detail.

This chapter also shows how the people working in the functional areas are organised differently according to the size and type of the business. The organisation of the people and the functions can be illustrated diagrammatically in the form of an organisation chart.

what you will learn from this chapter

- A business needs to carry out a range of different functions. These include:
    - *human resources* – looking after the employees
    - *finance* – managing the money coming in and out
    - *administration* – providing all the backup needed
    - *production* – manufacturing a product or providing a service
    - *marketing and sales* – finding out what products the customers need; promoting and selling the products to them
    - *customer service* – looking after the customers' needs
- These functions are organised to achieve the aims of the business and can be structured in a number of ways and illustrated by means of an organisational structure chart.
    - a *hierarchical* structure shows a number of 'layers' of people, eg directors, managers, supervisors, assistants
    - a *flat* structure shows people working on a more 'equal' basis

functions in business

what does this mean?

A function in business is an area of activity in the business.

It does not matter if the business is a sole trader or a public limited company, the functions (areas of activity) remain the same, for example: buying and selling, dealing with suppliers, dealing with customers, paying bills, making sure there is soap in the cloakroom. Someone has got to do these tasks. It is up to the business to organise them in an efficient way.

different functional areas

You will see from the two Activities which follow that business activities can be classified in functional areas, even if the business is a sole trader who does everything himself or herself. The main functional areas are:

human resources looking after the employees, for example keeping employee records, training and disciplining

finance managing the money coming in and out, for example paying bills, paying wages, keeping the books

administration providing all the backup needed – the day-to-day jobs that have to be done

production manufacturing a product or providing a service

marketing and sales finding out what products the customers need and selling those products to them

customer service looking after the customers' needs, dealing with their complaints

Activity 5.1

Functional areas in business
Your school or college

Your own school or college is an organisation which in many ways is run along business lines. You are the customer and your education is the product.

Make a list of the functions which you can identify at work in your school or college.

Activity 5.2

Style on Top
A day in the life of Tina Solo

Tina Solo runs a busy town-centre hair salon 'Style on top' as a sole trader business. She employs four stylists and also works in the salon herself. She works a long day but the business is profitable and she enjoys it.

Tina's working day

08.00	Arrive at salon and open post.
08.15	Sketch out text for new advert to go in the local evening paper.
08.30	Talk to senior stylist Tracy about training of new assistant who started this week.
08.45	Try to pacify customer who rings up and wants an appointment that morning. They are fully booked until the afternoon. Customer not pleased. Manages to arrange a 15.00 appointment. The customer is happy in the end.
09.00	Salon opens. Talk to new assistant about her work and training.
09.30	Deal with bills – write out five cheques.
10.00	Work in salon, styling hair.
12.00	Have sandwiches and make telephone call to book advert in local paper.
12.15	Telephone accountant with a query about tax position of new employee. Is she to be put on an emergency code?
12.30	Have to have words with one stylist about the shoes she is wearing. They are not suitable for the job.
13.00	Back to work in salon, styling hair.
15.00	Have a ten minute chat with the new assistant during her coffee break – how is she getting on? Then back to work again in the salon.
17.00	Salon closing time. Door locked.
17.30	Salon alarm set. Go home.
19.00	Tina spends an hour at home writing up the cash book.
20.00	To the fitness centre for a workout. Suggest to a friend that she visits the salon for tinting.

activities

1 Draw up 6 columns on an A4 sheet of paper and head them up as follows:

human resources	finance	administration	production	marketing and sales	customer service
		08.00 *Open post*		*08.15* *Sketch out* *advert*	

2 Go through the list of Tina's activities during the day and write each business activity in the appropriate column, together with the time it takes place. Two of the activities are already entered to give you a start.

3 Do all the business activities take place on the business premises? What does your answer tell you about the life of a sole trader?

departments in business organisations

Tina in the last Activity was a sole trader who undertook most of the business functions herself. Many sole traders are able to cope with the workload of the back-up functions such as finance and human resources because the scale of their operations and the number of people they employ are limited.

If the workload gets too much it is always possible to pay someone else to do the specialised work. The sole trader could always employ a book-keeper to deal with the financial records or a bureau or an accountant to manage the payroll.

the need for departments

If the business is a large company with many employees, customers and suppliers, each business function is likely to be carried out by an individual department. There is no hard and fast rule about what the departments should be. It will all depend on the nature and size of the business. Set out on the next page are diagrams showing the departments which might be found in a manufacturing business and a services business.

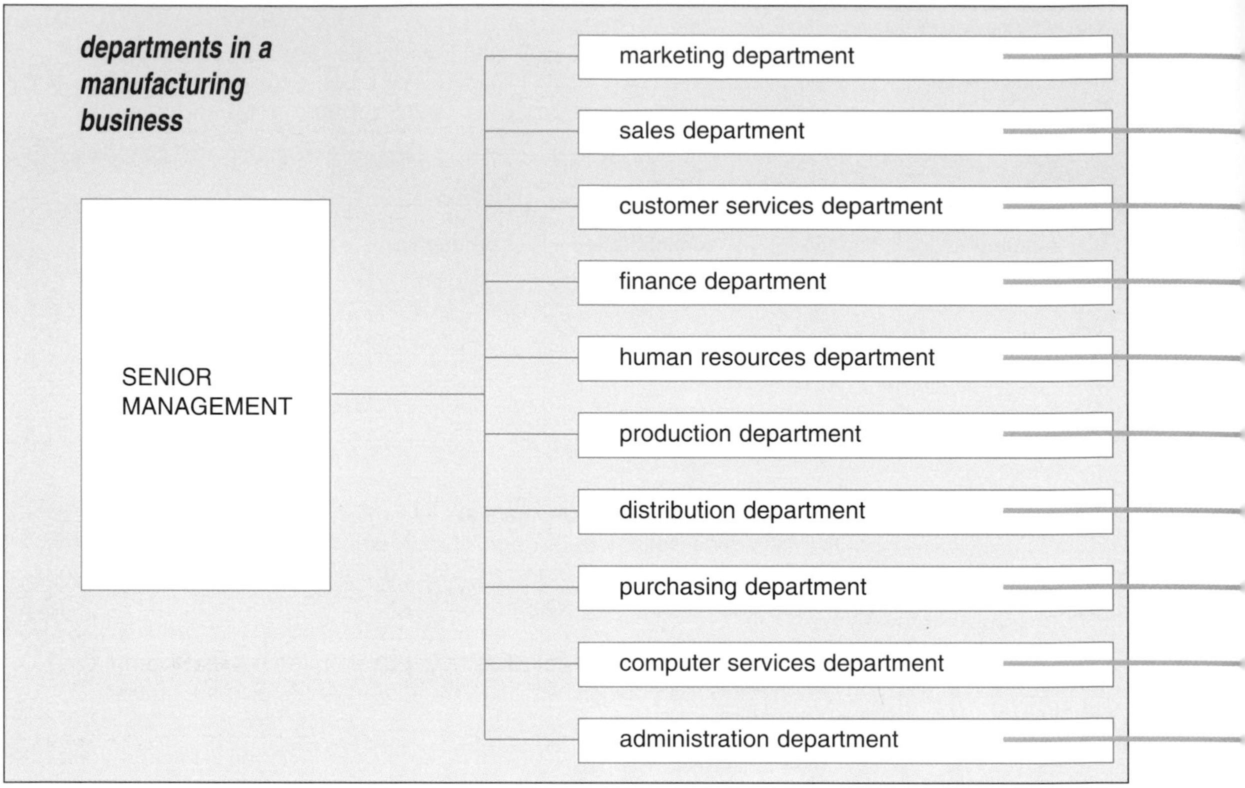

departments in a manufacturing business

SENIOR MANAGEMENT

- marketing department
- sales department
- customer services department
- finance department
- human resources department
- production department
- distribution department
- purchasing department
- computer services department
- administration department

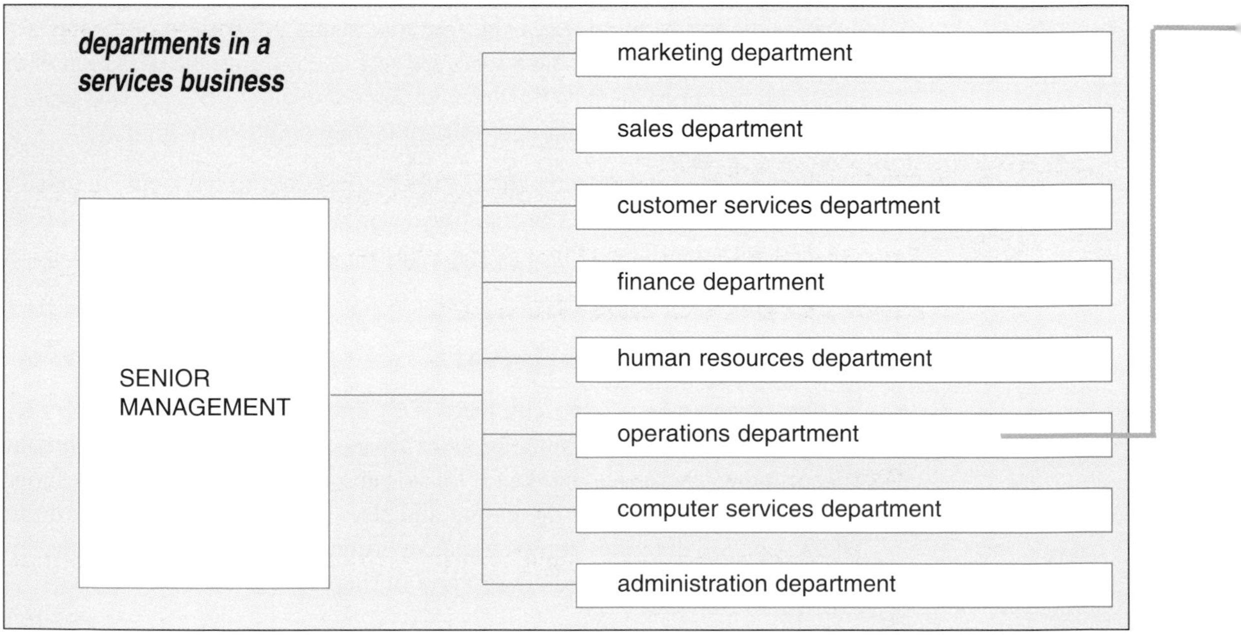

departments in a services business

SENIOR MANAGEMENT

- marketing department
- sales department
- customer services department
- finance department
- human resources department
- operations department
- computer services department
- administration department

| MARKETING | finds out what customers want, fixes a price, promotes the products |

| SALES | sells the goods – using sales reps, telephone sales, internet sites |

| CUSTOMER SERVICES | deals with customer enquiries/complaints, provides after-sales service |

| FINANCE | keeps accounts, sets financial targets, raises money |

| HUMAN RESOURCES | keeps employee records, carries out hiring, firing and training |

| PRODUCTION | research and development, product manufacture, quality control |

| DISTRIBUTION | sends out the manufactured goods by most efficient method |

| PURCHASING | buys the materials and services used, looking for value-for-money |

| COMPUTER SERVICES | looks after the computers used in production and in the office |

| ADMINISTRATION | provides the back-up needed by other departments, security, premises |

| OPERATIONS | organises and co-ordinates the providing of services to the customers |

Activity 5.3

Departments in manufacturing and services businesses

Study the diagrams on these two facing pages.

1 What departments are to be found only in a manufacturing business? What do these departments do?

2 What department is to be found only in a services business? What does this department do?

organisational structures

sole trader – flat structure

Let us take as an example Asaf Hussain, the owner of a small shop. He is a sole trader who employs four part-time sales assistants. The structure of his business will look like this:

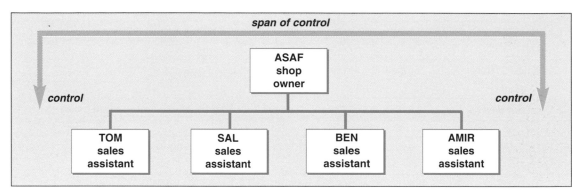

You will see from this diagram that:

- the structure is *flat* in shape; there is only one level of command – Asaf himself tells the assistants what to do

- Asaf has a span of control which extends over the four assistants; if he had more assistants, it would extend over those as well; a 'span of control' is the number of people over whom you have control – often the wider the span, the more difficult it is to keep control (ask any teacher!)

- Asaf presumably carries out the main functions of the business – finance, administration, human resources, marketing; his sales assistants do the selling

Activity 5.4

Flat structures
Asaf opens a new shop

Asaf decides to open a new shop in another neighbourhood. He has taken on four new sales assistants Pip, Dot, Sue and Jon and has recruited Hughie to manage the new shop.

1   Draw up a structure chart for the new shop.

2   Do you think that the new shop will cause any problems for Asaf's running of the business? Will Asaf have to manage all the employees?

other examples of flat structures

The flat structure is not confined to sole traders. Your own class is a flat structure with many students and one teacher or lecturer in charge! Your school or college is also likely to have a flat structure.

A current trend in large business organisations is for each operating area to be independent and to take its own decisions. 'Operating areas' could include:

- regional divisions, eg North, South, Midlands, London, East Anglia
- product divisions, eg Honda cars, bikes, garden power tools

Look at the charts in the Activity below.

Activity 5.5

Identifying flat structures

1   What types of business or organisation do these structure charts illustrate?

2   Try and find more examples of flat organisational structures – for example in the manufacturing and services sectors

3   What problems of control do you think might face the person (head, manager or managing company) at the top of a flat structure?

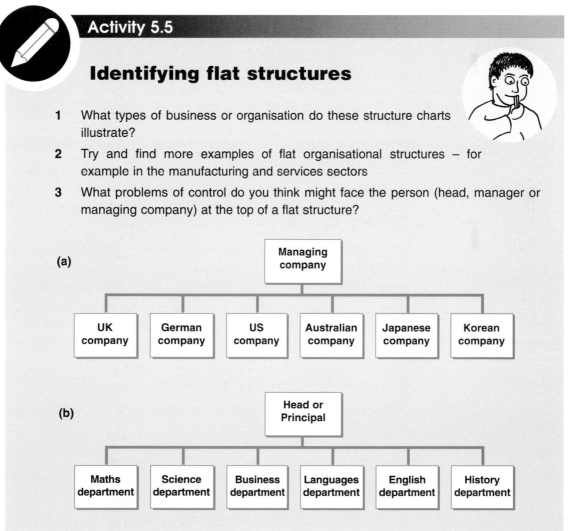

(a)

Managing company

| UK company | German company | US company | Australian company | Japanese company | Korean company |

(b)

Head or Principal

| Maths department | Science department | Business department | Languages department | English department | History department |

'tall' hierarchical structures

what is a hierarchy?

A hierarchy is a series of levels of people, each level controlled by the level above it.

Large organisations, public limited companies, for example, may have thousands of employees. They are likely to have a more elaborate and 'tall' organisational structure which has:

- more levels of hierarchy
- more division into functional areas such as sales and finance

The structure chart set out on the next page is that of a manufacturing company. As you will see it is very different from the flat structure of the sole trader business shown on page 96. It is 'tall' and has many layers.

structure of the hierarchy

Each horizontal level represents a step in the level of importance and responsibility of the staff:

- the managing director is responsible for communicating company policy and making sure it is carried out
- the other directors are responsible for making decisions affecting their function areas (eg sales, finance, production) and communicating those decisions to the people working in the function areas
- the company secretary is the director responsible for the administration of the company
- managers are in charge of the departments and answer to the directors; there may be different layers of managers in the hierarchy; they are responsible for carrying out or delegating the directors' decisions
- supervisors are in charge of the day-to-day running of the departments and normally work alongside the production and administrative staff; sales representatives and design staff are also on this level
- production, administrative and support staff carry out the day-to-day routine work of the company

up and down the hierarchy

Each horizontal level represents a level of authority. These are seen in action in cases of:

- *instructions* – passed down from one level to another

- *problems* – referred up to a higher level
- *disciplinary matters and complaints* – also referred to higher levels

functions in the organisation

You will see from the structure chart that the company is subdivided into vertical columns, each representing a particular function or group of functions, eg sales and marketing, finance, production and distribution. Generally speaking the larger the business, the more specialised function areas it will have.

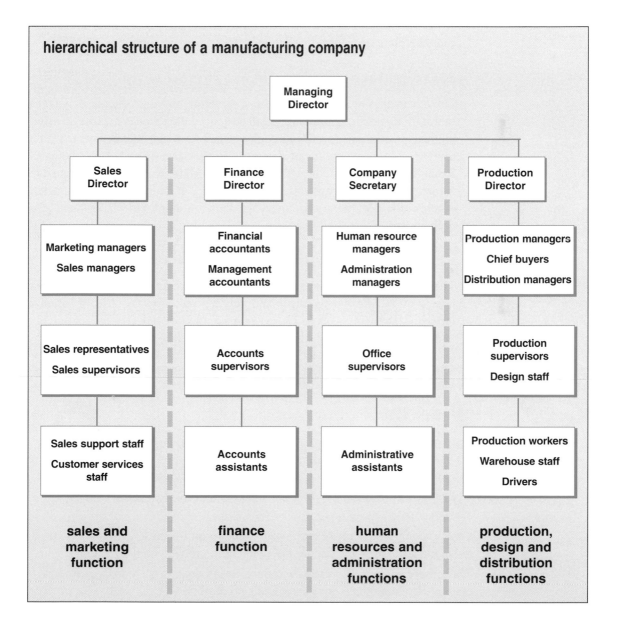

'flat' and 'tall' structures compared

advantages of a 'flat' organisation

A good example of a flat organisational structure is the sole trader who employs a number of staff. The owner is – or should be – in control of the way the business is run. He or she makes the decisions, supervises staff and deals with customers. He or she can pick up any problems immediately and do something about them. For example a sole trader can rapidly take decisions: to make a product, to change suppliers and to change prices. The other advantage of a flat structure is that staff are often more independent and can take more decisions themselves – this makes the job more interesting.

disadvantages of a 'tall' organisation

The advantages of a flat organisational structure highlight the disadvantages of a 'tall' hierarchical structure. A tall structure often means that the decision making process has to pass through several layers of management, which involves a loss of time. It can also result in the decision makers not being in touch with customers or with lower level staff, the source of valuable feedback about company sales and products. It must be said that a tall organisation does have the advantage that the employees have their jobs defined very clearly and that there is a clear 'line of command'.

why are organisations becoming flatter?

There is a trend for businesses to streamline their operations by stripping out layers of middle management and relying more on the use of smaller independent business units. These can make their own decisions, act quickly and achieve the sales the 'taller' businesses may lose out on.

Activity 5.6

'Flat' or 'tall'?

State whether the comments quoted below are likely to come from a flat or a tall business. Give reasons for your decision.

1   'I think we should drop our prices tomorrow. We should sell more that way. Just change the price tickets and the computer stock records.'

2   'I told my supervisor about the quality problem on Product x. It has gone up to his manager now, but we are still getting the problem coming through.'

3   'Customers seem to like the new orange lollies best, but Production are still churning out the purple ones like there's no tomorrow!'

matrix structure

Another form of structure which needs to be examined is the matrix or 'project team' structure.

Sometimes in an organisation it is necessary to take people out of their specific function areas – finance, sales, production – to form teams to work on specific projects. The project team or 'matrix' concept originated in the aerospace industry where new projects were essential to keep manufacturers in business. Project teams needed to work quickly in order to launch a new product first, before competing businesses brought out their version.

The matrix concept involves a different form of organisational structure chart. Look at the example below which sets out a traditional functional structure which is used to staff two project teams.

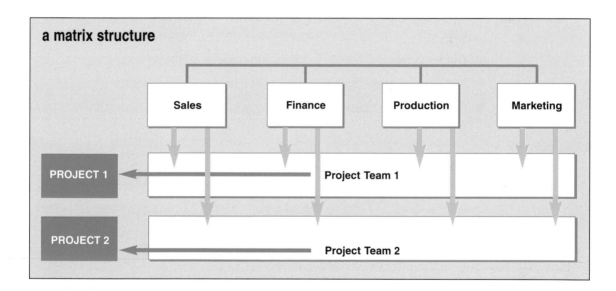

a matrix structure

Activity 5.7

Matrix structures

Tangerine PLC manufacturers computers. It wants to set up a project team for a new design of laptop computer, the Pip. The company is divided into finance, sales, marketing and production departments. Draw a suitable matrix structure chart showing how the project team could be set up.

CHAPTER SUMMARY

- Businesses organise themselves into areas of activity – these are known as functional areas.

- Whatever the size of the business the functions remain largely the same:
  - *human resources* – looking after the employees
  - *finance* – managing the money coming in and out
  - *administration* – providing all the backup needed
  - *production* – manufacturing a product or providing a service
  - *marketing and sales* – finding out what products the customers need; selling the products to them
  - *customer service* – looking after the customers' needs

- Organisation of businesses into functional areas enables them to achieve their aims.

- Businesses are structured in different ways according to the type and size of business. Business structures can be shown by means of structure charts.

- Common types of structure are flat organisations and tall organisations.

- Flat organisations have fewer levels of management than taller organisations.

- Communication within businesses is generally speaking more difficult in taller organisations.

KEY TERMS

functional area	a type of activity carried out in a business, eg finance, sales, marketing
department	a division in a larger business which looks after one or more functional areas
human resources	the business functional area which looks after the employees
production	the business functional area in which the product (which can be a manufactured item or a service) is produced
flat structure	a structure in which people work on a more 'equal' basis with few levels of management
hierarchical structure	a structure with a number of 'layers' of people, eg directors, managers, supervisors, assistants
matrix structure	a structure showing the use of project teams

MULTIPLE CHOICE QUESTIONS

1   The business decision to place an advert for a new product in a magazine will take place in which functional area of the business?
    A   human resources
    B   finance
    C   marketing
    D   production

2   The business decision to place a job advert in a local newspaper will take place in which functional area of the business?
    A   human resources
    B   finance
    C   marketing
    D   customer service

3   Which functional area of the business will deal with setting up a new alarm system in the business premises?
    A   human resources
    B   administration
    C   finance
    D   customer service

4   A span of control is best described as
    A   the length of time a manager stays in his or her post
    B   the number of people a manager is controlled by
    C   the number of people a manager has to supervise
    D   the number of layers of management in a hierarchy

5   A business which has a single manager and 40 assistants has a
    A   flat structure
    B   matrix structure
    C   tall structure
    D   hierarchical structure

6   Communication between top management and assistants is best achieved in a business which has
    A   a matrix structure
    B   a hierarchical structure
    C   a tall structure
    D   a flat structure

6

Marketing and sales

what this chapter is about

No business can survive without its customers. Many businesses nowadays set out to be 'customer-focused' or 'customer-centred'. These terms mean that their main aims are to find out what customers want and then to produce and sell those products in the most 'customer friendly' way.

In this chapter we will see how the marketing and sales function in a business is central to these aims.

what you will learn from this chapter

- The marketing function in a business aims to:
  - provide products that customers want
  - at a price that they will pay
  - promote the products effectively
  - making them easily available to the customer

- Marketing involves a number of different stages:
  - market research – finding out what customers need and want
  - product design – a manufactured item or a service
  - pricing the product at the right level – high enough to make a profit and low enough to attract sales
  - promoting it to the customers using advertising and other publicity methods
  - selling it and getting customer feedback
- The sales function is part of the marketing process. Some businesses have a separate sales department.
- There are many different methods of selling, ranging from the traditional sales 'rep' through to e-commerce (the use of the internet for on-line purchasing).

what is marketing?

some definitions

Marketing has been described as:

Getting the right product to the right people at the right price

The marketing function is therefore crucial to the success of any business. Products which have been 'flops' can often attribute their failure to poor marketing:

- a product which nobody wants – obviously the market research in this case has not been very thorough
- a product at the wrong price – not necessarily at too high a price – sometimes a product can be priced too low – people think of it as cheap
- a product aimed at the wrong type of person – motor bikes for grannies
- a product which is difficult to get hold of to buy – the business has not thought about distribution

Successful marketing results from concentrating on what is known as the '4 Ps':

Product

Finding out and producing what the customer wants, for example a type of car or a type of holiday. This will require detailed market research to see what people want and what demand there is for the product.

Price

Fixing a price at which the customer will buy the product. This will require research into what the competition are charging and what the customer is prepared to pay.

Promotion

Deciding how you are going to promote the product using advertising, publicity and special offers.

Place

Deciding on where and how you are going to sell it – locally, nationally, over the counter, by phone, over the internet?

---

the marketing process

The marketing of a product follows a number of stages. These apply equally if the product is a manufactured item like a car or a service like a holiday. Study these stages in the diagram below.

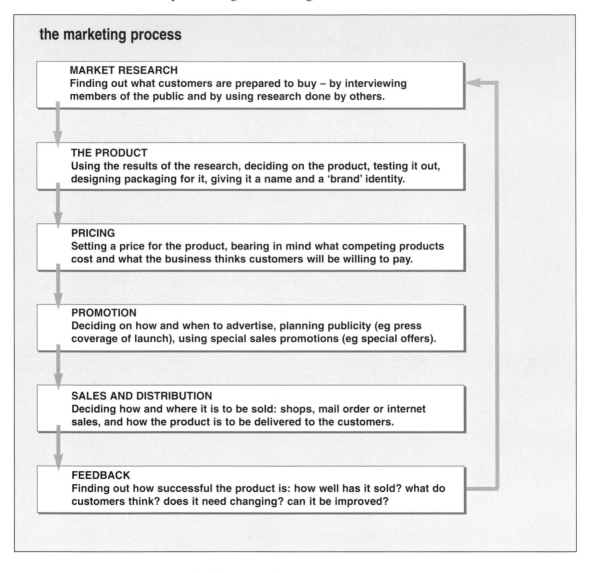

the marketing process

MARKET RESEARCH
Finding out what customers are prepared to buy – by interviewing members of the public and by using research done by others.

THE PRODUCT
Using the results of the research, deciding on the product, testing it out, designing packaging for it, giving it a name and a 'brand' identity.

PRICING
Setting a price for the product, bearing in mind what competing products cost and what the business thinks customers will be willing to pay.

PROMOTION
Deciding on how and when to advertise, planning publicity (eg press coverage of launch), using special sales promotions (eg special offers).

SALES AND DISTRIBUTION
Deciding how and where it is to be sold: shops, mail order or internet sales, and how the product is to be delivered to the customers.

FEEDBACK
Finding out how successful the product is: how well has it sold? what do customers think? does it need changing? can it be improved?

a marketing cycle

You will see from the diagram that the marketing process is in fact a cycle – it goes round in a circle. The feedback stage (at the bottom) has an arrow going back to the market research stage at the top. A business will not normally just launch a product and then let it remain unchanged. People will soon get tired of it and want something new.

A business selling a car or a holiday will want to get feedback from the customer – often from a questionnaire – so that the product can be modified and improved over time. Marketing starts and ends with market research – finding out what the customer needs or wants.

customers and consumers – needs and wants

So far in this chapter we have talked about 'customers'. You will also come across the term 'consumers'. What is the difference?

A *consumer* is a member of the general public who receives and makes use of goods and services. The *customer* is the individual who has to buy and pay for the goods or services. These are not necessarily the same person. Take, for example, a kid sister who watches TV commercials for toys at weekend breakfast-time viewing. The child is the *consumer*, the parent who has to go off to buy the Barbie Doll is the *customer*.

Businesses sell their products because there is a *demand* for them. In the example of the Barbie Doll the toy company has carefully targeted the child and cleverly created a demand for the product. But is the doll needed?

You need to be able to tell the difference between

- a consumer's *needs* – items that are essential, eg clothes, bread
- a consumer's *wants* – items that the consumer can be persuaded by clever marketing to buy, eg body lotion, a video

Activity 6.1

Customer or consumer?

Needs or wants?

Either individually or in small groups make a list of the products you or your family have bought over the last week – say about ten in all. These products can be items such as food or services such a bus journey or visit to the cinema.

1   For each product identify who is the customer and who is the consumer.

2   Identify whether each product is a need or a want.

Individually construct a table on a piece of paper (or wordprocessor file) listing the products down the page and setting up 4 columns headed 'Products needed' ,'Products wanted', 'Customer' and 'Consumer'. Tick the columns against the appropriate product.

Make comments about your lists. Did you find it easy to decide what was a want and what was a need?

How are the products made attractive in order to appeal to our wants?

market segments

The buying public is not one single market, it is made up of a number of different market *segments* – different types of consumer.

Businesses need to classify consumers into market segments so that they can direct their marketing effort towards the right people. There would be little point, for example, trying to sell expensive holidays to people who cannot afford them. Common methods of *segmentation* of consumers is by:

- age
- gender (male or female)
- wealth and income
- geographical area
- lifestyle (fashion and taste)

We will look at all these in turn.

classification by age

Producers of goods carefully distinguish between different age groups when marketing their products, as we saw in the case of the Barbie doll. Commonly accepted age groups include:

age	buying group
0 – 10	child
11 – 17	teenager
18 – 35	young working person
36 – 59	mature working person
60 plus	retired person

Not only do these different age groups have different needs and wants, they also have different amounts of money to spend. The following figures show the 'wealth' – the value of what individuals in different age groups own:

age	average wealth (£)
16 - 19	300
20 - 29	2,200
30 - 39	27,000
40 - 49	66,900
50 - 59	104,900
60 - 69	133,500
70 - 79	119,300
80 plus	92,700

Activity 6.2

Market segments
customer age groups

1   Make lists of the products which are specifically aimed at the
    following age groups (for example – types of footwear, types of
    holiday, drinks):

    11 - 17 years

    18 - 25 years

    60 + years

2   Draw up a simple bar chart showing the average wealth for different age groups.
    Use the figures from the bottom of the previous page. If you can, use a computer
    spreadsheet to process the figures and produce a suitable chart.

    Why do you think businesses produce products and provide services that are
    targeting retired people as a market segment?

classification by gender

Although we are supposed to live in an age where the sexes are equal, there
will always be differences between what men want and what women want.
Producers will always exploit those differences by marketing products 'for
him' and products 'for her'. These differences can be obvious as in the
clothing, cosmetics and perfumes industries. They can also be more subtle,
as you should be able to find out in the next Student Activity.

Activity 6.3

Market segments
products for 'him' and 'her'

Divide into groups of three or four students and find examples of the
following products which are more attractive to one sex than to the other. Try
not to argue too much! Compare your findings with those of other groups.

(a)   types of car

(b)   brands of drink

Discuss in class what it is about the products that makes them appeal to one sex rather
than the other. Does advertising have anything to do with it?

classification by geographical area

Businesses are able to classify customers according to the type of area in which they live. Country and city areas will clearly have different types of consumer living in them. Classification is also possible by postcode. You will know that in your locality certain areas are different from others.

One form of computer database classification is ACORN:

A Classification Of Residential Neighbourhoods

As a postcode covers a relatively small number of households, it is possible to classify each postcode area into a specific neighbourhood 'type'.

classification by lifestyle

This type of classification is less straightforward than the examples of segmentation already given. The basis of this type of classification is to view each consumer as a 'type' which will combine elements of social class, personality and attitude. One example is the 'Values and Lifestyle' (VALS) approach which classes various types of adult into groups, including:

achievers	the 'my life is a success story' people who are well-off and conscious of status symbols – big houses, smart cars
strivers	people who are on the way to being achievers but are less well-off and very conscious of what others think about them

All of these lifestyle types need products that indicate status and levels of wealth. Further lifestyle types are described in the Activity which follows.

Activity 6.4

Market segments
lifestyle types

Listed below are three more lifestyle types. Suggest four or more specific products (items or services) for each type of consumer which you think would be suitable for that lifestyle.

YAKS (Young, Adventurous, Keen and Single)

Aged 18 to 24, status seekers, no large financial commitments, with modest income.

EWES (Experts With Expensive Style)

Aged 25 to 34, with high income, large mortgage, no children. The high life.

OWLS (Older With Less Stress)

Aged over 55, mortgage paid off, children left home, healthy and wealthy.

market research methods

It is the role of the Marketing Department in a business that is making a product or providing a service to be aware of the different classifications of consumer – the segmentation of the market described on the previous pages. Different types of consumer will require contrasting types of product, eg different types of cars, clothing, holidays. Producers are also aware of changing patterns of consumer behaviour: certain products will stop selling well, other products will suddenly 'take off'. Market research involves the collecting of information about what is happening in the mind of the consumer and in the market segments to which the consumer belongs. Information can be gathered in two ways – field research and desk research.

field research

Field research, also known as primary research, means communicating directly with consumers – in the street, over the telephone, through the post – by means of interviews and questionnaires. The questionnaire on the next page is part of an extensive national shopping survey.

Nowadays more sophisticated shopping information can be obtained by retailers who issue 'loyalty cards' to their customers. Each time a shopper uses a 'loyalty' card every single item purchased is recorded, which when linked with the purchaser's address, enables the seller to build up a very accurate picture of who buys what, and where they live.

desk research

Desk research, also known as secondary research, involves looking at published material – reference books, statistics, and marketing reports by specialist companies. This allows the Marketing Department to find out about trends relating to consumers' income and expenditure.

One source of statistical information is the Government Statistical Service which publishes through The Stationery Office a number of annual reports, including:

* *Family Spending*
* *Social Trends*

These publications, which are normally available in reference libraries, make fascinating reading. *Social Trends* in particular is a mine of information about income and consumer spending, covering areas such as population changes, household and family income and spending and leisure activities.

The extract on the next page relates age groups and ownership of mobile phones.

13. YOUR INTERESTS

01 How many times in the last year have you bought goods/services via the mail?
1 ☐ 1   2 ☐ 2-3   3 ☐ 4-5   4 ☐ 6 plus   9 ☐ None

02 What types of music do you regularly listen to?
1 ☐ Classical/Opera   3 ☐ Light Classical
2 ☐ Rock and Roll   4 ☐ Eighties
5 ☐ Easy Listening

03 Does anyone in your household buy, or would anyone consider buying books/videos/magazines/software in the following interest areas:
01 ☐ History   09 ☐ Health Foods
02 ☐ Ancient History   10 ☐ Slimming
03 ☐ Science Fiction/Fantasy   11 ☐ Railway
04 ☐ Military/Aviation   12 ☐ Classics
05 ☐ Children's Interests   13 ☐ Art
06 ☐ New Age   14 ☐ Computers
07 ☐ Mystery/Myth   15 ☐ Golfing
08 ☐ Crime/Thriller

04 Please tick all the newspapers that are REGULARLY read by your family: 99 ☐ None

	Daily	Sunday		Daily	Sunday
Express	01 ☐	21 ☐	Guardian	11 ☐	
Independent	02 ☐	22 ☐	Star	12 ☐	
Mail	03 ☐	23 ☐	Sun	13 ☐	
Mirror	04 ☐	24 ☐	News of the		29 ☐
Sport	05 ☐	25 ☐	World		
Telegraph	06 ☐	26 ☐	Observer		30 ☐
Times	07 ☐	27 ☐	People		31 ☐
Other/Local	08 ☐	28 ☐	Post		32 ☐
Daily Record	09 ☐		Sunday Mail		33 ☐
Financial Times	10 ☐		(Scotland)		

05 How often do you buy your main Sunday newspaper?
2 ☐ 1-2 times a month
1 ☐ 3-4 times a month   3 ☐ Less often

06 Is your main daily newspaper delivered?
1 ☐ Yes   9 ☐ No

07 On what day(s) do you buy your main daily newspaper? (If not everyday, please tick all that apply)   9 ☐ Do not buy
1 ☐ Every day   5 ☐ Thursday
2 ☐ Monday   6 ☐ Friday
3 ☐ Tuesday   7 ☐ Saturday
4 ☐ Wednesday

08 Do you subscribe or would you consider subscribing to any of the following?

	Currently subscribe	Would consider
Which?	01 ☐	17 ☐
Gardening Which?	02 ☐	18 ☐
New Scientist	03 ☐	19 ☐
New Statesman	04 ☐	20 ☐
Newsweek	05 ☐	21 ☐
Britannia Music	06 ☐	22 ☐
Reader's Digest	07 ☐	23 ☐
Spectator	08 ☐	24 ☐
The Softback Preview	09 ☐	25 ☐
Books for Children	10 ☐	26 ☐
Time	11 ☐	27 ☐
Disney Book Club	12 ☐	28 ☐
Red House Books	13 ☐	29 ☐
House of Grolier	14 ☐	30 ☐
National Geographic	15 ☐	31 ☐
The Economist	16 ☐	32 ☐

09 Do you have or are you considering buying a mobile phone?
1 ☐ Yes   2 ☐ Considering   9 ☐ No

10 If you have a mobile phone, which network are you connected to?   1 ☐ Orange
2 ☐ Cellnet   3 ☐ One 2 One   4 ☐ Vodafone

11 When did you purchase your mobile phone?
1 ☐ 0-3 mths   3 ☐ 7-9 mths   5 ☐ 12 mths +
2 ☐ 4-6 mths   4 ☐ 10-12 mths

field research – extract from National Shopping Survey

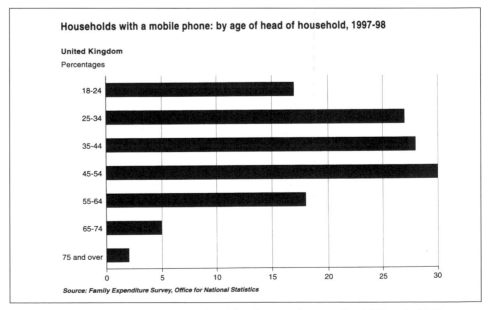

Households with a mobile phone: by age of head of household, 1997-98

United Kingdom

Percentages

Source: Family Expenditure Survey, Office for National Statistics

desk research – ownership of mobile phones, Source: Social Trends 1999,
Office for National Statistics © Crown Copyright 2000

Activity 6.5

Field and desk research
mobile phones

On the previous page are an extract from a field research questionnaire and a table from from 'Social Trends 1999' (desk research). Both are sources of market research which provide information about mobile phones.

Assume that you work in the Marketing Department of a business which wishes to sell mobile phones by mail order.

1   Which of the two forms of research – field or desk research – will be cheaper?

2   Which of the two forms of research will be more up-to-date?

3   What have been the trends in mobile phone pricing since the Social Trends data was published?

4   What do you think have been the trends in the age groups of people owning mobile phones since the Social Trends data was published?

5   Bearing in mind all these factors what market segments – eg male/female, age group, social class – would you aim to sell your mobile phones to?

6   Suggest some ways of reaching those market segments.

Portfolio activity: Find out from the Marketing Department of the business that you are investigating for your Portfolio what field and desk research it uses when investigating the market for its products.

pricing – fixing the 'right price'

So far the Marketing Department has carried out its market research and decided on its product and the market segments it is targeting. It will now need to fix a price. It is important that it gets the price right. There are a number of different factors it will need to consider. Many of them relate to the basic aims of the business:

making a profit

The business will want to cover the cost of its product, or it may make a loss. If it is producing a hi-tech product such as a minidisc player or digital TV it will want to recover not only the cost of manufacturing the product but also the cost of research and development – which can be very high.

beating the competition – maximising sales

The Marketing Department may be able to get people to buy its product rather than a competing product by pricing it *below* the price of the competing products. This is done to achieve the business aim of maximising sales. When it is carried out on a large scale by competing businesses it is known as a 'price war' and can often have the effect of dramatically cutting business profits. It has happened in products areas such as car fuel, mobile phones and internet provision.

providing a quality product at a quality price

A business should always make sure that it is not undercharging for a product, particularly if it is a quality product. People sometimes buy a product:

- *because* it is expensive and it is seen by other consumers as being a quality product – eg a Mercedes car or a designer label jacket

- because a high price indicates that it is a quality product and *worth buying*

Activity 6.6

Pricing the product
getting the price right

1   The price of mobile phones has dropped dramatically in recent years. Why do you think this has happened? What business aim is being followed when prices are cut?

    Can you think of any other products (including services) where the prices have been 'slashed'? See if you can find evidence of how this has affected business profits in the businesses which have cut their prices.

2   Investigate the price of 'cut-price' sliced bread in your local supermarket and compare it with the price charged at your nearest small food store. Write down your findings in a suitable table format. What is the difference in price? What effect do you think this pricing has on

    (a)   the profits on supermarket bread?

    (b)   the profits of other products in the supermarket?

    (c)   the profits of the small food store?

3   The Ferrari is a high performance quality car built in limited numbers in Italy. Many models cost over £100,000 each.

    Why do you think people will spend so much on a car when there is not even room to put their shopping in the boot?

Portfolio activity: Investigate the pricing policy of the business you are studying for your Portfolio. How does the business achieve its main aims (eg profit or sales maximisation) through the way it prices its products?

promoting the product

the promotion process

It is sometimes thought that promotion is the same as advertising. People often think of a major product promotion as being a combination of TV commercials, roadside hoardings, and newspaper adverts. Advertising is, in fact, only part of the process of promotion which brings the product to the attention of the consumer. The overall promotion process involves the Marketing Department of a business in a number of different stages:

- advertising – informing the public about the product
- branding – creating an image of the product at the point of sale
- packaging – presenting the product in an attractive way
- publicity in the media, special promotions and sponsorship

We will deal with these in turn.

advertising

Advertising involves:

- identifying the right market segment(s) for the product and making sure that the group(s) of consumers targeted need or want the product
- identifying the right media for the advertising – newspapers, magazines, TV, radio, cinema, leaflets
- creating the right message
- getting the timing right (eg advertising sunshine holidays in winter!)
- getting the cost right – making sure that you are getting value for money for your promotion

Activity 6.7

Advertising
getting the message across

Video a selection of TV adverts to show to the whole class.

Discuss in class:

(a) whom was the advert aimed at?

(b) how did it appeal to its target audience?

(c) how much information did it actually provide?

(d) did it need to provide much information?

branding

Branding is the process of identifying a product in the minds of consumers by creating a name or logo for that product which will persuade the consumer to buy it.

Examples of branding include:

- a product name which is well known, eg Coca-Cola, Persil
- using the manufacturer's name to indicate quality, eg Nike, Mercedes
- using the retailer's name to suggest value for money, eg supermarket 'own brands'

People buy branded goods because they know what they are getting. There have been bitter disputes about branding, particularly when 'own brands' from the supermarkets have copied the packaging (colour and shape) of the major independent brands. Next time you are in a supermarket, compare 'Head and Shoulders' shampoo, instant coffee or a Cola drink with the shop brand.

Activity 6.8

Branding
creating an identity

Find your own examples of brands from adverts and labels. Create a collage using these examples and add comments saying what type of brands they are (product name, manufacturer's name, retailer's name) and how effective you think the brands are.

Portfolio activity

Does the business you are studying for your Portfolio have its own branded products ? Products may be items for sale or services. How successfully do you think it uses brand names. Add them to your collage. How successful do you think they are?

packaging

Packaging means more than just the box or wrapper a product is sold in – it involves all aspects of presentation. The Marketing Department has to ensure that the packaging gives the consumer the 'right image' of the product. This can involve:

• its shape and size and general appearance

• colour (look at the use of white for hygiene products)

• ease of use (can it be opened easily – sometimes a problem with modern packaging!)

• environmental factors – is the material bio-degradeable?

Activity 6.9

Packaging
what makes it successful?

Collect examples of what you think is

• good packaging

• bad packaging

'Good' and 'bad' can relate to the materials used, appearance, ease of opening, and whether the packaging is 'environmentally friendly'. Discuss in class what factors make packaging successful or unsuccessful. Make a list of what is good and bad about the packaging that you have investigated.

publicity and public relations

Publicity means appearing in the news. Publicity is always the objective of any producer of goods and services, and will help greatly with promotion – for example, the lady climber rescued in the Scottish Highlands, who when dug out of a snowdrift said 'I could just do with a glass of Guinness.'

Public relations, on the other hand, is the area of the Marketing Department which looks after the public image of the business, making public statements when things go well or badly.

special promotions

Promotions involve a business marketing a specific product, or range of products, by using special offers and techniques which will attract the interest of the consumer. These methods can include:

• money off this purchase – two for the price of one, coupons, bulk packs

• extra benefits – eg 'air miles', free gifts, money off next purchase

TWO FOR THE PRICE OF ONE

BUY TWO – GET ONE EXTRA FREE

COUPON
5p off your next purchase of Britax furniture polish

5% discount for purchases of 6 or more bottles of wine

sponsorship – 'cause-related' marketing

Sponsorship is a well-known means of promoting the name of an organisation. Many sports and arts organisations rely on support from sponsors: in return for a money payment, the name of the sponsor is mentioned prominently on publicity material and at the sponsored event. The best form of sponsorship for a business is where there is TV coverage. Many televised sports events carry the sponsor's name prominently.

Famous sports personalities are also sponsored, and as part of the deal wear clothes or footwear with the sponsor's name: for example David Beckham with Adidas boots, Ronaldo and Nike.

Charity sponsorship is a well-established practice. 'Cause-related marketing' is the phrase used to describe the way a business uses sponsorship to help its marketing effort. Many well-known companies have 'adopted' a charity or worthy cause, help to fund it and use its name prominently in its publicity material.

Activity 6.10

Sponsorship
sports and causes

1   Collect examples of business sponsorship of sport. This can take the form of sponsorship of a team, an event, or a personality. What evidence can you find of a link between the sponsor's products and the sport? Write down the advantages to the business and to the sportsperson of the sponsorship deal.

2   Find examples of 'cause-related' marketing – businesses adopting and helping a particular charity. Make a list of the examples that you find. What benefits are there for the businesses in this type of arrangement?

organising marketing in a business

The way the marketing function operates in a business will depend on the size of the business. If the business is a sole trader, the owner is likely to do all the marketing. If the owner sees the business as 'customer centred' and is a capable salesperson, the product marketing should be successful. If marketing is neglected by a sole trader the chances of the business surviving are considerably reduced.

A larger organisation – such as the business you may be investigating as part of your coursework – is likely to have a marketing department along the lines of the type we have seen so far in this chapter. A typical structure showing the marketing functions in a limited company is shown below. This business could equally be a manufacturer or a services provider – a biscuit company or a bank. Some marketing job descriptions are set out on the next page.

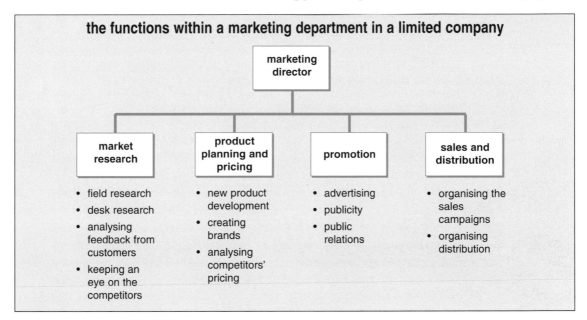

the functions within a marketing department in a limited company

marketing director

market research	**product planning and pricing**	**promotion**	**sales and distribution**
• field research	• new product development	• advertising	• organising the sales campaigns
• desk research	• creating brands	• publicity	• organising distribution
• analysing feedback from customers	• analysing competitors' pricing	• public relations	
• keeping an eye on the competitors			

Activity 6.11

Marketing roles

Portfolio activity

Produce a questionnaire to ask the Marketing Manager from the business you are investigating how the different individuals with different job roles communicate and work with each other to achieve the marketing objectives of the business. Write up your findings in a similar way to the examples on the next page.

Jobs in the Marketing Department of a limited company

FRANK HANCOCK, MARKETING DIRECTOR

"I am in charge of all of the marketing sections, such as marketing research, product policy, promotion, sales and the distribution of goods. I also liaise with the accountants on what prices to charge. All of the managers of these sections meet with me regularly to make sure that we are all working to the same goals. We call this maintaining the 'corporate image'. All in all there are about thirty people working for me.

Once a month I discuss company policy at a board meeting with the managing director, (my boss), and the directors of production, human resources and finance so that we can coordinate our policies into a strategy for the whole company."

JANE SEYMOUR, MARKETING RESEARCH MANAGER

"I am responsible for finding out what the public thinks about our present products, and what they want in the future. My staff do this by looking at the way our products and those of our competitors have sold in the past, and asking questions about consumer opinions, usually using questionnaires. All this information is collected is brought together and analysed so that I can make recommendations to the Marketing Director about the future. We call this forecasting. Sometimes we do industrial research into what the 'trade' thinks. This means asking the retailers we sell to for their opinions, about our products, our advertising, and our delivery service. You see, marketing research looks at everything we do. This gives my job great variety, and my staff are not doing the same things every day. I have six people working for me directly, although if we have a big job to do I might go to an outside research agency for help."

ANDREA LLOYD, PUBLIC RELATIONS ASSISTANT

"I help the PR manager to establish a good image for the firm in the eyes of the outside world, whether they are customers, suppliers or the public at large. We do this by making sure that good news about the firm is well spread and that bad news is explained away. I need good writing skills for this because we send press releases to the TV, radio and newspapers. To be successful I will also need to be able to speak effectively to reporters and maybe go on the radio and TV. At present my boss does this. At the moment a lot of my work involves cutting articles from the press and keeping records about ourselves and our competitors' activities for future use."

the sales function

direct and indirect selling to the customer

Sales is an important part of the marketing function. The Marketing Department may be in charge of selling, as in the diagram on page 119, or selling may be carried out by a separate Sales Department.

Direct sales are made when the provider of the product sells direct to the consumer without any middle person such as an agent or wholesaler being involved. Remember that a product can be a manufactured item or a service.

Indirect sales are made when the provider of the product sells to the consumer through a middle person such as an agent or wholesaler.

Look at the diagrams and the examples :

direct selling

Examples:

• a manufacturer sells to a consumer through its factory shop

• a taxi takes you to the station

• you buy a book direct from our website www.osbornebooks.co.uk

indirect selling

Example: you buy a box of Kelloggs Cornflakes from Asda.

Example: you buy a daily newspaper from your corner shop.

Example: you book a package holiday through an independent travel agent.

other sales methods

Some businesses do not sell through shops:

- they sell services rather than make goods
- they sell goods and services used by other businesses and so sell direct to those businesses using 'reps'

Businesses are increasingly selling to their customers using methods which by-pass the traditional shop. Some common sales methods are described below. E-commerce is described in more detail in the next section.

direct mail

Businesses obtain databases of names and addresses and send catalogues to selected market segments so that customers can buy direct by mail order. This method is used both for selling to the public and to other businesses. Much of this sort of sales material can end up in the bin!

telesales

Selling by telephoning the customer direct – telesales – has become very common, both when selling to the public and to other businesses. It is used extensively by organisations like financial services companies and also by business suppliers.

network selling to the public

This involves an individual agreeing to sell a product and then recruiting new salespersons who in turn recruit new salespersons who in turn recruit new salespersons, and so on . . . Commission and rewards are paid on direct sales and also on the sales made by the new recruits. This form of selling can prove very rewarding for the person who first started the 'network'. Networks are often developed by 'party selling'. Parties are held in private homes with the 'host' or 'hostess' selling the product – clothing, perfume, children's books, for example.

the growth of e-commerce

Selling through websites is now the fastest growing sales method worldwide. Manufacturers and mail order companies are easily accessed on-line and through net 'searches'. Popular products sold using this method include books, CDs, cars and holidays. If you have access to the internet try the on-line bookstore www. amazon.co.uk or shopping sites available through the web search engines such as Yahoo. This form of selling by 'e-tailers' poses a serious threat to the traditional retailers. Read the newspaper article below.

Internet threat to town centres

By Anita Howarth

Town centres, already hammered by out-of-town developments, face a devastating new attack from home shopping on the internet, according to a top retail boss.

Barry Gibson, chief executive of mail-order and pools firm Littlewoods, says towns will have to reinvent themselves as places for leisure and entertainment rather than shopping centres if they are to survive.

Though the government has closed the planning doors that allowed out-of-town superstores, it is encouraging the growth of internet shopping.

Gibson says this will tear the heart out of many town centres, just as superstore developments have done.

He believes that 'e-tailing' could be the straw that breaks the back of many shopping districts. Some have already suffered up to a 3 per cent fall in turnover because of out-of-town retailing.

The e-tail revolution could snatch between 2 per cent and 5 per cent of their remaining customers, Gibson believes.

He revealed his gloomy view to a conference of the British Council of Shopping Centres last week.

He admitted that the drop in custom might not sound much to many people.

But with retailers having already driven down costs, any further reduction in turnover could have a disproportionate impact on profits'.

It could become a landslide, he added.

Leading retailers are already looking for ways to cut back on their outlets in towns, concentrating on the largest regional centres and on the most profitable retail pitches there.

Source: The Mail on Sunday

Some retailers have now responded positively to this threat by "if you can't beat them, join them' and have opened their own on-line shopping and home delivery facilities.

Tesco Direct is an example. You can order your weekly shop on-line and have the goods delivered to your door.

Now carry out the Activity on the next page.

Activity 6.12

E-commerce
the selling revolution

Investigate examples of businesses which have set up websites for selling their products on-line. You can do this either by reading articles in the press about IT developments, or by looking at sites on-line. Most search engines such as Yahoo give easy access to on-line shopping.

1　What are the advantages to customers of buying on-line?

2　What could be a disadvantage in terms of the customer's security of buying products in this way?

3　What other disadvantage can you see if you are a customer buying goods such as clothes on-line?

4　What are the advantages to a business of selling on-line?

5　What are the implications of on-line shopping to traditional retail businesses which have shops in town and city centres and retail parks?What are some traditional retailers doing to compete with E-commerce?

7　Does the business you are investigating for your Portfolio have a website and an on-line shop? How could e-commerce benefit the business?

the sales function in a business

The way a function such as sales or marketing operates in a business depends very much on the size and type of business. A sole trader will do most things him/herself. The reason you are studying a large or medium-sized business for your assessment is that the structure will be more complex and will give you an better insight into the different job roles. If you look at a business which operates over a wide geographical area the sales function can be organised by region. A business with very distinct types of product might organise sales by product. Look at the two structure charts on the next page.

job roles in sales

The chart on the bottom of the next page shows the types of job role which you are likely to find in the larger type of retail business. This business is a limited company, so the structure is headed by a sales director.

The job descriptions which follow on page 126 are all related to sales and customer service (which is covered in greater detail in the next chapter). They should give you ideas for the descriptions you will need to write for your Portfolio.

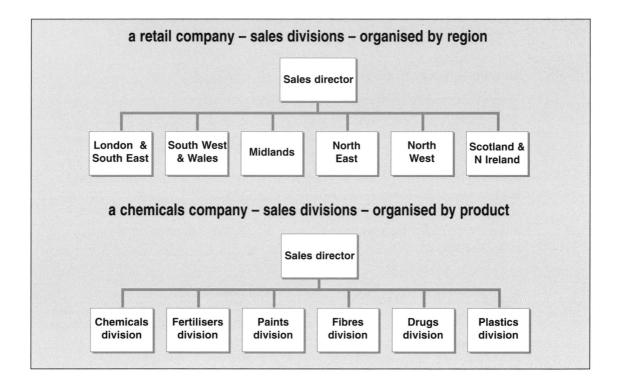

a retail company – sales divisions – organised by region

Sales director

- London & South East
- South West & Wales
- Midlands
- North East
- North West
- Scotland & N Ireland

a chemicals company – sales divisions – organised by product

Sales director

- Chemicals division
- Fertilisers division
- Paints division
- Fibres division
- Drugs division
- Plastics division

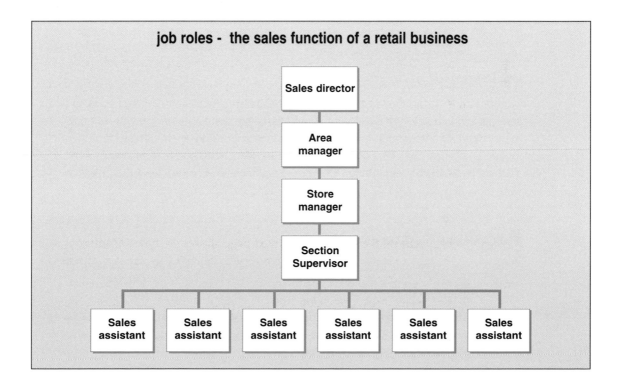

job roles - the sales function of a retail business

Sales director

Area manager

Store manager

Section Supervisor

- Sales assistant
- Sales assistant
- Sales assistant
- Sales assistant
- Sales assistant
- Sales assistant

Jobs in Sales in the retail trade

Jo Grundy, Sales Representative

– who visits shops to sell his company's products

"I sell my company's products to existing customers, but I also try to find new customers. I work a region of the country all by myself, but I report to an area manager. He gives assistance when a big customer is involved. I also get good back up from the marketing research people and the sales administration team. I enjoy the challenge of trying to sell to new customers, and I like the independence of travelling around in my company car, although it is good occasionally to go to sales meetings at Head Office and meet the rest of the sales team, to swap experiences. I get paid commission on sales, and this keeps me working hard."

Tess Rosso, Area Sales Manager

"I work for the sales director and I am responsible for all sales activities in the six stores in my area. Each one has a sales manager, who is in charge of all the sales staff within that store. I visit each store to discuss any problems and to make sure that sales targets are being met. The store sales managers meet me at my office every three months to discuss current recruitment and training of sales staff, sales targets, and any new Head Office initiatives. Once a year I discuss new sales targets and other matters with my director and the other area managers. This information I pass down the line to my six stores."

Jim Pentry, Sales Assistant

"I work in one department of the store, getting to know all about the products so that I can explain things to the customers. I have had sales training at the store and I now understand the importance of listening to the customer rather than just talking at him or her. I get a real buzz from gaining a sale (plus I get commission as well). Next month I will move to another department for more experience. This is hard work but I need to widen my experience if I want to gain promotion to being a supervisor."

Paula Crawford, Sales Demonstrator

"I work for a manufacturer of goods which I demonstrate to the public in a variety of retail outlets like supermarkets and department stores. I love the travel and the regular change of work place, and I get great fun out of entertaining a crowd with my demonstrations. Now and then a product won't work properly, which is awkward and calls on my sense of humour, but I love the challenge. I get a steady wage, but I also receive commission, so I keep motivated."

JAN MUSGROVE, CUSTOMER SERVICES ASSISTANT

"I work in Customer Services on one of the telephone desks. I deal in the main with enquiries and complaints. There are five assistants in the store altogether, and our supervisor deals with the important customers and any major problems.

We sometimes have to help out with checkout duties.

The work is never boring – I am dealing with customers all the time, and get a lot of satisfaction from helping people. Of course you get the occasional awkward one – but that's life.

We do get a thorough training in telephone technique and dealing with people."

Activity 6.13

Investigating job roles the sales department

Portfolio activity

Read through the job roles on the last two pages and make sure that you understand the range of activities carried out in the sales department of a business.

Interview people who work in the sales department of the business that you are investigating and find out

- what they do to help the sales function in the business
- the ways in which they communicate with each other

Make notes on your interviews and write out job descriptions of the people you have interviewed, explaining what they do and how they fit into the sales team.

It would be useful if you were able to draw up a structure chart of the sales function in the business you are investigating.

CHAPTER SUMMARY

- Marketing is an important function in business as it is based around the consumer and getting the product right for the consumer.

- Marketing involves concentrating on the '4 Ps':
  - *Product* – providing what the customer wants
  - *Price* – making sure that the price is fixed at the right level
  - *Promotion* – making sure the customer knows about the product
  - *Place* – deciding how and where the product will be sold

- There are many different types of consumer; they can be divided up by age, gender, income and wealth, geographical area and lifestyle.

- Market research involves finding out what different types of consumer want so that the product can be designed accordingly.

- Fixing a price for the product will involve balancing the factors of profit, maximising sales and providing quality.

- Promotion is not just advertising, it also involves creating a brand image for the product, packaging and creating publicity so that the consumer is aware of it.

- Sales can be direct or indirect. Direct sales involve the product being sold direct to the customer; indirect sales involve selling through another business.

- Sales methods include direct mail, using sales reps, telephone sales, network selling and e-commerce.

KEY TERMS

marketing	getting the right product to the right people at the right price
segmentation	classifying the consumer in different ways, eg age, sex
lifestyle	seeing a consumer in terms of personality and attitude
field research	finding out about consumer needs and wants by asking the consumer direct
desk research	finding out about consumer needs and wants by studying published sources
branding	creating a name or a logo for a product or organisation
publicity	appearing in the news in some way
public relations	the function in a business which looks after its public image
telesales	selling direct to customers by telephone
e-commerce	selling direct to customers through the internet

MULTIPLE CHOICE QUESTIONS

1   The 4 Ps of marketing stand for
    A   purpose, product, price, place
    B   product, price, promotion, place
    C   purpose, product, price, publicity
    D   product, price, promotion, publicity

2   A business importing and selling keep fit equipment is most likely to be interested in which type of market segmentation?
    A   classification by sex
    B   lifestyle
    C   geographical area
    D   income and wealth

3   A business organising customer questionnaires is carrying out
    A   segmental research
    B   desk research
    C   field research
    D   publicity research

4   The main benefit of a 'loyalty' card issued by a supermarket to its customers is:
    A   the customer will always pay the lowest prices
    B   the supermarket will know exactly what the customer has bought
    C   the customer will be able to obtain cash at the checkout
    D   the supermarket will know what other shops the customer visits

5   A business which fixes its price below that of its competitors will be giving priority to which business aim?
    A   making a profit
    B   creating a brand
    C   ensuring product quality
    D   maximising sales

6   Branding of a product is best described as
    A   giving it a low price so that customers will buy it
    B   giving it a high price so that customers will buy it
    C   giving it a name or logo which will make customers buy it
    D   making sure that it appears in the news

Customer service

what this chapter is about

'Customer service' is an important part of the sales function which we looked at in the last chapter. 'Customer service' means the ways in which businesses look after their customers by putting them first.

As part of your Assessment you will have to give an oral presentation of the way in which customer service meets the needs of the customers of the business you are investigating. You will also be asked to make suggestions for improvements in customer service, if they are needed.

As preparation for this talk you will need to study this chapter carefully and to collect evidence in an organised way from the business you are investigating.

what you will learn from this chapter

- Many businesses pay a great deal of attention to looking after their customers, particularly in the selling process – this is known as 'customer service'.

- Although businesses may have a customer service department with specialised staff, customer care should be in the mind of every employee from the managing director to sales assistant.

- Quality customer service – 'customer care' – involves providing information, advice, delivery, making sure the product is safe and reliable, providing credit (so that the customer can pay later) and providing after-sales service.

- Businesses need to be able to measure the success of their customer service by setting targets and then finding out how well the targets have been met. They will then be able to improve the level of customer service as they need to.

customer service

your assessment

Part of your assessment involves you investigating customer service in a business. You will have to make a presentation about the way the customer service in that business meets the needs of its customers. You will also be asked to make suggestions about how customer service might be improved.

what is customer service?

Businesses need their customers to buy their products or to use their services in order to survive and make a profit. The way that they treat their customers is therefore very important. Many businesses have a policy of 'customer service' which involves putting the customer first in all situations. Customer service involves:

- making sure the product range is available to the customer
- making sure the product range can be delivered if necessary
- making sure the product is safe and reliable
- providing information about products and being able to give advice
- providing credit facilities where appropriate (allowing the customer to pay over a period of time)
- providing after-sales service – guarantees, spare parts, help-lines

It should be the aim of every business to provide the highest level of customer service.

There are laws which provide protection to consumers buying products. Businesses should know what their obligations are under these laws; it will help them maintain a high level of customer service.

why is customer service so important?

The initial impression of a customer dealing with an organisation – whether as a shopper, a visitor or when speaking over the telephone – is based on the level of customer service he or she receives. Is the person who deals with the customer polite and helpful, or is the person unhelpful and not interested in the customer's request? The result will be a good impression – or a bad impression – of the whole organisation. If the impression is good, the person will want to do business again; if the impression is bad, the organisation will probably have lost a customer for good. Many organisations have a customer services department, and shops often have a customer services desk, as in the picture on the next page.

a customer services desk

customer care

Customer care is the application of customer service. If you get a part-time job in an organisation or a work placement, you may have to deal with customers, over a counter, at a reception desk, over the telephone, or elsewhere on the premises. Many business organisations run special customer care training programmes, spending much time and money ensuring that their staff provide a high level of customer service.

What is a customer care scheme? It is a focusing of the whole business on the needs of the customer rather than the needs of the business or the employee. It is an attitude which should run through the whole organisation from the managing director to the most junior sales assistant.

customer service at work – external customers

Customer service should be provided wherever the customer meets the business organisation: over the counter, or on the telephone. There are many examples of job roles involving customer service:

- shop assistants
- doctors' receptionists
- bank assistants
- bus drivers
- swimming pool attendants
- telephone sales staff (mail order firms)

customer service at work – internal customers

Many business organisations train their staff to think of other employees as 'customers' and treat them as such. For example a person in charge of the stationery stores or photocopier should provide materials and copying promptly and with the same courtesy that they would give to an outside customer. The same principal applies to quality in production – many Japanese companies train production line workers to treat the people in the next stage in production as their customers.

Activity 7.1

Customer service
assessing local businesses

Over a period of two or three days (a weekend for example) carry out a survey of the situations where you were a customer of a business organisation (eg a taxi ride, a disco, buying a cup of coffee). Draw up a survey sheet to cover the following:

1   Was the impression you received good or bad? Were the goods or services provided quickly and courteously?

2   Were you aware of a customer care scheme in operation?

Portfolio activity
Make notes on the aspects of customer care which you considered to be 'good practice', eg courtesy, speed of service, the way you were greeted and treated.

the need for information and advice

Many customers need information and advice. They may be about to make a purchase, or they may just be 'shopping around' for a product and looking for the best price or after-sales service. Whatever the situation the sales assistant must:

know the product range

Know the price, product description, availability, and details of after-sales service (guarantees and policy on 'money back'). Knowing the product ideally also means knowing the competitor's product: 'Oh yes, I know they are cheaper at Underwoods, but look at the quality we have here – this will last a long time.' The assistant must, however, beware of making false or over-ambitious claims: the customer will soon see through them.

know other sources of information

If the assistant is unable to provide all the information required, someone else in (or outside) the organisation may be able to help the customer. For example the question may be very technical: 'Will this hair dryer work off the mains electricity supply in Kuwait?' The question may have to be referred to the technical department of the manufacturer. The customer will not necessarily expect the shop assistant to know the answer, but may be very unhappy if the assistant does not know how to find out.

Some customers do not just need information, they need very specific assistance. The shop assistant in a department store, for example, should be prepared to point out where the toilets are, where the coffee shop is, or where the childrens' play area is located. They should also have the skills necessary for the area in which they work, eg measuring feet for shoes.

the need for care

Apart from the obvious general application of customer care skills, one of the factors which motivates staff is the fulfilment of a customer's need for 'care' in a very specific sense. 'Care' is more than 'help,' it means anticipating a customer's needs. Consider the following examples:

- a sales assistant sees that a pregnant woman is exhausted with tramping around the shops and provides her with a chair to sit down on

- a sales assistant sees that an elderly lady is confused and tired, and spends more time serving the lady and helping her to make simple decisions

- a sales assistant sees a child screaming and calms him by giving him or her something as a distraction

In all these cases, the employee goes out of his or her way to provide care for the shopper, who will then think of the organisation in a good light.

Activity 7.2

Customer service
meeting customer needs

You work as a shop assistant in the stationery department of a large store. What would you do in the following circumstances?

1   A customer wants to know how much 'The Times' and 'The Independent' newspapers cost.

2   A German tourist comes in and asks for 'Die Welt' You are not sure what she means.

3   A pregnant woman comes in with two screaming children who are demanding all the sweets and toys that they can see. She looks very pale and anxious.

Portfolio activity
Investigate and write a short report on the ways in which the business you are studying for your Portfolio trains its staff to provide good customer service.

customer types

In the last section we saw how different customers have different needs. Every employee providing customer service should be able to anticipate these needs. There are many different types of customer, for example:

• the customer who needs information and advice

• the child

• 'special needs' customers, eg people in wheelchairs, blind customers

We have dealt with the person who needs information and advice. We will now look at the child and the special needs customer.

the child

Ask any parent, nanny or child-minder and you will find that taking children shopping, or placing them in any situation which involves waiting, can be a considerable problem! Of course, some children are not a problem, and a smiling face normally means that everyone can relax.

If you are working in a business and are dealing with the public, you may encounter the following problems with children:

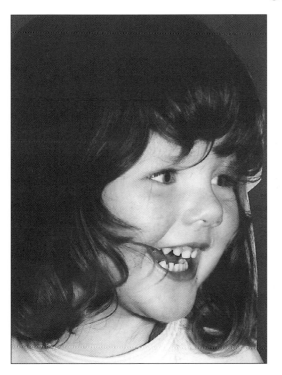

• children disrupting the course of business – creating a disturbance, destroying displays of goods

• children helping themselves to goods, tampering with telephone equipment

• lost children

• children trying to pay for goods

Whatever the situation, remember that it is the person in charge of the child who is primarily responsible and who will have to be approached in the first instance if there is a problem. Only if there is a threat to safety – eg a lost child or a collapsing display – should you take direct action.

You should be sympathetic in situations where 'care' is needed – eg a distressed or bored child – you may be able to help the parent in a difficult situation. Through this you should get a satisfied customer.

special needs customers

Customers with special needs include:

the physically handicapped and disabled

People in wheelchairs and with walking frames will need special treatment and patience; the organisation should be equipped with suitable lifts and ramps.

the mentally handicapped

People who are slower than normal in carrying out the simplest transaction will need a high degree of care and understanding. Do not treat them disrespectfully.

the deaf ('hearing-impaired')

Some customers may be completely or partially deaf and will be skilled in lip reading and may be equipped with hearing aids. Do not shout at them.

the blind ('visually-impaired')

Blind people will be used to getting about in public, so ask them if they need help. Talk to them. There is nothing more frightening than being grabbed unexpectedly by a complete stranger, however well-meaning that person may be.

Activity 7.3

Customer service
dealing with special situations

You work as a shop assistant on the till in the stationery department of a large store. How would you deal with the following customer types?

1   You suspect a three year-old child of slipping a Mars bar into her mother's shopping bag.

2   A blind person approaches you and asks for a Robbie Williams CD. The music department is on the next floor.

3   A customer in a wheelchair asks for this month's issue of 'Cosmopolitan'

Portfolio activity

Investigate a local supermarket or department store. What special facilities are available for the special needs customer and for children? Write notes for your Portfolio about the facilities available. These can then be compared with the facilities (if there are any) in the business you are investigating.

providing credit

A customer who is given *credit* is a customer who is supplied with an item or a service and is then allowed to pay at a later date. This is common practice in business-to-business dealings. When a business sells to the public – eg a shop selling a product to a customer – it normally expects immediate payment, unless a credit card is used.

credit cards and shop cards

A credit card is a plastic card which allows you to buy goods and services and pay for them later on the receipt of a statement from the credit card company. If you do not settle up the full amount of the statement by a given date you will be charged interest on the amount you still owe. This is often measured by an Annual Percentage Rate (APR), eg 20%.

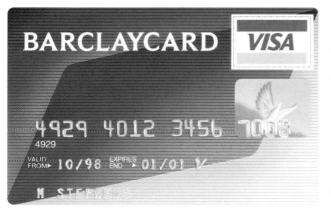

The credit card can either be a general credit card, eg Visa or Mastercard, which can be used anywhere, or you can apply for a shop credit card which can only be used at that particular shop. A shop card may give you extra benefits such as discount on purchases and previews of their Sales.

The card shown on the left is a Visa card issued by Barclays Bank. It can be used in most outlets worldwide.

Activity 7.4

Customer service
providing credit

Investigate and compare **one** type of general credit card (eg a Visa card or a Mastercard) and **one** type of shop credit card.

Identify any special benefits available for the card user and also the Annual Percentage Rate (APR) on each card.

Which would you choose, and why?

Obtain leaflets for both type of card – complete the application forms and add the leaflets to your Portfolio.

after-sales service – knowing your rights

An important part of customer care is the after-sales service. This involves:

- providing guarantee schemes for which the customer pays a premium, for examples three years' on-site servicing and repairs for a washing machine
- advising on the way a product works if it is brought back by the customer

One important role of customer services staff is dealing with complaints. It is therefore essential that the staff know about the rights of customers when they buy goods or services. Sales staff will not be required to have a detailed knowledge of the law – they will need to know how to answer customers' questions and avoid saying the wrong thing! What are the main laws?

Trade Descriptions Act

The Trade Descriptions Act makes it a criminal offence:

- to make false statements about goods offered for sale
- to make misleading statements about services

Examples of offences include:

- stating that a car for sale has clocked up 15,000 miles, when in fact the figure is 25,000 miles
- making a misleading statement about a service, eg 'our dry cleaning is guaranteed to remove every stain' when it does not, or 'our apartments are within easy reach of the sea' when they are fifteen miles away

Sale of Goods Act

This Act states that you are entitled to expect any goods that you buy from a shop to be:

of 'satisfactory quality'
This means they must meet the standard that a 'reasonable' person would expect given the description and the price

'fit for the purpose'
The goods must do what they are supposed to do, or what the shop claims they can do: an umbrella should keep the rain out, a watch should keep accurate time.

'as described'
The goods must be what they are claimed to be: a 'leather coat' must be made of leather, a 'stereo TV' must provide stereo sound.

If any of these three above conditions is not met, the consumer is entitled to a full or a part refund, depending on how soon the fault appears, how serious it is and how quickly the matter is taken up. Note also:

- the buyer can accept a replacement, but can also insist on a refund if a replacement is not wanted

- the buyer does not have to accept a credit note for spending on other purchases

- a shop is not entitled to put up a notice saying 'No Refunds!'

The Supply of Goods and Services Act protects the consumer in the same way as the Sale of Goods Act when a service is provided by a business.

Consumer Protection Act

The Act falls into three parts:

- you can take to court a manufacturer, producer or importer who supplies a defective product which causes loss or damage

- it is a criminal offence for a trader to sell unsafe goods – 'unsafe' means in breach of the safety regulations which apply to that product (eg to toys, pushchairs, food) and also in relation to what is reasonably expected of the product (you would expect a kettle to boil water, for example)

- it is a criminal offence for a trader to mislead consumers about the price of goods or services, eg saying '£50 off' when there is no reduction at all

For further information about consumer rights, log onto www.oft.gov.uk

Activity 7.5

Customer service
knowing customer rights

What are your rights in the following situations? What would you say to the shop in each case? Write down a summary of what you would advise, mentioning the law as appropriate.

1   You buy a tape of your favourite band. When you open the box at home you find a tape of Cliff Richard songs. The shop has run out of the tape you want and offers you a credit note.

2   You buy a new pair of jeans and the next day find that the zip is faulty. You take them back to the shop, but the assistant points to a notice saying 'No refunds'.

3   You buy a new pair of shoes which are sold as 'leather effect'. A friend tells you that they are not real leather. You take them back to the shop and demand a refund.

4   You buy a teddy bear for your young brother at Christmas from your local store, and get a real bargain. On Boxing Day your brother is admitted to hospital having swallowed both the teddy's eyes.

measuring the quality of customer service

Part of your assessment asks you to judge whether the customer service you have investigated is of good quality, and if it can be improved. But what is good quality?

how businesses measure success
Business organisations can measure the success of their customer service by collecting statistics, for example:

positive signs (customer service is successful)
- an increase in the number of customers who approach them with an enquiry
- an increase in the number of customers who buy their products
- repeat business – an increase in the number of customers who come back again to buy their products
- an increase in the overall sales figures
- a reduction in the number of complaints and returned products

negative signs (customer service is not successful)
- an increase in the number of complaints
- an increase in the number of products returned as faulty
- a reduction in the number of customers
- a reduction in the sales figures

monitoring success
Monitoring can take a number of forms:

sales performance
As we have seen, an improvement in customer services for a profit-making organisation should result in an increase in the number of customers, and a better sales performance leading to increased profits.

feedback
Many organisations organise customer questionnaires to find out what is right and what is wrong with the customer service. Shops often put questionnaires by the checkout and holiday companies circulate them on return charter flights. See the next page for an extract of a W H Smith questionnaire on service. Feedback can also be achieved simply by staff talking to customers about their needs and the level of service provided.

Q5 Below is a list of statements about service. Can you please indicate whether you strongly agree, agree, disagree or strongly disagree with each statement for this shopping occasion at W H Smith. If the comment is not applicable to this trip please tick the 'not applicable' box. **Please tick the box which applies to each statement** (✓)

	Strongly Agree	Agree	Disagree	Strongly Disagree	Not Applicable	
Staff had time to help with my enquiry	❑	❑	❑	❑	❑	(9)
Staff were friendly	❑	❑	❑	❑	❑	(10)
Staff were approachable	❑	❑	❑	❑	❑	(11)
I did not have to queue to seek assistance	❑	❑	❑	❑	❑	(12)
Staff wanted to help me	❑	❑	❑	❑	❑	(13)
Staff were happy	❑	❑	❑	❑	❑	(14)
Staff were interested in serving me	❑	❑	❑	❑	❑	(15)
I did not have to queue too long to pay	❑	❑	❑	❑	❑	(16)
Staff were knowledgeable	❑	❑	❑	❑	❑	(17)
Staff were understanding	❑	❑	❑	❑	❑	(18)
Staff helped me make my decision	❑	❑	❑	❑	❑	(19)
I enjoyed shopping at W H Smith	❑	❑	❑	❑	❑	(20)
Staff were there if I needed them	❑	❑	❑	❑	❑	(21)
It was easy to find what I was looking for	❑	❑	❑	❑	❑	(22)
The shop is well laid out	❑	❑	❑	❑	❑	(23)
The signs helped me find my way around	❑	❑	❑	❑	❑	(24)
I could browse in peace	❑	❑	❑	❑	❑	(25)
It was fun to shop there	❑	❑	❑	❑	❑	(26)
I knew I could exchange goods easily	❑	❑	❑	❑	❑	(27)

Q6 Was there any member of staff you thought offered a very high level of service? Can you remember their name?

Please write in _____

W H Smith – "Customer First" questionnaire
Reproduced by kind permission of W H Smith Ltd and David Young & Associates

Activity 7.6

Customer service
dealing with the questionnaire

Choose four of the statements from the questionnaire on the previous page and assume that a significant number of people completing the questionnaire have strongly disagreed with them.

If you were responsible for customer service, how would you deal with the complaints? Put your suggestions into a memo addressed to the manager of the store. You can make up the names and use today's date.

How does the business you are investigating monitor customer service? Ask for examples to include in your Portfolio.

Our own service targets

We aim to prove our commitment to top-class service by measuring performance against our own, tougher standards. We'll publish details of how we're doing:
Our own targets are:

Answering phone calls: We aim to answer calls within 15 seconds and make 30 seconds the maximum wait. However, for billing queries at peak times we will try to limit the maximum wait to 45 seconds.

Letters: We'll respond to your letters in writing, by phone or face-to-face within five working days 75 per cent of the time, and certainly within ten working days.

Appointments: Whenever we make an appointment to meet you we will agree to come either in the morning or the afternoon.

Customers who visit our offices: We always aim to make sure you see the right person within five minutes.

codes of practice

Some businesses operate a code of practice for customer service. They may publish a document (sometimes called a 'charter') which sets out for the public its targets for customer service. Many businesses, railway companies for example, regularly publish tables showing how well they have met their targets. A business which serves the public and is shown to have met high standards of customer service may be awarded a Charter Mark. This can be displayed on publicity material. The extract on the left shows the targets set by a public utility.

Activity 7.7

Customer service
a students' charter

Obtain and study examples of customer service charters issued by public service businesses.

1   Devise your own 'Student's Charter' setting out the standards of service you would expect from your school or college.

2   Ask your teacher/lecturer to devise a short 'Tutor's Charter' setting out the standards expected of students, eg work handed in on time, attendance in class.

improving customer service

Your assessment asks you to make suggestions for improvements in the customer service of the business you are studying. You will have to be careful how you do this as it would not be diplomatic to criticise your chosen business too openly – they have after all given you a lot of time and assistance. Some of the following suggestions might be a starting point:

- the *reliability* of products or services – do they perform?
- the *friendliness* of staff – do they smile or not?
- the *availability* of goods and services – are the opening hours satisfactory? are the goods in stock when needed?
- *speed of delivery* – are the goods delivered on time and to the right address?
- *exchanges and refunds* – is the policy made clear to customers? is it fair and legal?
- *access to buildings* (for special needs customers) and *customer safety* – do the premises comply with Health & Safety regulations?
- *environmental policy* – customers like environmentally friendly businesses – does the business have a published policy?

Some businesses run 'quality circles'. These are discussion groups made up of employers and staff which suggest ways of improving quality in the business. 'Quality' here applies both to the product and to the way it is sold.

Activity 7.8

Customer service
making the presentation

As part of your Assessment you will have to stand up and make a presentation on the way the business you are investigating tackles the issue of customer service. The information you gather for your Portfolio will depend on the type of business involved. Here is some guidance:

1   Make a list of the various customer service initiatives and explain them in your presentation.

2   Find out and explain what customer service training is given to staff in the business.

3   Collect written information such as any charter, guidance notes to staff, training material.

4   Find out how the business aims to improve its levels of customer service and explain this to your audience.

5   Collect examples of good practice from other businesses you have investigated and keep them to compare with the standards of the chosen Portfolio business.

CHAPTER SUMMARY

- Many businesses pay much attention to looking after their customers, particularly in the selling process – this is known as 'customer service'. Some businesses treat their own employees as 'customers'.

- A business may have a customer service department with specialised staff. Whatever the set-up, customer care should be in the mind of every employee from the managing director to sales assistant.

- Quality customer service involves providing information, advice, delivery, making sure the product is safe and reliable, and providing credit (so that the customer can pay later).

- After-sales service involves knowing the rights of the seller and the buyer as set out in consumer law.

- Businesses need to be able to measure the success of their customer service by setting targets and then finding out how well the targets have been met. They will then be able to improve the level of customer service as appropriate.

KEY TERMS

customer service	looking after the customer and always putting the customer first
customer care	customer service in action
special needs	customers who need an extra degree of care because they have some disability
credit	allowing a customer to buy a product – often with a credit card – and then to pay at a later date
APR	Annual Percentage Rate (APR) is the comparative cost of credit to the customer – it is not an interest rate
Code of Practice	a set of targets for customer service published by a business
Charter Mark	a 'kite mark of service' awarded by the Government to public service businesses which have adopted and keep to a 'Charter' of excellence of service

MULTIPLE CHOICE QUESTIONS

1   Customer service means

   A   putting the customer first

   B   putting the customer last

   C   providing a service rather than goods

   D   asking the customer to complete a questionnaire

2   The advantage of a Visa credit card issued by a bank is that:

   A   it can only be used in the shop where it was issued

   B   payment is made from the bank account straightaway

   C   payment can be made by the customer at a later date

   D   the customer can be identified when entering the shop

3   APR stands for

   A   Average percentage rate

   B   Annual purchasing rate

   C   Annual percentage rate

   D   Average purchasing rate

4   You are working at a customer service desk in a clothes shop. A customer brings back a T shirt with a major defect in the fabric and asks for a refund. You should say:

   A   'Sorry, we don't give refunds.'

   B   'That should be fine. Can I see your receipt please?'

   C   'We can only give you a credit note.'

   D   'This item is now discontinued, so we can't do anything about it'

5   A shop advertises a stereo for sale at £149.95. The ticket says 'previously sold at £199.95'. You know for a fact that this is not true. The shop will be in breach of:

   A   The Trade Descriptions Act

   B   The Sale of Goods Act

   C   The Supply of Goods and Services Act

   D   The Consumer Protection Act

6   A quality circle is:

   A   a chartermark given to businesses with excellent customer service

   B   a range of high quality products on display in a shop

   C   a discussion group set up to improve quality in a business

   D   a round symbol placed on high quality products

8

Production and finance – using business resources

what this chapter is about

Two other important functions in business are the production function and the finance function. Production is responsible for producing the manufactured item or service. Finance is responsible for raising the money to pay for production, for recording transactions and for planning what money is needed for resources in the future. This chapter is therefore about business resources – the resources a business needs to manufacture a product or to provide a service.

what you will learn from this chapter

- Many different types of resource are needed to manufacture a product or provide a service:
  - land and buildings to house the business
  - machinery and equipment to produce the product
  - people to manage, make and deliver the product
  - raw materials (for manufacturers) and stock (for retailers)

  These resources are known as 'factors of production'.

- The aim of the business in using these resources – is to 'add value' to the resources so that the final product can be sold at a profit.

- There are a number of ways in which a business can improve the way it uses its resources so that it can increase the profit it makes.

- The finance function is closely involved with production. It involves:
  - raising money to obtain the resources it needs
  - recording transactions, keeping accounts, paying wages
  - preparing financial reports so that the business can keep planning ahead and can buy the resources that it needs in the future

business resources

When a business manufactures a product or provides a service it will need a variety of resources which include items it owns and people. These resources will vary with the type of business involved but could include:

land and buildings used by the business

. . . for example farmland, mines, fisheries, offices, factories, warehouses, shops, hotels, keep fit centres

machinery and equipment used by the business

. . . for example production line machinery, vans, cars, computers, communication equipment

people who work in – and for – the business

. . . for example managers, supervisors, assistants, specialists, consultants, accountants, solicitors

materials and stock used by the business

. . . for example goods bought in by a shop to sell to customers, raw materials and components bought in by a manufacturer to produce the finished product

Now look at and compare the diagrams which follow.

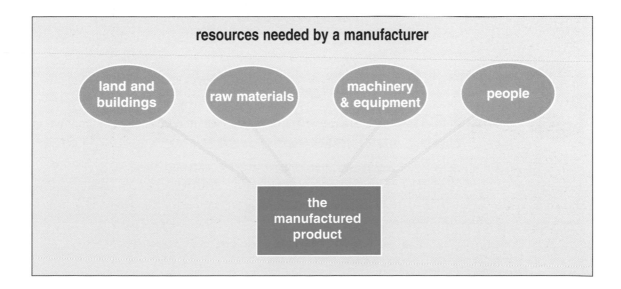

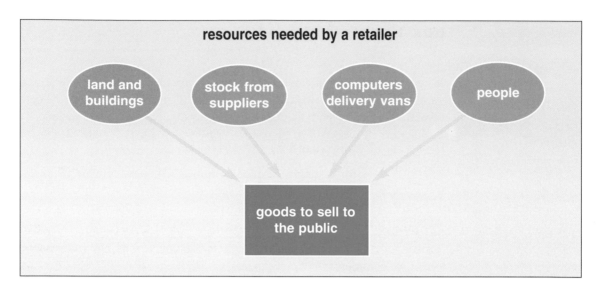

resources needed by a retailer

land and buildings

stock from suppliers

computers delivery vans

people

goods to sell to the public

resources needed by a travel agent

land and offices

holidays air tickets

computers

people

holidays to sell to the public

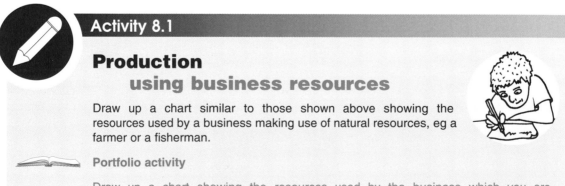

Activity 8.1

Production
using business resources

Draw up a chart similar to those shown above showing the resources used by a business making use of natural resources, eg a farmer or a fisherman.

Portfolio activity

Draw up a chart showing the resources used by the business which you are investigating for your Portfolio.

the production process

what is production?

'Production' is the process of turning all these resources into a product – a manufactured item or a service – which can be sold by the business. These resources are sometimes known as the 'factors of production' – they are combined to produce the product.

production costs

The resources used by a business will have to be paid for. They result in costs for the business which have to be covered – wages, rent, cost of materials, stock, electricity, phone bills and so on. All of these have to be controlled by the Finance Department.

adding value

When a business manufactures an item or provides a service it uses its resources to 'add value' to those resources. This means that the product can be sold at a higher price when it has gone through the production process.

Take, for example, a farmer who grows apples. He is combining the resources of his land, the trees, the labour cost of maintaining them and picking them. He could sell the apples at 70p a kilo to the passing public. But he could also add value to them by processing them further and selling the final product for more money. He could use his resources to:

adding value

sell the apples

make apple pies and sell them

pulp the apples into juice and sell the juice

make cider from the pulp, bottle it and sell it

making a profit

When a business is planning to produce a product – whether it is a manufactured item or a service – it will need to make sure that the day-to-day costs will be covered by the money received from sales. The greater the added value, the greater the possible profit:

PROFIT *equals* MONEY FROM SALES *less* DAY-TO-DAY COSTS

Clearly if the money from sales does not cover running costs, the business will make a loss. See Chapter 14 for more on business profits.

Activity 8.2

Production
adding value

How do you think you could add value to the following basic resources by using them in some form of business venture? State what extra resources you might need to add value and make a profit.

1   A pile of seasoned timber.

2   A lake stocked with fish.

3   You find you are a genius at writing computer games.

Portfolio activity

Write down the ways in which the business you are investigating adds value to the resources it uses in order to make a profit.

methods of production

The way a business manufactures a product will depend on the type of product involved. There are three main methods of production.

job production

With this method one item is completed at a time. It is suitable for large or 'one-off' projects such as ships, buildings and anything that is built to order.

batch production

A 'batch' is a term used in baking. Batch production involves completing a group of items – a 'batch' – at the same time and then moving onto the next group. A tray of bread rolls or loaves being prepared and then baked in the oven is a common example. Batch production therefore involves a series of operations repeated time and time again.

continuous production

Continuous production is the commonly accepted idea of 'production line' manufacture. A product is assembled on a continuous moving line and parts and processes added as it moves along. The processes can be carried out by hand or by robots. The modern car production line is a common example and is highly automated. For many products such as food products the process ends with wrapping and packaging.

The illustrations on the next page show the manufacture of Cadburys Dairy Milk chocolate bars.

Cadbury's
Continuous production of Dairy Milk chocolate bars

computer control of the production line

chocolate being mixed

**formed into slabs
– on the production line**

. . . being wrapped

points for class discussion

- Why is this particular method of production suited to chocolate bars?

- What other products would be suited to this method of production?

methods of improving production

being efficient

You will know that you need to be efficient to achieve good results. This means that you have to make the most of your resources. If, for example, you are producing a piece of work, you should make the most of your notes, your textbooks, your tutor and your time. Businesses also need to make efficient use of their resources. Efficiency is often measured by comparing the average cost per unit. This is calculated by dividing the total cost of making the product by the number of units produced.

productivity

Efficiency shows how well all the resources are being used. It is also useful to look at how many items have been produced (or how many services have been sold) by the employees. This is one measure of productivity. Some employees are paid a bonus if they produce (or sell) more than a given number of items – so it is in their interest to be productive!

One way of calculating productivity is to divide the number of items produced by the number of people employed. If a car factory produces 30,000 cars a month and employs a workforce of 1,500 over the month . . .

productivity = 30,000 ÷ 1,500 = 20 cars per employee per month

Activity 8.3

Production
measuring productivity

A factory producing TV sets records the following staffing and output levels for three months production:

	employees	output of TV sets
Month 1	1,250	200,000
Month 2	1,100	187,000
Month 3	1,300	195,000

1   Calculate the productivity (the number of TV sets per employee) for each of the three months.

2   Is productivity at its highest when the output is at its highest level? If not, why not?

a quality product

Businesses sell their products in a competitive market. A business producing a quality product can be reasonably confident that it will sell.

Quality control on the production line of a manufactured item involves a process of inspection of a set number of items. Any faulty items will be rejected and the cause of the problem investigated. Quality control of a service product is equally important and involves monitoring of the service and feedback from customers received by the Marketing Department.

It is important to appreciate that quality is not only desirable in the finished product, it should also be applicable in every process and system within the business. This is known as **Quality Assurance.** Businesses which show that they can match up to and maintain high standards may apply for one of a range of internationally recognized certificates of Quality Assurance (the BS EN ISO 9000 range). Anyone dealing with a business with this certificate can be confident that it is dealing with a 'quality' organisation.

Activity 8.4

Production
achieving quality

The following note is packed with every pair of childrens shoes which leaves Start-rite Shoes Limited in Norwich. Read it through and answer the questions which follow.

QUALITY POLICY STATEMENT

It is the policy of Start-rite Shoes Limited to provide footwear which will give total satisfaction to our customers with their fit, fashion, comfort, service and price. To help achieve this objective the Company has established and will maintain a Quality Management System designed to meet all the requirements of BSEN ISO 9002. This programme complements and co-ordinates the Company's overall manufacturing strategy which includes:

* Providing materials and components of an approved specification.
* Up-to-date fashion interpretation.
* Modern, well maintained machinery and support systems.
* On-going training at all levels.

---

1   What is the specific business aim relating to customers set out in the statement?
2   How will the company meet the requirements of BSEN ISO 9002?
3   What are the four main aims of the company's manufacturing strategy?
4   Which department would be responsible for producing this statement?

Portfolio activity

Write down the ways in which the business you are investigating applies Quality Control or Quality Assurance. What functions within the business are directly and indirectly responsible for quality?

managing stock

management of stock levels

'Stocks' are items held by a business on a temporary basis, either to sell or to turn into manufactured goods. Stock is normally managed by the Sales Department in the case of a shop or a Production Department in the case of a manufacturer. The Finance Department will keep a record of its value.

The problem for businesses is that holding stocks is expensive. If a car manufacturer needs to keep £1 million of stocks in the form of body panels, tyres, seats and other components this has to be paid for. The Finance Department will have to raise the necessary money from somewhere. Also, stock needs to be stored in buildings – businesses will then have to pay for rent and rates, security and insurance costs – in order to keep that stock.

Businesses need to balance two needs:

• the need to keep stock levels low to save money

• the need to have enough stock available to avoid running out

How do they do this? A common method is known as 'Just-in-Time'.

Just- in-Time (JIT)

Various methods of achieving reductions in stock levels – and costs – have been tried, one of the most successful is 'Just-in-Time' (JIT), a system of stock ordering that originated from Japan, and is now used extensively by both manufacturers and retailers in the rest of the world. The basic idea is that the components that are needed by the manufacturer at each stage of the production process (or goods needed by a retailer) are delivered to the right place and in the right quantities – just in time – and then to the final consumer.

Manufacturers who use JIT often try to attract component suppliers to the same area. Some car manufacturers have gone a step further than this by building a car factories with the component firms on the same site.

Retailers who use JIT – the major food supermarkets, for example – have arrangements with their suppliers to supply goods more or less on demand. Information technology systems used by these businesses helps them to anticipate the quantities they have to order: electronic tills provide up-to-the-minute stock usage for each 'line' and so stock levels are constantly monitored. Orders are sent to suppliers, often through EDI (Electronic Data Interchange) computer systems, and delivered within a short space of time. If there is a run on a particular item – eg soft drinks in a heat wave – the system will ensure that new stock is delivered very rapidly.

Case Study

Nissan in Sunderland
modern production methods

NISSAN

COMPANY PHILOSOPHY

Nissan's Sunderland plant aims to build profitably the highest quality cars sold in Europe, to achieve the maximum possible customer satisfaction and thus ensure the prosperity of the company and its staff.

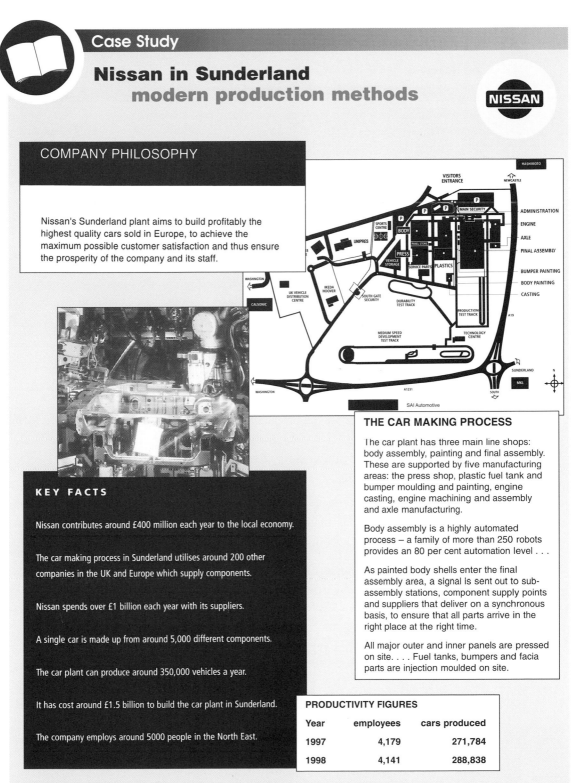

KEY FACTS

Nissan contributes around £400 million each year to the local economy.

The car making process in Sunderland utilises around 200 other companies in the UK and Europe which supply components.

Nissan spends over £1 billion each year with its suppliers.

A single car is made up from around 5,000 different components.

The car plant can produce around 350,000 vehicles a year.

It has cost around £1.5 billion to build the car plant in Sunderland.

The company employs around 5000 people in the North East.

THE CAR MAKING PROCESS

The car plant has three main line shops: body assembly, painting and final assembly. These are supported by five manufacturing areas: the press shop, plastic fuel tank and bumper moulding and painting, engine casting, engine machining and assembly and axle manufacturing.

Body assembly is a highly automated process – a family of more than 250 robots provides an 80 per cent automation level . . .

As painted body shells enter the final assembly area, a signal is sent out to sub-assembly stations, component supply points and suppliers that deliver on a synchronous basis, to ensure that all parts arrive in the right place at the right time.

All major outer and inner panels are pressed on site. . . . Fuel tanks, bumpers and facia parts are injection moulded on site.

PRODUCTIVITY FIGURES

Year	employees	cars produced
1997	4,179	271,784
1998	4,141	288,838

read this through and then answer the questions on the next page

Activity 8.5

Modern production methods
Nissan in Sunderland

Read the Case Study on the previous page and answer the following questions.

1. What are the main business aims of Nissan in Sunderland as set out in the company philosophy? Write them out in a list.

2. What type of production process is used by Nissan in Sunderland?

3. Approximately how many components go into each car produced?

4. To what extent is the production process automated?

5. What components are manufactured on site? What is the main advantage of doing this?

6. What is the productivity figure per employee over the two years?

7. How many outside suppliers of components does the Nissan plant have?

8. What benefits has Nissan brought to the North East?

organisation of the production function

The organisation of the production function in a business will vary widely, depending on the size and type of business:

- is it a manufacturer, a retailer, a service provider?
- how large is it?

The diagram below shows the different tasks carried out in the production department of a manufacturing business. On the next page are some descriptions of jobs in a production department.

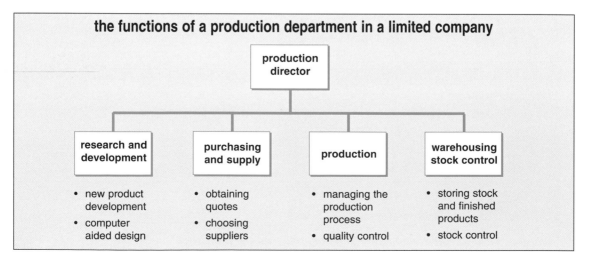

the functions of a production department in a limited company

Jobs in the Production Department of Carcare Limited, manufacturer of car accessories

SEAN O'CASEY

PRODUCTION MANAGER

"I am in charge of the production lines of the business. I report directly to the production director. I also work with Rick Brunson, the sales manager, who lets me know about any problems. I also talk regularly with other departmental managers – particularly the purchasing manager who buys in all my raw materials and components. I also deal with the Finance Manager who keeps an eye on cost levels and discusses production budgets with me on a regular basis.

I am in charge of sixty production line workers. We are a fairly happy bunch – we rarely have any disputes. Carcare is a good employer and looks after its workforce."

JANINE LEGRAS

PRODUCTION LINE EMPLOYEE

"I have worked on the production lines here at Carcare for two years now. At the moment I make the covers for car seats. They like women on this job because you have to be nimble-fingered. There are twenty of us on this line, and a supervisor who keeps her eye on us and the work we do."

Activity 8.6

Production
dealing with departments

Portfolio activity

1   Draw a structure chart of the production function of the business you are investigating for your Portfolio. If the business produces a service the chart should show the 'operations' function – the area in the business which organises the way the service is provided to the customer.

2   Explain, with examples, how and why the production (or operations) function communicates with other function areas in the business.

the finance function

There is detailed coverage of business finance in Chapters 11 to 16 of this book. The remainder of this chapter explains the finance function with descriptions of some of the jobs in a typical finance department.

finance and other function areas

The finance function in a business is closely involved with the production of goods and services and so links up with other function areas in the business, including the senior management. Look at the table of activities below.

FINANCE DEPARTMENT ACTIVITIES	FUNCTION AREAS INVOLVED
Sales of products have to be recorded ⟶	Sales
Costs relating to production have to be recorded ⟶	Production
Money has to be raised for production ⟶	Production
Bills have to be paid ⟶	Administration
Wages have to be paid ⟶	Human Resources
Accounts have to be kept to calculate profit or loss ⟶	All departments
Financial planning reports have to be prepared ⟶	Senior Management

finance department structure

Set out below is a structure chart of a typical finance department showing the main functions that it carries out.

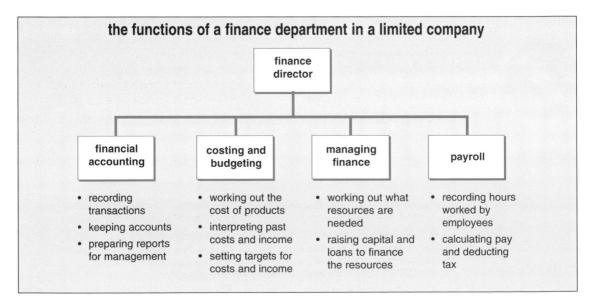

the functions of a finance department in a limited company

finance director

financial accounting	costing and budgeting	managing finance	payroll
• recording transactions • keeping accounts • preparing reports for management	• working out the cost of products • interpreting past costs and income • setting targets for costs and income	• working out what resources are needed • raising capital and loans to finance the resources	• recording hours worked by employees • calculating pay and deducting tax

financial accounting – the accounting system

The box on the left-hand side of the structure chart on the previous page shows the financial accounting function.

the financial accounting system

Later in this book (Chapter 15) we will be looking in detail at the financial documents involved in buying and selling. These documents form the first part of a process which ends up with the production of financial reports such as profit statements. These are used by the management of the business in seeing how well the business is performing and meeting its objectives. The stages in the process are shown in the diagram below.

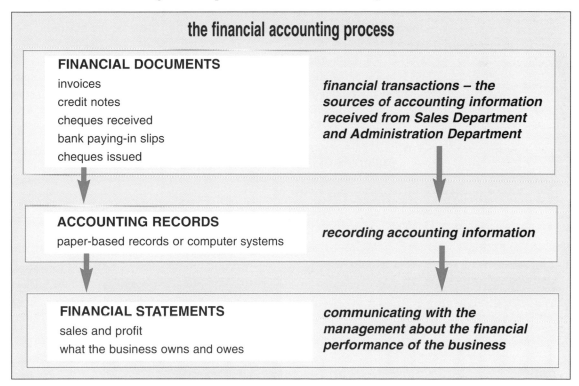

accounting records

Financial transactions of all types are recorded in accounts. In most accounting systems there will be separate accounts for:

- sales and purchases
- each type of expense
- debtors (people who owe the business money)
- creditors (people to whom the business owes money)

the ledgers

Because of the large number of accounts involved, there are a number of different *ledgers* in an accounting system. A ledger is a book into which you write figures. Look at the examples shown in the diagram below.

sales ledger

Accounts of debtors, ie customers who owe the business money – this information is provided by the Sales Department.

purchases ledger

Accounts of creditors, ie suppliers to whom the business owes money – this information is provided by the Production and Administration Departments.

cash books

A book which records cash and all payments in and out of the bank account – this information relates to most of the function areas of the business.

general (or nominal) ledger

The remainder of the accounts: eg sales, purchases, expenses, and items owned by the business – this information also relates to most of the function areas of the business.

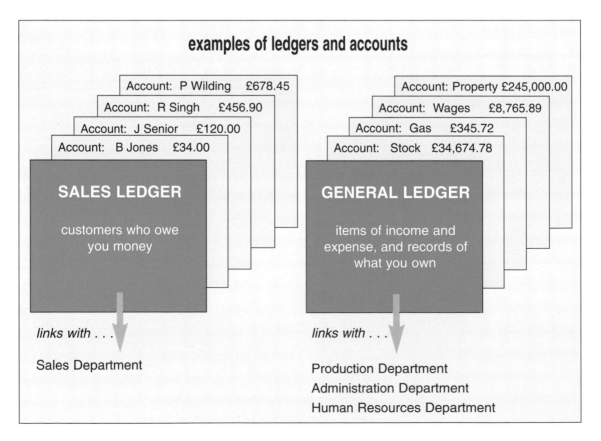

examples of ledgers and accounts

Account: P Wilding £678.45
Account: R Singh £456.90
Account: J Senior £120.00
Account: B Jones £34.00

SALES LEDGER

customers who owe you money

links with . . .

Sales Department

Account: Property £245,000.00
Account: Wages £8,765.89
Account: Gas £345.72
Account: Stock £34,674.78

GENERAL LEDGER

items of income and expense, and records of what you own

links with . . .

Production Department
Administration Department
Human Resources Department

double-entry accounting

The basis of many accounting systems is the double-entry book-keeping system. You do not have to study double-entry for your course, but it is useful to know what the system involves. Double-entry book-keeping means making two entries in separate accounts for each transaction. For instance, if you are paying for wages by cheque you will make an entry in *bank account* (because you are paying out money) and an entry in *wages account* (because you are recording the amount you are paying for wages). If you are using a manual accounting system you will make the two entries in separate accounts by hand (the accounts are set out below). If you are operating a computer accounting system you will make *one* entry on the keyboard, but indicate the other entry with a code number (see the example at the bottom of the page).

Bank Account	
	30 Nov Wages £1553.46

Wages Account	
30 Nov Bank £ 1553.46	

computer accounts

As noted earlier, many small businesses and almost all large businesses use computers to handle their business transactions. If you use an accounting program, you input the transactions into the computer where they are stored on disk. The principles of double-entry book-keeping remain the same – when you input the data you use input codes to identify the two accounts involved in each transaction, eg 1200 = bank account, 7500 = stationery account, as in the example shown below from a Sage computer accounting program screen.

Bank Payments

Bank Payments

Bank: Bank current account   Tax Rate: 17.50
N/C Name: Stationery   Batch Total: 53.46

Bank	Date	Ref	N/C	Dept	Details	Net	Tc	Tax
1200	17/12/1998	234234	7500	3	Copy paper	45.50	T1	7.96
						45.50		7.96

financial statements

The finance department regularly draws up financial statements for management. These report on areas such as sales and profit and so monitor the main objectives of the business. These are prepared from the information held in the accounting records. Some computer accounting programs will print out these statements automatically.

The two main statements are the profit statement and the balance sheet:

- the *profit statement* shows the sales figure, the expenses and profit
- the *balance sheet* shows how much a business owns and owes

Read the Case Study below and answer the questions in the Activity which follows.

Case Study

Bentom Music
financial statements

Set out below are figures from the balance sheet and the completed profit and loss statement of Bentom Music, a business which sells mail order CDs.

The figures have been taken from the accounting records of the business at the end of the year.

BENTOM MUSIC	
Balance sheet figures	
	£
Property	80,000
Vehicles	25,000
Computers	20,000
Other equipment	15,000
Stocks of CDs	40,000
Bank deposit	2,000
Bank loan	22,000
Owners Capital	160,000

BENTOM MUSIC
Profit and Loss Statement

	£	£
Sales of CDs		260,000
less purchases of CDs		100,000
equals		160,000
less expenses		
rent and rates	5,000	
postage	2,500	
insurance	1,500	
telephone	2,500	
wages and salaries	80,500	
electricity	3,000	
advertising	25,000	
Total expenses		120,000
PROFIT		40,000

Activity 8.7

The finance function
financial accounting

1   The balance sheet shows you what the business owns. What is the total value of what the business owns?

2   Where has the money come from to finance the business?

3   The profit and loss statement lists the money from sales and expenses of the business. What is the sales figure?

4   Where has the sales figure come from?

5   Apart from the CD purchases figure, what is the largest item of expense for the business? Where has this figure come from?

6   What is the profit of the business over the period of the profit and loss statement? Which groups of people and functions in the business would be interested in this figure?

costing and budgeting

costing

Another function in the finance department is *management accounting*, which will be looked after by *management accountants*. It is the job of this department to find out information about the cost of producing a product – whether the product is a manufactured item or a service. Costs can involve a wide variety of resources:

- the raw materials purchased (if the product is a manufactured item)
- the cost of stock (if the business is a shop)
- the cost of paying the wages for the employees producing the product
- other expenses known as 'overheads' which have to be paid anyway, for example electricity bills, advertising, rates, stationery for the office

It is up to the management accountants to liaise with the various function areas and calculate the cost of producing the product to ensure that:

- there is sufficient finance to cover the cost
- the business is making the most efficient use of its resources

budgeting

It will be the responsibility of the management accounting function to set budgets (targets) for future periods. For example:

- a *sales budget* to forecast the income that will be received by the business from sales (see the example on page 86)
- a *production budget* to plan the number of items produced and to work out what they will cost

As time goes on the management accountants will monitor actual figures against the budgeted figures. They will see, for example, if sales of the product in January are on target with the budget. If the sales are below target, the reasons will have to be investigated. Perhaps the price is too high or the packaging is not attractive. Discussions will take place with Production and Marketing management – possibly to change the price or the packaging.

raising finance

Money is the lifeblood of any business. Money is required by a business for:

- *long-term needs* such as investing in premises, machinery, computers
- *short-term needs* such as buying stock and raw materials, paying bills, paying wages

It is the job of the Finance Department to co-ordinate the raising of money for the different function areas of the business, eg Production, Marketing.

The finance raised is normally either short-term or long-term:

- *long-term* in the form of investment from the owner (known as 'capital') and bank loans repayable over a period of time
- *short-term* in the form of
  - money received from sales of the product
  - credit from suppliers (the money is available because the suppliers have not yet been paid by the business)
  - short-term borrowing from the bank on overdraft

Look at the diagram below.

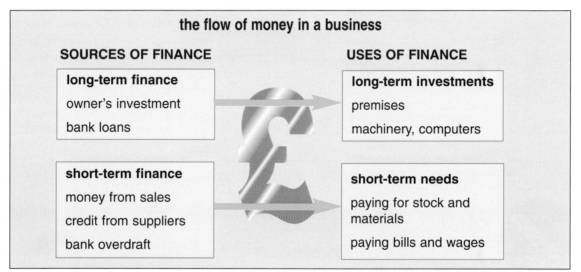

the flow of money in a business

SOURCES OF FINANCE

long-term finance
owner's investment
bank loans

short-term finance
money from sales
credit from suppliers
bank overdraft

USES OF FINANCE

long-term investments
premises
machinery, computers

short-term needs
paying for stock and materials
paying bills and wages

Activity 8.8

The finance function
raising finance to meet costs

1   What sorts of cost are taken into account when a management accountant calculates the cost of a product?

2   What is a sales budget? What departments or functions in the business would be affected if a sales target had not been met?

3   What sources of finance might a business use if it
     (a)   wanted to buy some new premises?
     (b)   needed extra stock?

payroll

Payroll is the function in the business which works out the pay and deductions (income tax and National Insurance) of its employees. The size of the business will largely dictate how many employees in the finance department will work on payroll. Some businesses 'farm out' payroll and pay specialist bureaux to do the job for them. Most businesses process payroll within the Finance Department, which gets its information from the Human Resources Department.

Payroll can either be done manually using the forms and instructions provided by the Inland Revenue, or it can be done by computer using programs such as Sage Payroll. More and more businesses are now using computer payroll programs as they are faster and very accurate.

Personal | Employment | Banking

Reference	6
Title	Miss	Initials A
Surname	Brown
Forenames	Angela
Address	66 Grassfield Crescent Mereford
Postcode	MR4 2JX	Director

N.I. Number AB763491B
Works No. 6
Sex Female
Marital Status Single
Date of Birth 29/06/1981
Telephone

On Hold

employee record screen from a Sage Payroll program

Activity 8.9

Job roles in finance

Read through the information on payroll (see above) and the Job Roles set out on the next page and answer the following questions:

1   Where is a payroll assistant working in the Finance Department likely to get his or her information from? Can you see any problems this type of information might cause, if, for example, it was left lying around on a desk?

2   What department or function in a business is the credit controller likely to deal with on a regular basis? Why?

Portfolio activity

3   Draw up a structure chart showing the jobs in the Finance Department or function in the business you are investigating for your portfolio.

4   Talk to people working in the Finance function of your chosen business and write down examples of the ways in which people working in Finance deal with other departments and function areas. Explain why this communication is important to the running of the business.

Jobs in the Finance Department of Carcare Limited, manufacturer of car accessories

KERRY SMITH

PAYROLL ASSISTANT

"I work as a wages clerk in the finance office. There are ten clerks altogether, and our supervisor.

Although we occasionally have to work out wages manually, most jobs are computerised now – all we have to do is to enter the hours worked by each employee on the computer, and it automatically works out the pay and prints out a payslip. Some employees still get paid in cash – and I have to work out a cash analysis and get the right notes and coins from the bank. More and more employees now get paid direct into their bank account. I find the work interesting because I like working with figures."

NIGEL BURTON

CREDIT CONTROLLER

"I work at a supervisory level. My job in basic terms is to make sure that customers we sell to on credit will pay up. These customers are mostly shops and garages. The big shops are normally no trouble, but the smaller businesses often get into difficulties and the first we know about it is that they don't pay their bills. I have five assistants working under me. The job is an important one because if our customers don't pay up they become bad debts and the business loses money as a result. We have to vet new customers very carefully, taking bank references and normally two trade references as well – we often telephone those through. Our computer system printouts an 'aged debtor' report each week – this shows up any overdue accounts. We soon get onto them I can tell you."

JOHN CARDWELL

SALES LEDGER CLERK

"My main job is issuing invoices to customers who order goods from us. I have to check their purchase order forms carefully and also make sure they are good accounts and not bad payers. We used to type out the invoices ourselves but we now have a computer system which prints them out in batches. The computer does all the calculations, which is great, but we still have to check our work carefully."

CHAPTER SUMMARY

- Different types of business need a variety of resources to manufacture a product or provide a service. These can include:
  - land and buildings from which the business will operate
  - for a manufacturer – machinery and equipment to produce the product
  - people to manage, make and deliver the product
  - raw materials (for manufacturers) and stock (for retailers)

- Production is the process of turning these resources into a product. The aim of production is to 'add value' to the resources so that the final product can be sold at a profit.

- Production methods include job, batch and continuous production.

- Businesses can improve production through efficiency and quality measures and the management of stock levels.

- The finance function is closely involved with production. It can be organised in a variety of ways, including financial accounting, costing and budgeting, raising finance and payroll processing.

- A finance department will liaise with many other departments in
  - keeping accounts and preparing financial statements
  - analysing the costs of products and preparing budgets for forward planning
  - raising finance to pay for the resources needed by the other departments

KEY TERMS

adding value	using resources to add to the value of a product
productivity	a measure of the output of a business in terms of the resources used, eg the number of items produced per employee over a period of time
quality control	checking the quality level of a product as it is produced
quality assurance	the application of quality standards to all systems in a business – certifiable under BS EN ISO 9000
Just-in-Time (JIT)	a stock management system whereby resources needed in the production process are ordered as and when they are needed – 'just in time'
financial accounting	recording financial transactions, keeping accounts and preparing reports from them
management accounting	calculating the cost of products, preparing budgets for future periods, planning for raising finance

MULTIPLE CHOICE QUESTIONS

1   A factor of production is:

A   quality control on the production line

B   a form of short-term finance

C   the time it takes on average to make a product

D   a resource needed in the production process

2   Added value means

A   using resources to add to the value of a product

B   the profit percentage added to the product cost

C   buying in bulk so that the price comes down

D   putting up the price of a product to increase profit

3   The manufacturing process which involves completing a number of items at a time is known as

A   cost production

B   continuous production

C   batch production

D   job production

4   Ordering materials and stock so that it reaches a business when it is needed is known as

A   continuous production

B   quality assurance

C   productivity

D   Just-in-Time

5   The financial accounting system involves a process with a number of stages:

A   financial documents, accounting records, financial statements

B   accounting records, financial documents, financial statements

C   working out costs, accounting records, financial statements

D   working out costs, financial statements, budgets

6   A business raising money to buy new premises is most likely to obtain finance for this purpose from:

A   income from sales

B   bank long-term finance

C   credit card finance

D   bank overdraft

9 Administration and communication in business

what this chapter is about

Businesses need two basic support systems which will enable them to operate smoothly and efficiently and achieve their aims – good administration and good communication. Administration means making sure that the right resources are in the right place at the right time. Communication means making sure the right information gets to the right place at the right time.

what you will learn from this chapter

- Administration work involves back-up tasks such as:
  - dealing with the post and e-mail
  - keeping the records of the business up-to-date
  - dealing with enquiries
  - setting up meetings
  - looking after the premises – eg cleaning and security
- Administration can either be carried out by employees in each department or can be carried out by a special 'administration' department which looks after all the other departments.

- There are a number of ways people working in different functions in business can communicate with each other:
  - by word of mouth – by telephone, in meetings, in interviews
  - in writing – memos, letters, messages, adverts, notices
  - using information technology, for example e-mail (inside and outside the business), fax

- Communication flows within a business can be affected by the structure of the business.

- Efficient communication is important when dealing with people outside the business, eg customers, suppliers, the public.

administration – organising the work flow

all in a day's work

Whatever the size of a business, it is likely to have to deal with incoming, outgoing and internal communications. A sole trader is likely at times to have to work hard to manage to keep up with all that is going on. A larger business (such as the one you will be studying for your assessment) will need to be organised to deal with the flow of communications and also to provide all the back-up needed for the different business functions.

incoming

Information and messages – enquiries, orders, complaints – will come into the business by post, by fax, by phone and internet. Callers with appointments will arrive, callers without appointments will arrive.

outgoing

The business will also need to generate messages and information for external use – letters, quotes, catalogues, adverts, telesales – using a wide range of communication methods. It will also need to deliver its product – which may be an item or a service.

internal

The different functions within the business (eg sales, finance, production) need to communicate with each other in the day-to-day running of the organisation. The methods used can include paper documents, telephone, fax, intranet (internal e-mail) and meetings.

what is administration?

Clearly many of the activities listed above will be organised within the departments concerned and will be overseen by supervisors and managed by managers. For example a sales department will process orders received and the finance department is likely to process the payroll.

But there will be activities which do not *have* to be done within a specific department. These include:

- distributing the post when it arrives
- collecting and stamping the post going out at the end of the day
- operating the telephone switchboard
- dealing with callers to the premises
- photocopying and design and production of forms
- filing and database maintenance
- making sure the premises are clean and secure
- maintaining equipment such as computers

These activities are best described as 'back-up', and this is what we mean by 'administration' – making sure that the right resources are in the right place at the right time.

Activity 9.1

Administration
at your school or college

Find out what department or section is responsible for the following activities in your school or college. Draw up a structure chart showing these activities.

1 dealing with the post – incoming and outgoing
2 processing all the photocopying and teaching aids needed by teachers /lecturers
3 dealing with visitors during the day
4 operating the telephone switchboard
5 cleaning the premises
6 making sure all the computers are working correctly

Portfolio activity
Investigate the way administration is organised in the business you are investigating. Draw up a structure chart and compare it with the chart you have completed for your school or college administration (see above).

how to organise the administration function

There are a number of options available to a business with separate departments when it is organising its administration:

- each department can be made responsible for its own administration
- the business can set up its own administration department
- the business can use other businesses to carry out some of its administration work – examples of this include cleaning and security services and the use of outside telephone call centres which will take telephoned enquiries and orders on behalf of the business

The diagrams on the next page illustrate these three possibilities.

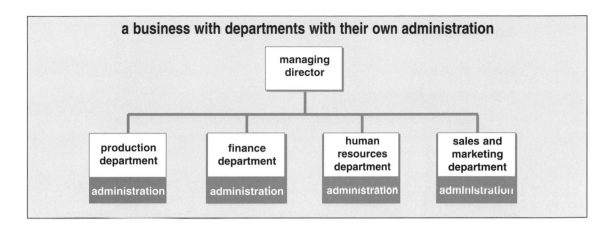

a business with departments with their own administration

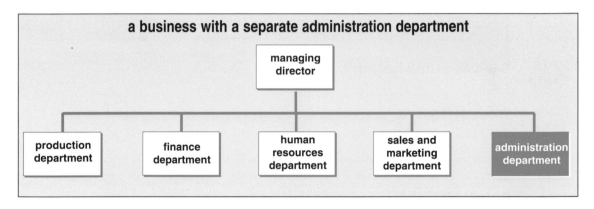

a business with a separate administration department

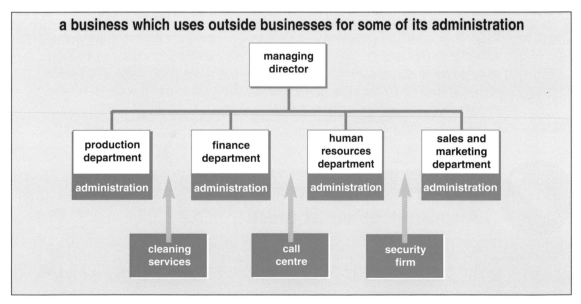

a business which uses outside businesses for some of its administration

Now read the descriptions of jobs on the next page. They give an idea of what is involved in working in administration.

Jobs in administration

SARAH WHITEMAN

ADMINISTRATIVE ASSISTANT

"I work in the administration department on a part-time basis. I work with fifteen other assistants and a supervisor.

The work is certainly varied. I do mostly word processing, filing and photocopying. We deal with all the paperwork involved with the running of the company, so we get to see what all the other departments are up to. I like working here, the atmosphere is good – the supervisor is strict, but has got a broad sense of humour!"

LEE CHEUNG

MAIL ROOM ASSISTANT

"I have worked in the mail room for three years now. We deal with all the incoming mail and packages, many of which have to be signed for. We open the mail, date stamp it and sort it into the various departments: anything to do with stock goes to production, cheques go to finance, job applications to human resources and so on. We have to make sure that the mail gets to the right person as quickly as possible.

We also deal with outgoing mail which involves collecting the post from the various departments, franking the letters and weighing any parcels. Parcels are more tricky because some go on a 24 hour delivery service and some 72 hours. The post is always collected from the office by the mail van and the carriers. The afternoons can be very busy with all the deadlines to meet."

Activity 9.2

Administration at work

Portfolio activity
Investigate the way administration is organised in the business you are investigating. Talk to people working in administration. Explain, with examples, how and why the administration function communicates with other departments in the business.

communicating in business

communication flow

Communication means getting a message across.

Businesses need to communicate on a very regular basis with people *outside* the business – with customers and suppliers, for example. They also need to communicate *internally*: departments need to pass information to each other, managers need to talk to supervisors, assistants need to complain to supervisors, and so on. As you will see from arrows on the diagram below, the communications flow in many directions:

- in and out of the business
- vertically – between the different levels of authority
- horizontally – between departments or functions

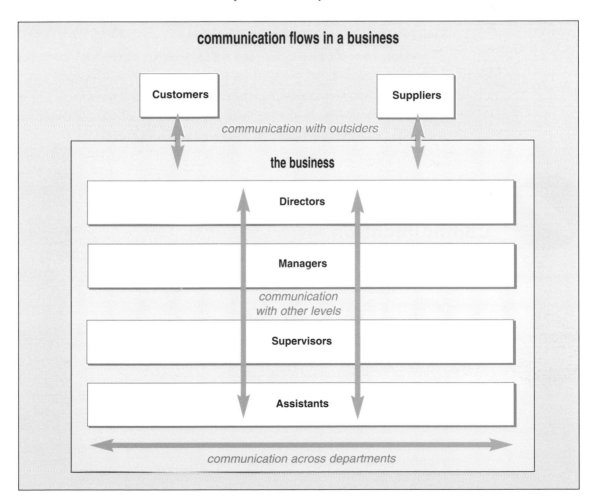

It is important to appreciate the different types of communication and see how they are used for different circumstances. You will then be able to choose the right type of communication for the appropriate situation.

When reading through the types of communication explained on the next few pages, put yourself in the place of a person working in business and think about the following points:

1   How appropriate is the means of communication for the person you are dealing with?

2   Should the message be kept private?

3   Will the message get to the person in time?

4   Should the content of the message be kept for future reference?

oral communications

Oral (word of mouth) communications include:

*   meeting someone face-to-face and talking to them, eg serving a customer in a shop, taking part in a meeting

*   having a formal interview, eg when applying for a job

*   talking to someone on the telephone, eg answering a customer enquiry

*   leaving someone a message on voicemail (answerphone)

Activity 9.3

Communication
oral communication

You are working in business. What form of oral communication would you use in the following situations, and why?

1   You have the following message on your voicemail from a customer "Hello. This is James Brand calling at 2.00pm on 01908 675245. Please can you let me have the prices of the new range of copiers as soon as possible?"

2   You suspect that one of your colleagues in the finance department is fiddling the books and taking money. You want to bring the problem to the attention of your supervisor.

3   You are told by the receptionist that one of your customers has called unexpectedly and is waiting in the reception area.

written communications – the letter

the letter – house style

If you work in a business or receive letters from a business, you will note that the appearance and format of each letter is in a uniform 'house' style, a style by which that organisation is known. The most common way of setting out a letter is in the style explained on the next two pages. The example letter has been prepared by a firm of double glazing contractors, Wyvern Double Glazing. A customer, Mr J Sutton, has enquired about the installation of windows for a new extension..

elements of the letter

printed letterhead
This is pre-printed, and must have up-to-date telephone numbers and e-mail.

reference
The reference on the letter illustrated - DH/SB/69 - is a standard format

- DH (Derek Hunt), the writer
- SB (Sally Burgess), the person who keyed the letter in
- 69, the number of the file where Mr Sutton's correspondence is kept

If you need to quote the reference of a letter to which you are replying, the references will be quoted as follows: Your ref. TR/FG/45 Our ref. DH/SB/69

date
The date is shown in date (number), month (word), year (number) order.

recipient
The name and address of the person to whom the letter is sent. This section of the letter may be displayed in the window of a window envelope, so it is essential that it is accurate

salutation

'Dear Sir. . . Dear Madam' if you know the person's name and title (eg Mr, Mrs, Ms), use it, but check that it is spelt or applied correctly - a misspelt name or an incorrect title will ruin an otherwise competent letter.

If you are dealing with another business and are not sure whether the person you are writing to is male or female (you may just have an initial and surname in your records) you can always ring the switchboard of the business and find out. The same applies if the person is female and you are not sure whether to write to them as 'Mrs', 'Miss' or 'Ms'.

heading

The heading sets out the subject matter of the letter - it will concentrate the reader's mind.

body

The body of the letter is the main text of the letter. It must be:

• laid out in short precise paragraphs and short clear sentences

• start with a point of reference (eg thanking for a letter)

• set out the message in a logical sequence

• avoid jargon and slang expressions

• finish with a clear indication of the next step to be taken (eg please telephone, please arrange appointment, please buy our products, please pay our invoice)

Note that the body of the letter is the only part which has punctuation!

complimentary close

The complimentary close (signing off phrase) must be consistent with the salutation:

'Dear Sir/Dear Madam' followed by 'Yours faithfully'

'Dear Mr Sutton/Dear Ms Jones' followed by 'Yours sincerely'

name and job title

It is essential for the reader to know the name of the person who sent the letter, and that person's job title, because a reply will need to be addressed to a specific person.

enclosures

If there are enclosures with the letter, the abbreviation 'enc' or 'encl' is used.

Activity 9.4

Letters

Collect examples of letterheads and design your own (on a word processing file) for an imaginary business you are setting up. Draft out the text for some model letters, for example:

• a letter asking for information or a request for a quotation

• a letter of apology for something your business has done

• a letter of complaint to a supplier

If you have the opportunity ask someone who works in a business to comment on the letters for you.

elements of the letter

Wyvern Double Glazing Contractors
107 High Street
Mereford
MR1 9SZ
Tel 01605 675365 Fax 01605 765576

reference ⟶ Ref DH/SB/69

date ⟶ 14 December 2000

name and
address of ⟶ Mr J D Sutton
recipient

23 Windermere Close
Crofters Green
Mereford MR6 7ER

salutation ⟶ Dear Mr Sutton

heading ⟶ Double Glazing of 23 Windermere Close

Thank you for your letter of enquiry dated 11 December.

body of
the letter ⟶ We are pleased to enclose a brochure with details of our double glazing units, all of which comply with the most up-to-date building regulations.

We will be happy to give you a quotation for glazing your new extension. In order to do this we will need to send our surveyor to measure up your property. We shall be grateful if you will kindly telephone us to arrange a visit at a convenient time.

We look forward to hearing from you.

complimentary
close ⟶ Yours sincerely

signature ⟶ *D M Hunt*

name and job
title ⟶ Derek Hunt
Sales Manager

enclosures ⟶ enc

the memorandum

The memorandum (memoranda if you are referring to more than one) is a formal written note used for internal communication within an organisation. It may be word-processed or handwritten, and will often be produced in a number of copies which can be circulated as necessary. It can be used for situations such as:

- giving instructions
- requesting information
- making suggestions
- recording of opinions

A memorandum is normally pre-printed by the organisation with all the headings in place, and can be half page or full page in size. A completed memorandum is illustrated and explained below.

MEMORANDUM

To	K Roach, Finance Manager		
From	Tim Blake, Sales Manager	**Ref**	KR/AC/1098
Copies to	Departmental Managers	**Date**	23 June 2000
Subject	Product A163 Launch SuperSucker cleaner		

Please attend a presentation of our new A163 SuperSucker cleaner on 24 July in the Ground Floor Conference Room. Details of the new product are attached and a fully working example will be demonstrated on the 24th.

enc

---

elements of the memorandum

Most of the headings on the pre-printed memorandum form are self-explan-atory, as they are also to be found on business letters. As the memorandum is an internal document it does not need the name or address of the business.

'to' and 'from'

The name and job title of the sender and the recipient are entered in full, and so the salutation 'Dear......' and 'Yours ....' are not necessary.

copies to

Memoranda are frequently sent (as in the example above) to a large number of people; the recipients will be indicated in this section of the document.

reference and date

As in a business letter the reference indicates the writer, inputter, and file number and the date order is day (number), month (word), year (number).

subject and text

The subject matter of the memorandum and the text must be clear and concise.

signature

A memorandum can be signed, initialled, or even – as is often the case – left blank.

enclosures

If material is circulated with the memorandum, the abbreviation 'enc' or 'encl' should be used.

You should note that a memorandum can also be sent electronically as a message on an intranet (internal computer network) – a practice that is becoming increasingly common.

the message

There is no set format for a written message, which often results from a telephone call. It can be a scribbled note on rough paper, or it can be on a printed form. A typical pre-printed telephone message form is shown below.

TELEPHONE MESSAGE

for ....

date ....time....................

caller's name...

caller's organisation.......................................

telephone no...

call taken by ....

message

notices and adverts

Businesses will also use notices and adverts as part of their day-to-day work. Examples of notices include:

*   warnings – 'Wet Floor!'
*   requests – 'Please turn this photocopier off when not in use.'
*   staff noticeboard items – 'Staff Balti Night Out'

An example of an advert is a job vacancy. Look through your local paper's Situations Vacant columns for examples. What are their main features?

For a notice or an advert to be successful as a communication, it must be clear and accurate and contain all the necessary information – it must get the message across.

Activity 9.5

Communication
written communication

You are working in business. What form of written communication would you use in the following situations, and why. In each case draft out and then print out a suitable text on a word processing package. Make up names, dates and other details where they are not supplied.

1   Refer to the letter from Wyvern Double Glazing Contractors on page 179. The surveyor has called and measured up the extension. Your estimating department has passed you a memo with drawings stating that the cost will be £4,500 plus VAT. You are to draft a communication in Derek Hunt's name to the customer setting out the cost and enclosing the drawings.

2   You are the manager of the Administration Department of a large company and have organised a staff night out on a riverboat for July 4, departing 8.00 pm from the South Quay, returning 11.30pm. The cost per head will be £9.50. Partners of staff will also be welcome (same cost). You need to let the departmental managers know these details and find out from them the number of people from their departments who will be coming.

3   You take a telephone call for your supervisor, who is at a meeting. His garage has telephoned to say that his car has been serviced and will be ready for collection at 4.00pm.

4   You are the supervisor of a number of staff who carry out data input in an office equipped with PCs. You notice that staff are placing mugs of hot coffee on top of the workstations, a highly dangerous practice, as coffee spilt in a computer could ruin it. You want to stop this practice by putting a notice on the notice board.

5   You work in the Human Resources Department and have been asked to draft out an advert for a vacancy for a part-time accounts clerk. You would like to recruit someone who has had experience of computer accounting on Sage programs.

electronic communication

The growth of information and communication technology (ICT) has resulted in a revolution in the way communication takes place between businesses and also inside businesses.

intranets and e-mail

Many businesses are now linked internally by an intranet. This is a network system whereby people working in a business are supplied with computer workstations which are linked together electronically. This means that they can all have access to information held on computer by the business, eg customer details, product details, diary systems. In addition to accessing all this data, they can send each other electronic messages. This is 'electronic mail', normally known as 'e-mail'. It can be very informal. You may find that your school or college has an intranet installed. An intranet will normally be linked up on-line to the internet (see below and next page), usually referred to as 'the net'. Note that *an intranet* and *the internet* are far from being the same thing!

the internet and e-mail

The internet, or 'net', is a rapidly expanding network of private, public, commercial and non-commercial computers linked via telephone lines by internet service providers (ISPs) who operate servers connecting their subscribers together. ISPs communicate with each other by telephone links, largely by satellite. Any person or business who is 'on the net' just has to dial up through the computer to be able to contact other internet users, anywhere in the world, e-mail or 'messenger' services.

websites

More and more businesses are coming on-line and setting up websites, not only for promoting their products but also for selling their products 24 hours a day, worldwide. A website is a series of interlinking pages set up on a computer server provided by an internet service provider (ISP). It is a 'shop window' for the business, and so successful have websites become that some businesses, for example the on-line bookshop www.amazon.co.uk trade only from their website.

A website normally has a 'contact' page which enables any visitor to the site to e-mail the business. A business with a website therefore has to deal with incoming electronic messages from the site in addition to the normal sources of e-mail.

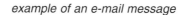

```
 rpnelson@goblin.com,,quotation                                              1
        To: rpnelson@goblin.com
      From: www.ritabooks.co.uk
   Subject: quotation

Dear Mr Nelson
Thanks for your e-mail enquiry of 1 December.
The title 'Bonzai for Beginners' ISBN 0 9510650 72 is available at £17.95. You can obtain it from most
bookshops and also from our website on mail order www.ritabooks.co.uk

Regards
H Bach
Customer Services
```

example of an e-mail message

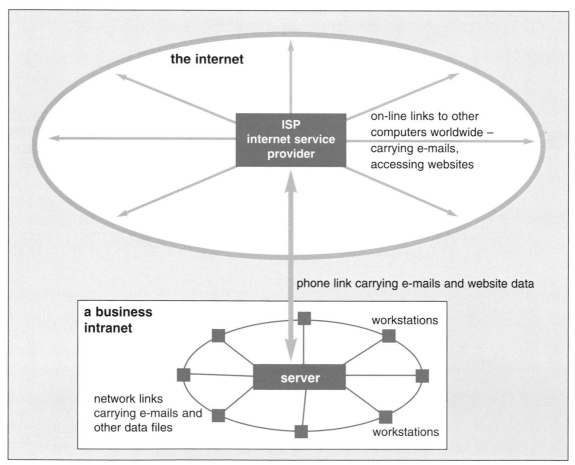

a business intranet linking up with the internet

fax

Another form of electronic communication is the fax (short for 'facsimile') which is a system whereby a sheet of paper is scanned by a machine in one location, transmitted down a telephone line and printed out by a similar machine at the other end. This is useful, for example, if you want to send a map, a price list or a drawing of a product to someone who wants it in a hurry. It is normal practice to send a fax with a 'fax header' which is piece of paper like a letterhead which sets out:

- the name and address of the organisation sending the fax
- the details of the person and organisation it is being sent to
- the date and the number of pages being sent

Faxes may also be generated on a computer file and sent direct down the telephone line from the computer. A typical fax header is shown below.

Osborne Electronics Limited

Unit 4 Everoak Estate, Bromyard Road
St Johns, Worcester WR2 5HN
tel 01905 748043 fax 01905 748911

facsimile transmission header

To: Jamie Milne, Buying Office, Zippo Computers

Fax number: 01350 525504

Number of pages including this header: 1   Date: 10 October 2000

message
Jamie
Just to let you know that the consignment you called about this morning was despatched last Thursday (5 October) and should be with you soon.
Regards
Jon Smart
Despatch Dept

---

videoconferencing

Videoconferencing involves an image generated by a camera on top of a computer being sent down the telephone line and displayed on a computer screen at the other end. This is useful for meetings where one or more of the people cannot be present. Modern technology is now making it possible for images generated by a small camera (webcam) to be sent over the internet.

videoconferencing in action

teleworking

Some businesses rely on electronic communications to such an extent that some employees work at home or in custom-built 'telecottages' in the country. 'Tele' means at a distance. They are usually linked on-line and communicate by telephone, fax and e-mail. They enjoy the advantages of a pleasant working environment and avoid the stresses and expense of travel.

work away from the city – a view of teleworking from BT

Activity 9.6

Communication
electronic communication

You are working in business. What form of electronic communication would you use in the following situations, and why? Assume that your business is equipped with fax , is on-line and has a website.

In the case of 1 and 2 draft on a word processor file the text of any message you might send. Make up names and dates and other details as appropriate.

1   You receive a telephone call from a customer who is coming to visit your business tomorrow. He does not know where your premises are. It is too late to send him a letter and the road systems around you are so complicated that it will take you a long time to give directions.

2   You receive an e-mail from a potential customer in Australia. She wants details of your products and their prices. Because of the time difference your office and the Australian office are never staffed at the same time.

3   One of your directors has to go to Paris for the day from London. The meeting is tomorrow. She wants to know very quickly if it is quicker and cheaper to get there by rail rather than by air. How could you find out from your office without having to contact a travel agent?

4   **Portfolio activity**
    What electronic means of communication are being used by the business that you are investigating? Make a list. Talk to people working in the business about the effectiveness of electronic communication. From their comments draw up a table comparing its advantages and disadvantages.

the choice of communication

So far in this chapter, the text and activities have provided an overview of the different types of communication and the ways in which they are used, both when dealing with outsiders and also when dealing other departments in the business. Obviously, certain types of communication are used because that is 'the way things are normally done'. It is important, however, to appreciate *why* different types of communication are used in different situations:

*   is it appropriate for the person you are dealing with?

*   should the message be kept private – is it confidential?

*   will the message get to the person in time?

*   is the communication needed for record keeping purposes?

On the next two pages are charts which highlight these points.

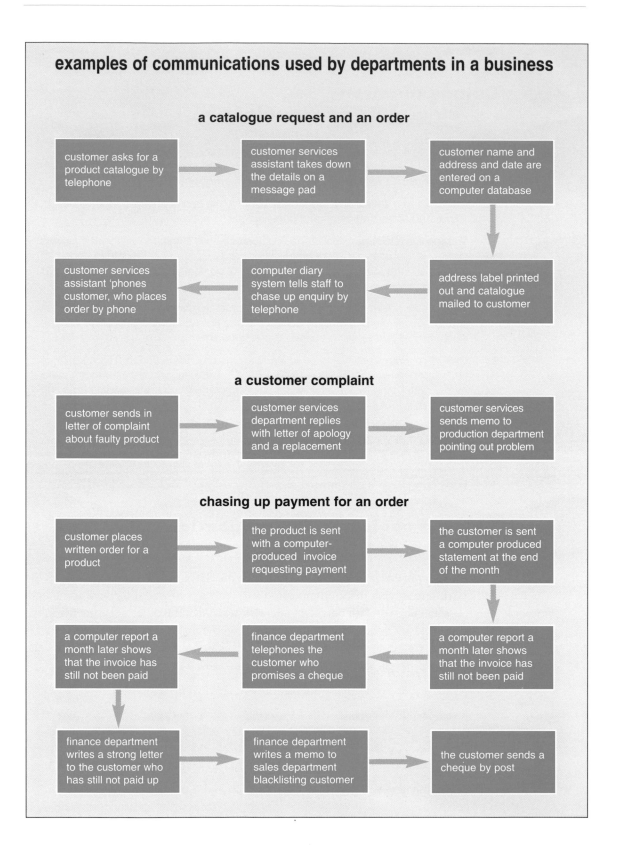

examples of communications used by departments in a business

a catalogue request and an order

customer asks for a product catalogue by telephone → customer services assistant takes down the details on a message pad → customer name and address and date are entered on a computer database ↓

customer services assistant 'phones customer, who places order by phone ← computer diary system tells staff to chase up enquiry by telephone ← address label printed out and catalogue mailed to customer

a customer complaint

customer sends in letter of complaint about faulty product → customer services department replies with letter of apology and a replacement → customer services sends memo to production department pointing out problem

chasing up payment for an order

customer places written order for a product → the product is sent with a computer-produced invoice requesting payment → the customer is sent a computer produced statement at the end of the month ↓

a computer report a month later shows that the invoice has still not been paid ← finance department telephones the customer who promises a cheque ← a computer report a month later shows that the invoice has still not been paid

↓

finance department writes a strong letter to the customer who has still not paid up → finance department writes a memo to sales department blacklisting customer → the customer sends a cheque by post

recruitment of new sales staff

human resources department meet to discuss the need for new sales staff → an advert is drawn up to go in the Situations Vacant column in the local press → human resources department meet to discuss the applications received

human resources department meet to discuss the interviews ← interviews are held with the job applicants ← letters are written to a shortlist of 5 people they want to interview

letters are sent to 2 successful applicants → when replies have been received, rejections are sent to the other applicants → memo to finance department setting out the payroll details of new staff

Activity 9.7

Communication
the right method?

Read through the flowcharts on these two pages.

1   Give at least three examples from these situations of:

   (a)   oral communication

   (b)   written communication

   (c)   communication using electronic means

2   Which of the four situations requires

   (a)   complete confidentiality

   (b)   a speedy response to the customer

3   Give at least two examples from these situations of:

   (a)   departments communicating with each other in connection with people outside the business

   (b)   the use of computers to help record the work of the departments

4   In the case of the chasing up of the payment, what other communication should take place within the business to complete the flowchart? What means of communication would you use?

achieving the aims of the business

the aims of business

The aims of a business are what it sets out to do. In Chapter 4 we saw that the main aims of a business should be:

- making a profit
- expanding the business
- increasing sales
- beating the competition
- providing quality in customer service and all areas of the business
- helping the community
- preserving the environment

the part played by communication

Effective communication within a business and in its dealings with customers is essential if these aims are to be achieved. Customer service is very important. Some businesses measure the success of customer service by the response rate to communications, for example:

- a same day reply to letters received through the post
- a defined maximum waiting time for answering the telephone
- same day response to e-mail

A good level of customer service and quality systems working within the business will ensure that customer enquiries are answered promptly and accurately. This in turn will lead to:

- customer loyalty and repeat sales
- increased sales – leading to better profitability and the opportunity to expand the business
- beating the competition

Efficient customer feedback through market research is another form of communication. Simply talking to customers will enable a business to learn of opportunities through which it can help the local community – sponsoring a local event or school, for example.

Listening to pressure groups will help a business to realise how it can help to protect the environment.

It is all a question of keeping the channels of communication open.

Activity 9.8

Communication
achieving business aims

Read through the situations set out below.

Work out in each case what has gone wrong with the communication channels

- inside the business
- between the business and its customers

How has this affected the business achieving its aims? Suggest how the problems could have been avoided.

---

1 musical chairs

A customer rings up a travel agent with an enquiry about a holiday. The telephone is answered after 20 rings. "Hang on please" is the answer and then a tape starts playing a Cliff Richard song. "Who was it what you wanted? Did you say Reservations? . . . . Oh OK - trying to connect you." More Cliff Richard for what seems like a very long time. "Sorry there's nobody answering. It's lunch time you see. I don't think there's anyone there. I'm not sure. Do you think you could try later? What was it you said? That's not very nice!"

---

2 a 'male' order problem

A customer rings up a business wanting to buy a shirt advertised in a mens clothing mail order catalogue. He gets through to the Sales desk and places his order, quoting the product code from the catalogue and his credit card number. Both numbers are read back to him by the Sales assistant who tells him the shirt is in stock and will be despatched that day.

A week later nothing has arrived by post. He telephones again and is told that the shirt should be with him in two days' time. Four days later the shirt arrives, but it is the wrong colour. He checks the catalogue and finds that they have sent a shirt with a different catalogue number.

He telephones the company, by this time very angry. "Sorry mate, I don't know what has gone wrong here. I think someone in the packing department has made a mistake. What colour did you want. Mulberry? I'm sorry, that's been out of stock for months. Didn't they tell you when you ordered?"

---

3 card games

A customer checking her credit card statement finds an item for £550 taken off the account by a jewellery store. She has bought from the store before, but knows that she has not spent £550 there, and certainly not on a day when she was away on holiday. She goes into the shop and queries the item. A trainee shop assistant deals with her. "Sorry madam, I really am not sure about this. Now you mention it we have had one or two people with the same problem recently. It's probably something to do with the computer. I expect Mr Perkins will know about it. He's in tomorrow, I think, or was it Friday? Anyway he'll know. Now did you want to buy anything while you were in?"

business structure and communications

The communication problems highlighted in the last activity point to the fact that the businesses were not being managed properly. Another factor which affects communications in business is the structure – the 'shape' of the business. In Chapter 5 we saw that businesses can either be 'flat' or 'tall'. Flat businesses are traditionally smaller, with few levels of authority. Tall businesses are traditionally larger and have many 'layers' of authority. A boss of a flat business is likely to know and communicate with staff more than the boss of a tall business, although, of course, there are exceptions to this.

Look at the structure charts below and their lines of communication. How do these lines affect the way a business can achieve its aims, eg profitability, quality customer service?

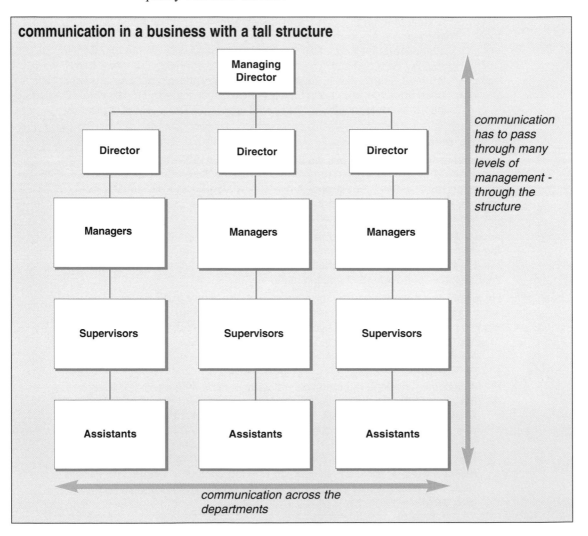

communication in a business with a tall structure

Managing Director

Director — Director — Director

Managers — Managers — Managers

Supervisors — Supervisors — Supervisors

Assistants — Assistants — Assistants

communication has to pass through many levels of management - through the structure

communication across the departments

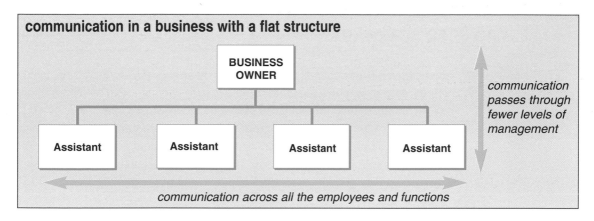

communication in a business with a flat structure

BUSINESS OWNER

Assistant   Assistant   Assistant   Assistant

communication passes through fewer levels of management

communication across all the employees and functions

communication in tall structures

Departments in a tall structure have to communicate with each other, as we have already seen in this chapter. If the business is to achieve quality customer service and so maximise sales and be profitable these horizontal lines of communication must work well. The problems in a tall structure can arise with the vertical lines of communication. Top management must know what is happening at Assistant level – what customers are saying about the products and about the business. The problem here is the decision-making process. Tall structures can be slow to react to market conditions because the major decisions have to be made at the highest level and it takes time for the information and recommendations to pass through the levels of authority.

communication in flat structures

The reason many tall structures are now changing into flatter structures is because the vertical lines of communication are so much shorter. Top management can react quickly to customers needs and so achieve the aims of the business more effectively. Employees in a flat structure will feel that they are part of the decision and will be motivated to work hard to achieve the business aims – good customer service, to sell more, to be profitable.

Activity 9.9

Communication and structure

Portfolio activity

Investigate the way communication is organised in the business you have chosen for your Portfolio and set out your findings in a written report. Then explain:

1   the way in which the shape of the organisation (flat or tall) influences the effectiveness of internal communications

2   the way in which effective communications help the business to achieve its aims and objectives – eg to maximise sales

CHAPTER SUMMARY

- Administration provides the back-up needed by all businesses. It involves tasks such as dealing with the post and e-mail, record keeping, dealing with routine enquiries and keeping the business premises clean and secure.
- Administration can either be carried out by employees in each department or can be carried out by a special 'administration' department which looks after all the other departments' needs. Some businesses use outside firms for tasks such as cleaning, security and telephone answering.
- Communication involves getting a message across.
- Communications in business can be internal (within the business) or external (for example, dealing with customers and suppliers).
- There are a number of different ways of communicating:
  - by word of mouth – telephone conversations, meetings, interviews
  - in writing – memos, letters, messages, adverts, notices
  - using information technology, for example internal and external e-mail, the internet, fax, teleconferencing
- Good standards of communication can help a business achieve its aims, eg quality customer service, increasing sales and profitability.
- Businesses with tall structures may have more difficulty with vertical lines of communication than businesses with flatter structures.

KEY TERMS

administration	the back-up activities needed for the efficient running of all businesses
call centres	operations centres which provide telephone enquiry and sales lines for businesses
memorandum	a formal written note used for communicating within an organisation
intranet	a computer communication network within a business
internet	a worldwide computer network linked by telephone lines
website	a computer file set up on the internet allowing 24 access – a 'shop window' for the business
videoconferencing	the linking of computers with cameras at different locations, enabling the users at either end to see and hear each other on-screen

MULTIPLE CHOICE QUESTIONS

1   Administration tasks in a business include:

A   dealing with the mail, photocopying, cleaning the premises

B   dealing with the mail, photocopying, market research

C   photocopying, cleaning the premises, production

D   cleaning the premises, security, quality control

2   A call centre is:

A   a reception area of a business where callers are greeted

B   a computer database which organises sales reps' visits

C   a centre which takes and makes telephone calls for businesses

D   a computer centre which sets up websites for businesses

3   Oral communications include:

A   telephone calls, faxes, discussions

B   discussions, interviews, e-mail

C   interviews, discussions, telephone calls

D   interviews, telephone calls, memoranda

4   The most appropriate communication method for sending detailed information to other departments within a business is:

A   telephoning each department

B   arranging a meeting for all staff

C   writing a letter to each department

D   writing a memorandum to each department

5   An intranet is:

A   a worldwide network of computers

B   a network of computers within a business

C   a telephone switchboard in a business

D   a meeting to help staff to get to know each other

6   Communication between top management and sales staff is likely to be better in:

A   a flat structure

B   a tall structure

C   a hierarchical structure

D   a vertical structure

10 Businesses and employees

Unit 1: Investigating how businesses work
Human resources

what this chapter is about

In this chapter we look at the Human Resources function which deals with the hiring and firing and well-being of staff. People are an important resource and businesses need to make sure that employees are treated fairly and are encouraged to work well. This will benefit the effectiveness of the business as a whole in achieving its aims.

what you will learn from this chapter

- There are many varying job roles in a Human Resources department (also known as Personnel) which deal with the different functions of the department.

- The main functions of Human Resources include:
  - recruitment of staff
  - disciplining and dismissing staff
  - training and developing staff
  - maintaining Health and Safety in the workplace
  - looking after employer/employee relations
  - maintaining staff records and administering the payroll

- Employers and employees have rights and responsibilities to each other. It is up to the Human Resources function to make sure that people know about them and to see that they are observed.

- The interests of employees are protected both by Trade Unions (which operate nationally) and by staff associations (many businesses have their own individual associations).

- The rights of employees are also protected by law. The most important of these protect employees against discrimination on the grounds of sex, race and disability.

This chapter forms the basis of your study of the Human Resources function in a business (Unit 1)

If you are also studying a Human Resources option unit, please refer to the section 'Individuals and the Organisation' on page 335.

job roles in a Human Resources department

'human resources' and 'personnel'

Most organisations, apart from very small ones, have a Human Resources department or section. Traditionally it is known as a 'Personnel' department although the term 'Human Resources' department is becoming more common, often in its abbreviated form 'HR'. In this chapter you will find references to 'Human Resources' and 'Personnel'. They mean basically the same thing – dealing with employees.

human resources and the organisation

Even in very small businesses a manager will include human resource management as one of his or her job roles.

As some HR departments are very small we shall look at a department that would be typical of a big company or local authority. In this case it belongs to Letchurch Garden Furniture Limited, a large company employing over 850 people. How is the Human Resources department structured? Look at the chart below and then read the job roles on the next few pages.

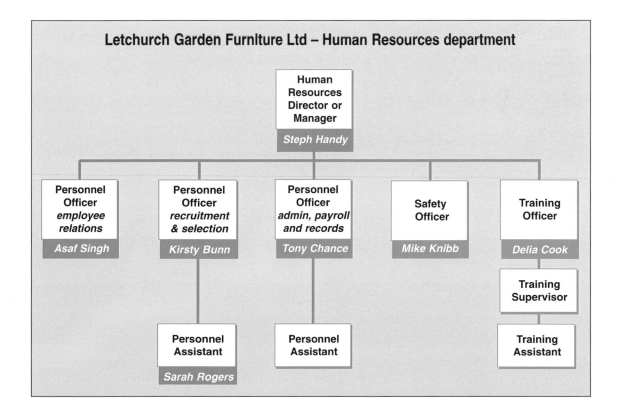

Jobs in the Human Resources Department of Letchurch Garden Furniture Limited

STEPH HANDY

HUMAN RESOURCES MANAGER AND DIRECTOR

"I have worked for Letchurch for 13 years, starting off as a personnel officer and then becoming personnel manager eight years ago. Three years later I was made a director of the company as well. My main roles include:

In the Human Resources department . . .

1   Carrying out the instructions of the Managing Director.

2   Ensuring all my staff work effectively.

3   Ensuring my department reaches its targets, eg in this department last year our target was to reduce the level of sickness absence from 6.5 days lost per employee per year to 4 days. We actually got it down to 3.5!

4   Ensuring my staff are motivated so that they do their jobs properly and enjoy what they are doing.

5   Carrying out the administration of the department – this includes the supervision of my five section officers.

6   Allocating work between the members of the department.

Then for the company as a whole I have these jobs to do . . .

7   Operating an effective communications system to ensure that all staff know what is going on .

8   Encouraging all our employees to say what they think and contribute ideas of their own (for example, when I was a personnel officer ten years ago I introduced a suggestion scheme which many of our employees have now used).

9   Ensuring that the company has a successful working relationship with all our employees."

Asaf Singh

Personnel Officer - Employee Relations

"We operate a large factory employing 850 people and 608 of these belong to the Transport and General Workers Union (TGWU). The 608 are represented by the TGWU representatives (known as "shop stewards"). My job is to make sure that the relationship between our employees and the company works effectively and without too many disputes. We have a series of agreements (sometimes called 'procedures') with our employees which set out how we deal with them from day to day. These include: Disciplinary Procedures, Grievance Procedures, and Redundancy Procedures."

Kirsty Bunn

Personnel Officer - Recruitment and Selection

"My main job involves the recruitment and selection of the right quality and quantity of staff. Firstly I have to talk to departmental managers who want to replace staff or recruit extra staff. They have to tell me exactly what they are looking for. I have to write out the job adverts and place them in the newspapers and at the job centres. Then I have to choose candidates to interview, often from hundreds of applications, and then invite them over for a "selection day". Steph (my manager) believes that it is too unreliable just to rely on a job interview so she expects all candidates invited in to do a series of job-related tests. Luckily, my personnel assistant, Sarah, sorts all that out!

Other parts of my job include looking after new staff and monitoring all employees' career progression. I also have to interview all people leaving the company to find out why they are leaving. This information provides very helpful feedback so that we can ensure that people are happy in their jobs."

Tony Chance

Personnel Officer - Administration, Payroll and Records

"I used to be a factory assembly worker but had to give that up fifteen years ago after a factory accident that permanently damaged my left arm. My job includes putting all newcomers onto the computerised payroll system and sorting out the pay arrangements for leavers. I handle all queries and complaints from staff about pay and I deal with the appropriate person in the company accounts department. I look after all the personnel records, including holidays and sickness. I deal with pension enquiries from staff and deal directly with the company pension scheme administrators. I also manage the company car fleet."

MIKE KNIBB

SAFETY OFFICER

"Being an ex-fireman like me means you pick up on unsafe workplace situations or dangerous equipment more quickly than other people. I have to ensure that Letchurch Ltd fulfils all of its duties under the Health and Safety at Work Act. This means I have to run a Safety Committee which consists of managers and employee-appointed safety representatives. I also have to run training courses for safety representatives and for supervisors and managers. More recently I had to carry out disability awareness programmes for all staff under the Disability Discrimination Act."

DELIA COOK

TRAINING OFFICER

"To carry out my role I have a Training Supervisor and Training Assistant to help me. My main role is the development and training of staff. My main concern is employee development. This means making sure that:

1   Staff are motivated to perform as well as they possibly can.

2   The organisation makes the best use of everyone's skills and abilities.

Basic training on the equipment in the factory is administered by the Training Supervisor, Pete Davis. Like most people in his position he had years of work experience as an apprentice, then as a fitter and finally as a team supervisor before taking on this role about four years ago."

SARAH ROGERS

PERSONNEL ASSISTANT

"In Human Resource departments like this one a personnel officer or a training officer will have an assistant to carry out much of the routine clerical work. I work as Personnel Assistant to Kirsty Bunn, who is in charge of recruitment and selection. Kirsty gives me loads of opportunities to do a wide range of personnel work. I joined Letchurch Ltd two years ago from the local college and I am using a lot that I learnt there on my Business Studies course – mind you, it never works out exactly like they tell you in the books! For example Kirsty gets me to look after all the lower grade vacancies. I have to plough through dozens of candidates, then short-list about ten candidates and fix up all the interviews for them. Sometimes I have to book hotel accommodation for those coming a long way. Then half of them don't even turn up . . . some don't even bother to ring in to tell you."

Activity 10.1

Human Resources at work
Letchurch Garden Furniture

Read through the descriptions of jobs on the previous three pages and answer the following questions, either through class discussion or in writing:

1   Steph Handy, the Human Resources Manager, has a wide range of responsibilities. In item 4 (of the list of things that she does) she wants her staff to be motivated and to work well. What does this mean? What sorts of things could she do to achieve this? Are there any of the items listed in her job description which might help her achieve this? Think about any jobs you have done and any ways in which you could have been motivated by your employer.

2   Asaf Singh deals with employee relations. Why is it important that he works to prevent disputes between employer and employees. What might happen if a dispute got out of hand – for example if there was a row between production workers and management over pay and working conditions?

3   Kirsty Bunn deals with recruitment and leavers. Why does she say that it is important to find out the reasons why people decide to leave the company?

4   Tony Chance is in charge of administering employee records. Why is it important that he is an accurate and efficient worker?

5   Mike Knibb is the Safety Officer. What experience has he had which helps him in this job? Why is maintaining safety in the workplace important when you have disabled employees or members of the public have access to the premises?

6   Delia Cook is the Training Officer. Why is her job so important to the way the company operates?

7   Sarah Rogers is Personnel Assistant to Kirsty Bunn. How does Kirsty make Sarah's job more interesting? What effect do you think this has on Sarah?

Portfolio activity

As part of your investigations into business you need to write descriptions of jobs in different functional areas. Write descriptions of <u>three</u> different jobs in a Human Resources department which you have investigated. You might be able to find out about the jobs from work experience, visiting speakers, visits to businesses, members of the family, or from careers resource centres at your school or college. If you can find out the information, draw up a structure chart of the Human Resources department in the business, using the chart on page 197 as a guide.

We have already seen in the last few pages the job roles of some employees in a Human Resources department. We will now look in more detail at each of the functions that they carry out.

recruiting and appointing staff

Recruitment is the first part of the process of filling a vacancy for a job. The recruitment process involves a number of stages.

deciding whether or not to fill a vacancy

If a vacancy for a job exists in an organisation it will be for one of several reasons:

- a new job is available because of the expansion of the organisation

- somebody in the organisation has retired or died

- somebody has gone elsewhere – there is a steady turnover of staff due to people getting other jobs elsewhere

- somebody has been promoted - the vacancy arises because the previous holder has been given a better job in the same organisation

- there is a restructuring of the business, which means there are gaps to be filled in the organisation

It may be that the business decides to save money by not filling the vacancy with a full-time employee. For example it may offer overtime to the remaining employees, it may employ part-timers, it may restructure the work flow or it may use machines and new technology to carry out the work. All these alternatives will need to be discussed carefully within the department.

filling the vacancy - finding the applicants

If the Human Resources department, after looking at all the alternatives, decides that the vacancy will need filling, then the next stage will be to look for candidates for the job. There are basically only two sources of candidate – candidates already working in the business and external candidates.

internal candidates

There will always be internal candidates who are interested in a vacancy because it is usually a promotion. The main benefits to the employer of internal appointments are:

- internal candidates know the business and what will be expected of them, and they can become effective in the new job very quickly

- the organisation will not need to rely upon external references which can be unreliable

- it is cheaper!

The disadvantages of appointing an internal applicant are that the successful candidates may become senior to people they used to work with as equals – there may be a problem for them in asserting their authority. Also, a person promoted internally may be expected to pick up the new job in an unreasonably short space of time.

external candidates

There are clear benefits from 'going outside' to fill a vacancy. These benefits are:

- a much wider range of people from which to choose

- newcomers to the organisation bring in new ideas and skills

There are also disadvantages in recruiting external candidates:

- it is more expensive

- it takes time for a newcomer to get used to his or her new employer.

- employers have to rely heavily on the references of other employers and these can be unreliable

Activity 10.2

Recruitment
sources of external candidates

The following are places where a business might find candidates for job vacancies: School and College Careers Services, Employment Agencies, University Career Services, Recruitment and Executive Consultants (sometimes referred to as "headhunters").

Which do you think is the best source for a business that is recruiting

1   a marketing manager?

2   a skilled computer operator?

3   an unskilled trainee assistant?

4   a trainee manager with no experience as yet?

Portfolio activity

Find out from the business you are investigating what their sources of recruitment are, and for what types of job.

Draw up a table of jobs and sources of recruitment.

after the appointment

terms and conditions of employment

Once the new employee has been appointed, he or she will be given a document known as 'Written Terms and Conditions of employment'. What does this include ?

1   The employer's name (this is usually a company name) and the employee's name.

2   The date when the employment begins.

3   A statement as to whether work with a previous employer counts as part of a continuous period of employment. An employee only gets employment protection after one year's continuous employment.

4   The job title - this can be a very broad title which may be to the employer's advantage. A new employee needs to be aware of this to ensure that they are not being taken advantage of. For example, a job as 'Secretary to the Managing Director' is not the same as an ordinary secretary's job and is far better paid.

5   The main terms and conditions relating to the job:

-    The pay rate - remember that this must be at least the Minimum Wage (you will need to find out what rate this is) and any special arrangements, eg overtime.

-    How it is paid (weekly, monthly, credit transfer, by cheque etc).

-    Hours of work - the number of hours required, eg 37 per week and the times of starting and finishing work each day, eg 9 am to 5 pm.

-    Holiday pay entitlement - at least 4 weeks a year plus public (or 'bank') holidays is a legal requirement (under the Working Time Directive 1996).

-    Sick pay entitlement (eg 3 months full pay and 3 months half pay). Remember that employers are not legally required to pay any sick pay other than the (rather low) Statutory Sick Pay (SSP).

-    Pension entitlement (better employers make a contribution to employees pensions). Note that no employer has to offer employees a pension.

-    The length of notice required, eg one month.

6   Details of how the grievance and disciplinary procedures operate must be provided. The statement need only state where the employee can refer to these procedures if he/she is interested in reading about them.

Activity 10.3

Terms of employment
employee rights

Why do you think it is important that an employee is given a contract of employment, or a 'Written Terms and Conditions'?

What are the rights of a 20 year-old employee who says the following to her employer?

1 "You've got to give me a pension - the law says so"

2 "I see you have only paid me £3.00 an hour in the first week. Is this right?"

3 "I am only getting three weeks paid holiday a year – my mate gets four weeks, plus bank holidays!"

retention – keeping the employee

'Employee retention' – which means keeping the employee once he or she has been appointed – is a major role of the HR manager. When people leave they have to be replaced. This is disruptive and can affect the effectiveness of the organisation. It is also expensive: at the time of writing replacing a manager using an executive recruitment agency cost between £5,500 and £6,500. Finding ways of keeping staff turnover as low as possible is therefore most important.

why do employees leave ?

the level of pay

Some employees leave because of poor pay. If pay rates for the particular job are better in another organisation then it is quite likely the job holder will consider moving. The convenience of the existing job and long standing working friendships will put some people off going elsewhere, but the cost of living and the need to provide the best possible lifestyle makes better pay very attractive.

lack of promotion

Where there are few opportunities for career progression people will leave. Some organisations prefer to recruit externally to fill more senior posts which means that anyone who wants to get on in their career has no choice but to leave.

lack of career development opportunities

Organisations which offer the chance to gain more qualifications and a wider variety of skills will retain people at least until the training is finished or the extra qualifications have been acquired. Organisations which do not offer these opportunities are less likely to retain their staff.

poor working environment

Working in unpleasant, dirty and unsafe conditions with poor canteen and social facilities will encourage people to leave if other organisations nearby offer something better. Today legislation such as the Factories Acts, the Health and Safety at Work Act and European Regulations mean that bad working conditions are fairly unusual.

personal treatment – discrimination

If an employee is treated badly, either by management or by fellow employees, then he or she will be more likely to try to get a job elsewhere. The commonest examples of bad treatment are discrimination against employees on grounds of race, sex, age or disability.

repetitive and uninteresting work

Boring work will encourage people to leave if there are more interesting alternatives elsewhere. Even when unemployment was high this was true and now that unemployment is far lower employers need to be aware of this point.

Activity 10.4

Employee retention
staying in the job?

Discuss in class people you know who have jobs. These people could include members of the class who have part-time jobs.

1   Identify the features of those jobs (such as low pay, poor promotion) which make the employees want to leave and get a job elsewhere?

2   Make a list of those features.

3   How could you make the jobs more attractive to the employees?

discipline and dismissal

No employer can afford to employ staff who are incapable of doing the job they are paid to do or who are behaving in a way which affects their job performance.

The main reasons for disciplining an employee are these:

1   being unable to do the job

2   being frequently late or absent

3   fighting or swearing or being drunk at work

4   stealing from the employer or from workmates

5   doing private work that is competing with the employer's business

If an employee is unsatisfactory in the job there is a laid-down procedure which is followed by most employers. This is designed to ensure that everyone is treated as fairly as possible.

the disciplinary procedure

There is a clear procedure to follow when disciplining an employee. Each stage must be carried out correctly, otherwise the employee has grounds for taking their case to an Employment Tribunal.

This procedure begins with . . .

an informal discussion with the employee

At this very informal stage the manager or supervisor will explain that he/she is unhappy with the employee's work and ask why this is so. At this stage the employee can request the organisation gives extra training, or a simpler lower-grade job, or the employee might want to tell the manager or supervisor about recent illnesses or personal problems that might have affected their work.

If this does not lead to an improvement in performance there will be . . .

a formal verbal warning

In most cases this formal 'telling off' is enough to get an employee to work harder. However, it will be formally recorded in the employee's employment records in case there is no improvement.

a formal written warning

If the quality of work has still not improved the employee will get a formal letter from the HR Department which will give details of the employee's performance, stating what is wrong with it, and threatening dismissal if the poor performance continues.

a final written warning

Some employers give a second written warning but others do not.

notice of dismissal

The final stage is to issue the employee with a letter stating they are dismissed (with notice as stated in the employee's written particulars) giving full details of the reasons for dismissal. Employees should be entitled to an interview with the personnel manager and they may have a trade union official or a personal friend with them to ensure that they are fairly treated.

examples of possible dismissal situations

Here are some sample situations where dismissal might apply, or could be prevented:

poor performance

An employee who is incapable of doing a job can sometimes be helped by being given extra training or being allocated a simpler, perhaps lower paid, job.

illness and absenteeism

An employee who has been ill or has been going through the problems of a divorce or a death in the family will be treated fairly by most employers. However, if the employee has been sick a long time and is not getting better the employer may have to ask him/her in a tactful way to leave – probably giving them an early retirement pension. In this type of situation the 'dismissal' is most likely to be agreed to by the sick employee.

poor punctuality

If the problem is lateness arriving at work it may be possible to rearrange work times so long as the lateness is for legitimate reasons, not just because the employee is too lazy to get out of bed !

The general rule is that whatever the problem is it is always best to be honest and 'straight' with the boss.

If the matter is extremely serious then the earlier stages of the procedure will be missed out. For example, theft from the business or from fellow employees is usually dealt with by the 'instant dismissal' of the employee concerned.

The employee may belong to a trade union (see page 216) in which case the union officials will be involved at the later stages of the disciplinary procedure. Usually union officials are sensible and will not cause difficulties for management if they can see that the employee has been fairly treated and given opportunities to improve the quality of his/her work.

Finally, if the dismissed employee is still unhappy about his dismissal he could complain to an Employment Tribunal.

Employment Tribunals

Employment Tribunals are 'employment courts' in which a professional lawyer, together with an industrialist and a trade unionist, decide whether or not an employee has been treated fairly by the employer.

If, after going through a disciplinary procedure, an employee still feels that the dismissal has been unfair he/she is entitled to complain to a Tribunal. After hearing both sides of the argument the Tribunal will decide which side has won.

If the employee has won then the Tribunal will either tell the employer to pay the employee compensation or give him or her their job back.

If the Tribunal decides that the employer has won then the employee has gained nothing except a lot of inconvenience and heartache. About one in three people who apply to a Tribunal win their case. Even when they do win the typical level of compensation is so low that it discourages many people from bothering to make a claim.

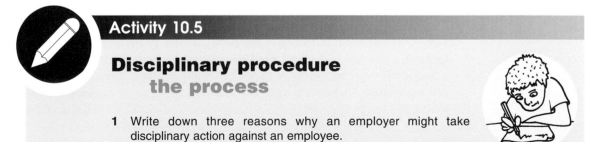

Activity 10.5

Disciplinary procedure
the process

1 Write down three reasons why an employer might take disciplinary action against an employee.

2 Draw up a flow diagram (boxes joined by arrows) showing all the possible stages in the disciplinary procedure. The first 'box' should be the informal discussion and the final 'box' should be an Employment Tribunal.

working conditions

Working conditions are an important part of the employer and employee working relationship. It is the job of the employer to introduce changes in working conditions when necessary. The main changes in working conditions have been as follows:

fixed short term contracts

Increasingly employers offer people work for one year or six months instead of permanently. This has the effect of making the employee feel insecure and therefore lacking in commitment to the employer.

pay and benefits

The main development in recent years has been the introduction of performance related pay (PRP) where the level of pay relates to the performance of the employee. 'Performance' can be the number of items produced by the employee (or the employee's team) or the level of sales achieved.

A very poor performance results in no pay rise or possibly even a pay cut.

flexibility in the way people work

The main areas in which flexibility has been introduced into working life are:

flexitime

Employees can, for example, alter the length of their working day so long as they do the set number of working hours each week. There is usually a 'core time' of hours, say from 10.00 to 15.00, but before or after these times employees can vary their day so long as they do, say, 37 hours in the week.

annualised hours

This takes the same principle of flexitime further. Assume that a business operates a 52 week year with 5 weeks holiday and a 38 hour week. This gives a total of 47 working weeks x 38 = 1786 hours per year. Employees could end up working 25 hours a week for a few weeks then 50 hours for a few weeks and so on. Clearly, such a system is only of use to a business where output varies greatly from season to season or from month to month.

flexibility in job location and skills required

Employers increasingly expect employees to be flexible in terms of where they work and what they do.

the place of work – teleworking

Employers require staff, especially at higher grades, to move around from one job location to another. Increasingly this can mean spending time in other countries, especially in the other EU nations.

Increasingly, employers are recruiting people to work at home using sophisticated computer technology which links into the employer's headquarters. This is attractive to employees who want to avoid travelling to work and to employers who save money because they need less office space.

the work itself – multi-skilling

Giving people a variety of jobs to do is known as multi-skilling. This means that employees are trained to do a variety of different jobs. Employers gain because:

- an employee can stand in and do the work of somebody who is absent through illness or holidays
- employees are more motivated because doing several jobs is usually more interesting than doing just one; where an employee is able to do several jobs it increases his/her value to the organisation and makes him/her feel more appreciated and more secure

Activity 10.6

Working conditions
flexible ways of working

Flexible ways of working include: flexitime, annualised hours, teleworking, multi-skilling. Which of these is the most suitable in the following four situations?

1   The business wants to cut down on staffing costs and is able to allow staff to work at home.

2   The business is very seasonal – busy in the Spring and Summer and quiet at other times of the year.

3   The business is open for long hours and has many employees who can work at different times of the day.

4   The business is able to increase the number of tasks each employee can do.

Portfolio activity

Find out if any of these methods of flexible working are used in the business you are investigating. Compile a questionnaire to find out what the employees and the Human Resources staff think of them.

training and development

the need for training

Firstly we will examine the importance of training employees. Then we will look at how employees might be developed to increase job satisfaction and improve their chances of promotion.

What is training? Training means acquiring knowledge and skills which can be used in a particular job.

These days it is assumed that people will change their job several times in a lifetime, often switching to completely different types of work. This may require them retraining at several points in their working lives.

It is also true to say that people who do keep the same job for a long time are required to update their skills regularly, or face redundancy because their old skills are made useless by the introduction of new technology.

Training is therefore much more central to peoples' lives as an ongoing process rather than just something they do at the start of their careers.

training programmes

Most larger organisations employ professional training officers to run training programmes for employees. In a large manufacturing company, for example, the training manager will have teams of training instructors to teach all kinds of courses to employees. Even in small businesses several types of training will still be necessary.

Types of training include:

- initial training for new employees – induction programmes
- updating training, particularly in new technology
- multi-skilling training (see the previous page)
- Government training schemes, eg 'New Deal' job schemes

We will now look at the main types of training course that organisations may run.

'In house' training courses

This is where employers run courses inside their own organisation. Courses run 'in house' will be ones where it is impractical and unrealistic to offer any other alternative – an obvious example would be the organisation's own induction programme when employees first join the organisation.

external courses

Sometimes it is necessary to send staff to do courses elsewhere. This may be with another employer or at a specialist training centre or at the factory of an equipment supplier.

vocational and professional courses

Internal and external courses such as NVQs and MBAs often have to be reinforced by courses provided by local colleges and universities. These courses provide the essential knowledge to support what is learnt in the workplace and on internal courses.

employee development

What is employee development? Employee development may be defined as a course of action which will enable an employee to realise his or her potential for growth in an organisation. In other words the employer does not just train people for now, but for the future as well.

How is this done? A good employer will have a system of identifying career potential in an employee. If there is no system to do this, the result will be that employees stay in 'dead end' jobs which may make them frustrated. Often they will leave for a better job where their potential is more likely to be recognised. This means that the employer will lose people who could have been a very great asset to the organisation.

A system to identify potential could include an analysis of every employees' performance and practical tests to assess employees' ability to handle the kind of work which more senior posts would involve.

methods of developing employees with potential

There are several ways to help employees to develop their abilities

- Job rotation – giving people a range of jobs in rotation widens their experiences and increases their skills.
- Job enlargement – this means expanding a job by adding on extra tasks. It gives managers a better idea of the employee's ability and stamina.
- Job enrichment – this means adding more interesting and more difficult tasks to the job. This might be done with a person of very great potential (often known as a 'high-flier') to see just how capable he or she really is.
- Understudying – this means that an employee will be attached to a very senior manager to act as an assistant. This gives the employee a better idea of what senior managers have to do.

One final important point - it is not a good idea to encourage employees to develop themselves in the ways listed above unless the organisation has got some career opportunities for them.

Activity 10.7

Training and development

Interview your teacher, a person who works in a factory and a person who works in a supermarket or department store. Ask them about the training they have had during the last year. Write a summary of your findings.

Portfolio activity
Find out about the training opportunities in the business you are investigating. Arrange a talk, if you can, by the person in charge of training and its administration.

Health and Safety at Work

employer responsibility

Employers have to observe the rules and regulations laid down in the 1974 Health and Safety at Work Act and in other related legislation. The 1974 Act states that the employer is responsible for making sure that the workplace is safe and healthy to work in. Examples of this are:

- safe entrances and exits

- safe equipment and machinery

- safe systems of work

- proper tuition and training to ensure that staff work safely

- proper and thorough investigation and recording of all accidents at work

- the employer also has a duty to discipline (or even dismiss) employees who injure other employees (either intentionally or simply by fooling about with equipment)

health and safety policy statement

The Health and Safety at Work Act requires that an employer should have a 'written statement' of its health and safety policy. This must be made available to all staff. A good employer will give copies of it to all new staff.

What will be in this statement?

- the procedure for the reporting of accidents by staff

- a list of all staff trained in first aid and details of where first aid boxes are located; some bigger organisations employ nurses and their details, names, and where they can be found must also be listed

- a list of all Safety Representatives - their job is to ensure that the employer is carrying out safety policies properly and they are required to carry out full three monthly safety checks; they have a duty to investigate complaints from staff about safety worries

- the name of a senior manager responsible for health and safety policies

As well as the 1974 Health and Safety at Work Act more recent legislation has brought further protection for employees. For example the COSHH regulations (1988). These letters stand for 'control of substances hazardous to health'. These regulations lay down very strict rules on how dangerous chemicals are to be handled, stored and recorded.

In 1992 European Regulations on the use of VDUs (visual display units) were introduced because of the problems they were known to cause (particularly eyesight problems). Repetitive strain injury (RSI) is also now covered by an associated European Regulation.

Activity 10.8

Health and Safety at Work

What hazards can you spot in the office shown below.

Portfolio activity

Interview the person who is responsible for Health & Safety in your school/college and the person responsible for Health & Safety in the business you are investigating. Compare the two jobs and write a job description for both of them.

Employee Organisations and Unions

Many of the employees at Letchurch Limited in the first Activity in this chapter (see page 201) belong to a Trade Union. In some organisations there is no union to represent employees at all, either because the employer does not want employees to have union representation or because the employees are not interested. Some organisations have 'staff associations' instead of trade unions. Some organisations have neither.

It is often the role of the HR Department to liaise with Trade Unions when important decisions are made about pay and conditions, redundancy, relocation, merger or a dispute.

Trade Unions

At the time of writing about 7 million people in the UK belong to a trade union. There are three main types of trade union in Britain:

Craft Unions

These were the earliest type of union – small organisations which brought together skilled employees to fight for good wages and conditions in the new industries of the eighteenth century. Nowadays craft unions are far larger and are found in the most modern industries such as aerospace, car manufacture and computers. The AEEU (Amalgamated Engineering and Electrical Union) is probably the best known.

General Unions

These recruited mainly unskilled and semi-skilled employees. Nowadays there are only a few of them but they cover a very wide range of industries. The TGWU and GMB are the best known in this category.

non-manual unions

There are now many union members in non-manual jobs. Unison, which operates in the public sector (eg local government) with about 1.3 million members is currently the biggest union in the UK.

what Trade Unions do

Most trade unions have basically the same aims, although the relative importance of each of them will vary. These are:

improvement in pay and conditions

Pay and conditions have steadily improved over many years and this is at least partly due to the action taken by trade unions. Trade unions are also involved in the improvement of health and safety standards in the workplace.

job protection

Nowadays, with jobs continually becoming redundant because of new technology, this is a very important role. Unions are constantly fighting to retain jobs, and where redundancy takes place, to negotiate the best possible redundancy compensation.

Staff Associations

Many employees are represented by staff associations rather than by trade unions. Their chief features are:

- each staff association is limited to the business where the staff are employed – in other words each organisation will have its own association

- staff associations are most common in non-manual areas of work such as financial services companies

- staff associations are usually financially supported by the employer

- staff associations provide an acceptable alternative to trade union membership for certain types of employee who for a range of reasons do not want to join trade unions

Because staff associations lack financial independence they have never had the power to fight for improved pay and conditions as trade unions have been able to do.

Activity 10.9

Employee organisations
investigating Trade Unions

Go to your local library or resources centre, or access the internet.

1 Find out the names of four different trade unions.

2 Find out which areas of work they represent.

3 Find out how many members they have.

4 Investigate what they provide for their members.

employment law

The relationship between employer and employee is regulated by law. All employees are protected by a variety of laws. It is the responsibility of the HR Department to ensure that these laws are complied with by the business. Some of the more important laws are described on the following pages.

Sex Discrimination Act 1975

This law states that employers may not discriminate between employees on the grounds that they are male or female. In other words an employer cannot prefer in favour of men or women, but must treat both sexes as equal.

what is sex discrimination?

The 1975 Sex Discrimination Act makes it illegal for an employer to discriminate against a particular sex when

- advertising for a job
- appointing an employee for a job
- promoting staff into better jobs
- deciding on the terms and conditions of the job
- offering employees opportunities for training and development

exceptions to the Act

There are a number of examples where the Act does not apply. These include:

- private clubs - for example some of the exclusive 'gentlemens clubs' in London can refuse to admit women
- the armed forces – recruitment of women can be restricted to specific areas – although these restrictions have been relaxed recently
- actors – it would be unusual to find a female James Bond, for example

Race Relations Act 1976

The 1976 Race Relations Act makes discrimination on grounds of race illegal in the same way as under the Sex Discrimination Act 1975, for example when advertising for a job and making job appointments.

exceptions to the Act

Again there are a few exceptions to the Act , for example

- ethnic restaurants can specify people of a particular race to work as waiters/waitresses (eg Chinese, Indian) to make the restaurant look more authentic
- social work departments can specify they want to appoint staff of a particular ethnic group where they have to deal with social problems of people of the same ethnic group – this is because they will have a better understanding of the client's culture and language

- actors of a particular ethnic group will be needed for specific roles; for example, a Chinese actress is unlikely to play Queen Victoria

direct and indirect forms of discrimination.

Both Acts state that there are two ways in which employers could break the law:

direct discrimination

This means that there is a positive decision to discriminate either against men or women. In one legal case a chief fire officer rejected a woman's application for aj ob as a firefighter without considering it seriously. This was direct discrimination.

indirect discrimination

Indirect discrimination is where the employer creates certain conditions of employment which make it harder for a particular racial group or for women or men to get the jobs advertised. For example a minimum height requirement might make it harder for large numbers of woman (or for certain ethnic groups) to apply for a job.

Activity 10.10

Employee protection
discrimination at work

Here are some extracts from adverts for job vacancies. Look at each of them and suggest whether they discriminate against certain people or not. If they do, state the Act of Parliament which is involved.

1   "Barmaid required at the Fox and Grapes Inn, Barchester."

2   "Man required to play the role of Santa Claus from 12th December onwards. Apply in writing to Sproggins and Smith Department Stores, High Street, Barchester."

3   "Englishman required to work in 'Ye Olde English Restaurant' 17 High Street, Barchester. Apply to the Manager."

4   "Female qualified teacher to teach French to 11-18 year old girls and to live in a school boarding house as a school housemistress. Contact the Headmistress, Barchester Girls School."

Disability Discrimination Act 1995

This Act provides protection for disabled persons in much the same way as the other laws discussed help prevent discrimination on the grounds of sex and race. It only applies to organisations employing twenty people or more.

The key aspects of the Act are:

no discrimination at work

The employer must not discriminate against disabled people when

- advertising jobs and inviting applications

- offering jobs after interviews have taken place

- deciding on the terms and conditions of the job when an appointment takes place

Once appointed, a disabled person must be treated the same as other employees when training or promotion or any other benefits are on offer. This does not mean that they must be treated more favourably than other employees: if five people are up for a promotion and there is only one post vacant the disabled person cannot expect favourable treatment.

a suitable workplace for disabled employees

The employer must take reasonable steps to ensure that a disabled person can work at the workplace. This includes making arrangements such as

- modifying the buildings (entrances, ramps, lifts, for example)

- changing working hours to suit the disabled person

- allowing time off for medical treatment

- allowing extra training so that the disabled person can carry out the job

- providing a reader or an interpreter, if required

- putting a disabled person in a more convenient work place (eg the ground floor rather than three floors up)

Employers only have to do what is reasonable. If modifications are very expensive than this would be unreasonable. There is some Government financial assistance available for modifications to buildings.

Where the employer will not make the necessary modifications the disabled person can make a claim to the Employment Tribunal. The employer will then have to convince the Tribunal that the modifications were not reasonable. If they cannot do this they must pay compensation to the disabled person.

Activity 10.11

Employee protection
disability discrimination

Here are some situations which might happen in the workplace.

State what you think are the rights of each of the employees under the Disability Discrimination Act.

1   Craddock Computers employs ten people. The MD advertises a vacancy in the local paper. A disabled man applies and receives a letter in reply stating "We regret that because of your disability we will not be able to offer you a job within our organisation."

2   Bellfield Foods employs 150 people in its factory. The company advertises a vacancy in the local paper. A disabled woman applies and receives a letter in reply stating "We regret that because of your disability we cannot consider your application for the current vacancy."

3   Jane Molesworth is a disabled employee and has worked in a large local government office with 75 staff for over seven years. She has successfully completed her in-house training and is doing professional exams, but has had no promotion, unlike her colleagues. The Human Resources manager has said to her "Sorry, Jane, you know that we cannot promote you at the moment. We are not allowed by law to show you favouritism."

4   John Martin is a disabled employee at a local insurance brokers which employs forty staff. He is confined to a wheelchair. The firm is planning to relocate to an out-of-town office complex. John, who is worried by the prospect, says to his manager: "You will have to lay on special transport for me to the new office. I cannot possibly get there myself. There is no bus service. Anyway the office will have to be on the ground floor as I can't get up any stairs."

Employment Rights Act 1996

This law covers a very wide range of employment related issues. It 'consolidates' and updates a number of previous laws:

- The employer must give a new employee 'Written Terms and Conditions of Employment' within two months of appointment (see page 204 for details).

- The employer must give an itemised pay statement, listing all deductions which have to be made from the wages (income tax, National Insurance, for example). In addition, the employer must only deduct extra payments which have been agreed with the employee, eg a monthly payment to the company social and sports club.

- Employers must pay a 'guaranteed payment' to all employees if there is a problem which means work cannot be carried out (for example if there is a shortage of raw materials to work on or if bad weather prevents work being carried out). This is at least £14.50 a day.

- Employers must give time off for people to

  - take part in public duties - as a Magistrate for example (but they not entitled to be paid when absent)

  - go to ante-natal care clinics (they are entitled to be paid as normal)

  - look for other jobs after being told that their job is redundant (again they are entitled to be paid as normal)

- Employers must give employees proper notice that they are to be dismissed, for example one weeks notice after one months service and two weeks after one years service.

- Where an Employment Tribunal decides that an employee has been unfairly dismissed the employer must pay the employee compensation or give the employee their own job back or give them a comparable job.

- Employees must get redundancy payments if they are made redundant.

- Where an employer has to go out of business because of insolvency (goes 'bust') employees have certain legal rights. As there is not often any money left to pay employees, the employees may be owed several weeks pay. The Act requires that the government will pay the employees compensation wages in these circumstances.

Activity 10.12

Employment Rights Act 1996
redundancy payments

Richard Talbot works for Letchurch Limited. He has just been made redundant. He says: 'I have worked at Letchurch Limited for ten years. I earn £275 a week before the taxman gets any of it. Last week they made five of us redundant doing the same job in the same department – we all get the same pay:

Me !	10 years service. I will be 47 in February.
Fred Parkin	2 years service. He will be 21 in January.
Sarah Smith	12 years service. She will be 36 in March.
Ted Wilson	15 years service. He will be 40 in March.
Ramjit Singh	20 years service. He will be 64 in May.'

The minimum Redundancy Payments due under the Employment Rights Act 1996 are set out in the table below.

Employment Rights Act 1996

Employees must get redundancy payments if they are made redundant. These payments are at least:

- Half a weeks pay for every year worked between ages 18 and 21

- One weeks pay for every year worked between ages 22 and 40.

- One and a half weeks pay for every year worked between ages 41 and 64.

The legal maximum payable is a total of 20 weeks pay.

What will the minimum Redundancy Payments bill be for Letchurch Limited under the Employment Rights Act 1996? Is this necessarily what they will pay?

Activity 10.13

Employee rights and the law

Portfolio activity

Write a summary entitled "Employee rights and Employment Law". The report should contain:

1   a description in your own words of the purpose of the four Acts explained in this chapter.

2   an example based on an actual employer/employee situation of how each of the four Acts protects the rights of the employee

CHAPTER SUMMARY

- When recruiting staff a Human Resources department can either fill the vacancy from within the organisation or advertise for external candidates.

- When an employee has been appointed, he or she should be given a written statement setting out the terms and conditions of employment; these will include details such as job title, pay, hours of work, holidays, notice period.

- The disciplinary procedure follows a number of stages ending in dismissal; these can include: initial discussion, verbal warning, formal written warning, notice of dismissal. If the employee thinks he or she has been unfairly treated, he or she can appeal to an Employment Tribunal.

- An employer has a responsibility to provide suitable working conditions for the needs of employees. This can involve flexibility in the hours of work, the place of work and the tasks which make up the job. The employer is required by law to make sure that Health and Safety regulations are observed.

- An employer has a responsibility to provide training and development programmes for employees. Training can be in-house or externally provided.

- The interests of employees are protected both by Trade Unions and by staff associations. The rights of employees are also protected by law. The most important of these protect employees against discrimination on the grounds of sex, race and disability.

KEY TERMS

Human Resources	the function in a business which deals with the needs of all the employees; it is also known as 'Personnel'
Minimum Wage	the minimum hourly rate which employers are required by law to pay to employees
Employment Tribunal	an 'employment court' to which an employee can take an employer if he/she has been unfairly treated
flexitime	a system which enables an employee to work a set number of hours but at times agreed with the employer
multi-skilling	employees trained to do a number of different tasks
Trade Union	a national organisation set up to protect the rights of employees and provide benefits
staff association	an organisation in an individual business set up to provide benefits for employees of that business
discrimination	giving preference to one employee over another

MULTIPLE CHOICE QUESTIONS

1   A Human Resources Department has overall responsibility for
     A   recruitment, payroll, training, production
     B   recruitment, payroll, training, sales administration
     C   recruitment, payroll, training, Health & Safety at Work
     D   raising finance, payroll, training, Health & Safety at Work

2   The written terms and conditions of employment given to a new employee
     must contain:
     A   employer's name, employee's name, job description, pay rate
     B   Trade Union's name, employee's name, job description, pay rate
     C   date work starts, holiday dates, job description, pay rate
     D   employer's name, employee's name, job description, tax rate

3   The disciplinary procedure can involve a number of different stages, but in
     the following order:
     A   Employment Tribunal, verbal warning, written warning, dismissal
     B   informal discussion, verbal warning, written warning, dismissal
     C   Trade Union discussion, written warning, verbal warning, dismissal
     D   informal discussion, written warning, verbal warning, dismissal

4   Annualised hours are suitable in situations where the employees
     A   want to fix the times of day in which they work
     B   work hours at the Minimum Wage pay rate
     C   work the same hours each day throughout the year
     D   work different hours at different times of year

5   An employee is allowed to have time off for ante-natal classes under the
     terms of :
     A   The Sex Discrimination Act
     B   The Race Relations Act
     C   The Disability Discrimination Act
     D   The Employment Rights Act

6   A Chinese Restaurant advertising for 'Chinese waiters' could be seen to be
     acting against the terms of:
     A   The Sex Discrimination Act
     B   The Race Relations Act
     C   no Act at all
     D   The Employment Rights Act

section three

BUSINESS FINANCE

introduction

In this unit you will investigate and learn about:

- how businesses find out the cost of products and their likely income before deciding to produce them

- what the main types of cost and income are

- how to set up a cash flow forecast – a table which estimates the future flows of money in and out of the bank account and shows if a project is feasible

- how to work out profit – using a table which calculates the difference between the income and running costs of the business

- how to work out if a business is going to 'break-even' on a product and make a profit

- how to use computer spreadsheets for these tables and calculations

- the way a business uses financial documents when it buys and sells

chapters in this section

assessment guide

Unit 3: Business finance

This Unit is externally assessed – you will have to sit a test paper set by your Awarding Body. Your Tutor will give you guidance about what to expect in the paper and is likely to give you practice papers.

In order to prepare for this external test you should collect material in your Portfolio for practice and revision. The following type of material will be useful, and will be produced if you do the Activities in the chapters . . .

1   Lists of start-up costs and running costs for different types of business – your test may give you examples and ask you to distinguish between the two types.

2   Lists of items which appear in a cash flow forecast and examples of how to work out the bank balance. Your test may ask you to fill in figures on a cash flow forecast table which they will provide – they are not likely to ask you to draw up your own table.

3   Lists of fixed and variable costs for a break-even calculation, together with examples of the calculation using the formula, plus examples of a break-even graph. Your test may ask you to work out a break-even point, but will give the formula; it may also ask you to comment on a graph.

4   Examples of a profit and loss statement. Your test could give you a format and ask you to fill in the figures, so you will have to know 'what goes where' and how to do the calculations.

5   Examples of the financial documents used by business. You will have to know what figures go where and how the documents 'work'. The test may give you blank documents and ask you to complete them and comment on them.

Now study the next page and appreciate what you have to do to achieve a Pass, a Merit or a Distinction in the external test.

to achieve a Pass in the test you must . . .

1   understand the difference between start-up costs and running costs and be able to put the costs into these categories; you will be able to tell whether the income comes from the sale of goods or services

2   be able to identify the flows of money which come into and go out of a business and recognize the main parts of a cash flow forecast

3   understand the difference between fixed and variable costs and create and interpret break-even charts

4   recognize the main elements of a profit and loss statement

5   understand how financial documents are used – this means knowing who uses them, why they are used, and when

6   be able to recognize each of the financial documents, complete them with details of the financial transaction and know how to check them for accuracy

7   be able to explain the advantages and disadvantages of using a computer spreadsheet for financial calculations

to achieve a Merit in the test you must also . . .

8   identify typical costs and revenues from specific types of business

9   accurately complete a simple cash flow forecast from given data and be able to check your workings – the inflows on the forecast are likely to include sales, loans, capital and grants, outflows will be the normal running expenses – you will not need to worry about VAT

10   accurately carry out a break-even calculation and construct a graph from given data

11   accurately complete a profit and loss statement from given data – this will include sales, purchases (the cost of sales), gross profit, overheads/expenses and net profit

12   understand the sequence in which the financial documents are used

13   be able to explain the advantages and disadvantages of using a computerised accounting system such as Sage to generate financial documents

to achieve a Distinction in the test you must also . . .

14   explain why it is important for a business to prepare a cash flow forecast

15   show how changes in fixed costs, variable costs and sales income will affect the break-even point and the level of profit that can be made; you will also explain the reasons why these costs and revenues might change

16   understand the significance of making errors in the completion of financial documents and in calculating the financial data which they contain – you should appreciate the consequences of these errors and what would have to be done to put things right

11 The costs of starting a new business

> **Unit 3 Business finance:**
> **covering the costs of a new product**

what this chapter is about

When a business starts up for the first time or launches a new product it has to work out carefully the costs involved. It also has to look at the money it will receive from the sale of the new product. The business will then be in a position to decide whether or not to go ahead – this will depend on whether it can cover its costs. This chapter explains and illustrates these costs. The next chapter looks in more detail at where the money comes from.

what you will learn from this chapter

- money coming in from the sale of the products of a business – the revenue – can come from the sale of manufactured goods or from the sale of a service

- a business starting up for the first time or launching a new product will need to plan what resources it needs, eg new staff, new premises, new machinery – these all involve an added cost for the business

- some costs are one-off 'start-up' costs, eg premises, machinery

- some costs are day-to-day 'running' costs, eg wages, advertising, rent

- different types of business will have different types of costs, eg a clothes factory (manufacturing), a supermarket (retailing), a travel agent (service)

business revenue

Businesses raise their money from a number of different sources – the owners putting money in, banks making loans and the receipt of money received from the sale of the products of the business.

The amount of money received from the sale of the products – the sales 'revenue' – can often make the difference between the success or failure of the business. Revenue can be from the sale of:

- a product manufactured by the business
- a product bought in – as in the case of a shop
- a service such as a holiday or a taxi ride

start-up costs for the new business

start-up costs

When a business starts up for the first time, or when it expands, the owner needs to plan what he or she will need to get going.

Start-up costs are 'one-off' costs you have to pay when you start a business.

There will be a number of 'one-off' costs involved. These can include*:*

premises

Premises could be a new factory (for a manufactured product), a shop or an office (for a service). You will probably point out that the owner of a business may not always have to buy premises – they can be rented, which is cheaper in the short term.

machinery and equipment

The business may need new machinery: production machinery (if it is a manufacturer), computers, photocopiers, delivery vans. Remember that these can also always be rented to save on start-up costs.

market research and advertising

Time and money can be spent in market research, finding out with questionnaires and interviews whether the new business idea will sell. People will need to be hired to do this, and this will cost money. Any new product will also need effective promotion and advertising, which can be expensive.

Activity 11.1

Ella MacPherson
start-up costs

Ella MacPherson has recently won some money on the Lottery and plans to set up a training business offering courses in office administration and computer skills. She has been working until now as a tutor at a local training college but is keen on being her own boss. She has drawn up a 'shopping list' of start-up costs:

Purchase of office premises	£95,000
Computer equipment and software	£22,500
Furniture and fittings	£9,500
Agency fee for market research	£2,500
Advertising in the local paper	£500
Advertising mailshot to local businesses	£2,000

1 What is the total of Ella's start-up costs? Use a spreadsheet if you can to calculate the total. Add in an extra number of rows (say 5) above the total row to allow for extra start-up costs.

2 Can you think of any other start-up costs that she might have to pay? Add these into the spreadsheet calculation.

3 She has thought about buying some premises. Can you think of any alternatives to this which might save her money?

4 What other costs, other than start-up costs, might she have to pay?

running costs for the new business

In addition to the *start-up costs* we have just looked at there will be a wide variety of *running costs* that a new or an expanding business will need to think about.

Running costs are day-to-day costs which a business has to pay

It is important to know the difference between running costs and start-up costs. The difference applies to personal finance as well as business finance. For example, if you think about buying a new walkman, the start-up cost is the price of the machine, the running costs are items like batteries which you buy from time-to-time to keep it playing.

Running costs in business are normally estimated for the period of a year.

types of running cost

You will know from the unit 'how a Business Works' that there are a number of functions or departments in a business. There are running costs for each of these areas:

production

The cost of manufacturing a product or producing a service, eg sheet steel for a car manufacturer, goods bought by a shop to sell to its customers, air fares and hotel charges for a travel company, food for a restaurant.

sales and marketing

The cost of making sure that the right products reach the right customers in the best possible way: advertising, getting customer feedback, providing customer care.

human resources

The cost of employing staff, eg wages, recruitment costs, staff perks, training, Health & Safety (making sure people are safe at work).

finance

The financial cost of running the business: paying interest to the bank if money is borrowed, bank charges, paying accountants' fees.

administration

The day-to-day costs of running the business: insurance, rent, rates, power, stationery, telephone bills, postage.

Activity 11.2

Running costs for businesses

Look at the images on the next page as prompts and write down individually (or in groups), as many different running costs you can think of for

- a services business
- a manufacturing business

Use one sheet of paper for each business and the format shown on page 225.

You do not need to write down any figures at this stage, just the *types* of cost, for example wages and 'phone bills.

What differences, if any, can you see between the two types of business?

Activity 11.2 use these images to suggest types of business running costs

description of business				
types of running cost				
production or service operation	sales and marketing	human resources	finance	administration

Activity 11.3

Ella MacPherson
running costs

Ella MacPherson (see Activity 11.1 on page 232) has now estimated her running costs for her computer training business for the first year. The list is as follows:

Training materials	£3,700
Advertising	£1,800
Staff wages	£28,000
Accountant's fees	£1,500
Bank charges	£400
Electricity bills	£450
Insurance	£1,800
Rates	£1,650
Telephone bills	£800
Stationery	£560

1 What is the total of Ella's running costs?

2 Draw up a chart with six columns in the format shown on the next page. Use an A4 piece of paper turned on its side, or, if you can, set up a suitable computer spreadsheet. Make sure the left-hand column is about twice as wide as the other five. Head up the columns as shown.

Using Ella's running cost figures shown above, enter the type of running expense (eg training materials, wages, bank charges etc) in the left-hand column and the money amounts on the same row in the column which best describes the type of expense (eg training materials = production cost of £3,700).

Add up each money column and write the totals on the bottom line.

Add up the column totals and then check the total with your answer to **1** above. If the amounts are different you will need to check your workings.

3 Can you think of any major running expense, not included on the list, which Ella's business will have to pay out on a regular basis?

Ella MacPherson

type of expense	production £	sales & marketing £	human resources £	finance £	administration £
TOTAL					

Activity 11.4

Red Alert Limited

Start-up costs and running costs

It is important to be able to distinguish start-up costs from running costs, because they will be dealt with differently in the financial records of the business.

Set out below are the figures for start-up costs and running costs of a new business that manufactures electronic security alarms. The figures are mixed up.

RED ALERT LIMITED – COSTS FOR THE FIRST YEAR

Electricity bills	£890
Premises purchased	£100,000
Office administration costs	£560
Equipment purchased	£45,600
Furniture purchased	£37,800
Rates	£2,190
Gas bills	£400
Insurance	£4,450
Wages	£120,000
Initial market research for business launch	£5,600
Electronic components used in production	£56,700
Cars and vans purchased	£55,650
Fuel and insurance for cars and vans	£7,400
Advertising during the year	£4,100

1   Sort the costs into start-up costs and running costs. You can do this by drawing up separate columns for start-up costs and running costs.

2   Calculate the totals of start-up costs and running costs.

3   How much money will the business need in the first year to cover these expenses?

costs in different types of business

Different types of business will have to pay different types of cost for the simple reason that they carry out very different types of activity.

manufacturing businesses

Businesses which make a product will need to invest in the resources for the manufacturing process.

Manufacturing start-up costs are likely to include factory or workshop premises, machinery and equipment.

Manufacturing running costs will involve wages of production workers, raw materials or components, the cost of running the factory as well as all the other normal business running costs such as office administration.

retail businesses

Retail businesses – eg supermarkets which buy and sell ready-made products – need resources to enable them to sell these products to the public.

Retail start-up costs are likely to include warehouses, shops, shop fittings, check-out equipment and delivery vehicles.

Retail running costs will include the stocks of the products that they sell, the cost of running shops, paying wages and all the other normal business running costs such as administration.

service industries

Service businesses such as travel agents and insurance companies provide a service and therefore do not need to invest in warehousing or to so great an extent in premises.

Service business start-up costs may be relatively low; they will need to invest in market research and also in the premises from which the business operates.

Service business running costs will include normal business running costs such as sales and office administration. The running cost of maintaining customer care will be important to service industries.

conclusion

As you will appreciate, no two businesses have identical costs. Generally speaking, it is more expensive and risky to set up a manufacturing business, but the rewards – in the form of profit – can be high.

Activity 11.5

Costs of different businesses

Set out below are the costs of three different businesses. They are a manufacturer of sports equipment, a shop and an employment bureau. Look carefully at the different types of cost and then carry out the tasks that follow.

expenses	Business 1	Business 2	Business 3
Factory premises	£2,200,000	-	-
Shop premises	-	-	£500,000
Office premises	£120,000	£150,000	£350,000
Vehicles	£67,000	£12,000	£155,000
Production line machinery	£145,600	-	-
Equipment	£6,000	£58,500	£176,500
Furniture	£37,800	£5,670	£67,000
Rates	£56,190	£1,870	£56,900
Electricity & gas	£5,400	£800	£23,000
Insurance	£24,450	£1,800	£56,000
Office administration	£8,560	£3,280	£98,000
Wages	£820,000	£86,000	£670,000
Raw materials	£556,700	-	-
Stocks of goods to be sold	-	-	£600,000
Advertising during the year	£4,100	£10,000	£120,000

1   Decide which business is the manufacturer, the retailer and the service business. Write a short paragraph about each of the three, giving reasons for your decision.

2   Calculate the total cost of each type of business. You could use a computer spreadsheet set out in the format of the table shown above with an additional row for the totals. Remember to head up the columns with the type of business.

3   Discuss in class why the totals vary so much. How might this variation affect the type of business chosen by someone starting a business for the first time?

Activity 11.6

Starting a small business

1   Divide into small groups of three or four.

2   Have a brainstorming session and decide on an idea for a small sole trader business. It could be in manufacturing, in retail or a services business. It could be an actual business you know, or one you have worked in. It could be a Case Study from your tutor.

3   Investigate the start-up costs of the business and draw up a list of the items you will need to buy. Calculate the total of the list.

3   Investigate the running costs of the business and draw up a list of the expenses you will need to pay for in the first year. Calculate the total of the list.

Remember that if you are investigating real businesses you will need to be careful when asking for financial information. Some people may not want to provide you with private financial details.

CHAPTER SUMMARY

● Money coming in from the sale of the products of a business – the revenue – can come from the sale of manufactured goods or from the sale of a service.

● A business starting up for the first time or launching a new product will need to plan what resources it needs: new staff, new premises, new machinery – all these involve a cost for the business.

● Start-up costs, eg premises, machinery, initial market research are one-off costs which are incurred when the business starts up or introduces a new product.

● Running costs are day-to-day expenses, eg wages, advertising, rent, electricity bills, and are normally estimated for a year at a time.

● Running costs can be related to areas of the business that you will be investigating on your course, such as production, sales and marketing, human resources, finance and administration.

● Different types of business will have different types of start-up and running costs, eg manufacturers need factories, retailers need sales outlets, and service industries need offices.

KEY TERMS

Start-up costs are 'one-off' costs incurred when you start a business or launch a new product.

Running costs are day-to-day costs incurred by a business.

Manufacturing businesses are businesses which make a product.

Retail businesses are businesses which buy manufactured products to resell to the public.

Service businesses are businesses which provide a service.

Product is a term which can describe a manufactured item or a service.

MULTIPLE CHOICE QUESTIONS

1 Which of the following is a start-up cost?
   A insurance premiums
   B payment of wages
   C payment of rent
   D premises purchase

2 Which of the following is a running cost?
   A premises purchase
   B machinery purchase
   C stationery purchase
   D vehicle purchase

3 A business pays the following costs in the first year of trading: computer purchase £3,000, computer insurance £450, wages of computer operators £18,000, computer printer purchase £1,200. The start-up costs total:
   A £22,650
   B £4,200
   C £18,450
   D £21,450

4 A business pays the following costs in the first year of trading: premises purchase £300,000, premises maintenance £1,450, forklift truck £12,000, premises fire insurance £3,200. The total running costs are:
   A £4,650
   B £313,450
   C £312,000
   D £15,200

5 A business which purchases a factory, machinery and raw materials in its first year of trading is likely to be:
   A a primary business
   B a retail business
   C a services business
   D a manufacturing business

6 The main start-up costs of a business are an office, a computer and a car. The business is likely to be:
   A a primary business
   B a retail business
   C a services business
   D a manufacturing business

12 Business finance and cash flow

Unit 3 Business finance:
using a cash flow forecast

what this chapter is about

A business needs money – finance – in order to cover the costs which you investigated in the last chapter. This chapter looks at where the money comes from. It also explains the way in which the flow of cash in and out of a business is set out in a table known as a cash flow forecast.

what you will learn from this chapter

- a business can be financed from a number of sources:
    - money received from the sale of its products or services
    - money contributed by the owner of the business
    - loans and overdrafts from the banks
    - grants from bodies such as the Local Authority
    - other income such as rent from property let to other businesses

- it is good business practice to plan so that business costs can be covered by the expected income from sales and other sources of income

- future flows of cash in and cash out can be set out in a table known as a cash flow forecast; this calculates the expected flows of money on a month-by-month basis

- the cash flow forecast also shows the business the likely bank balance at the end of the month; this tells the owner whether the business will have to borrow from the bank to make up any shortage in cash needed to keep the business running

financing a business

a comparison with personal finance

You will know from personal experience that you need to organise your finances carefully if you are to avoid running out of cash. You will have various sources of money: family, part-time earnings, savings, lottery winnings if you are lucky. You also have running costs: fares, food, books, entertainment. You will also have some 'one-off' costs from time-to-time: holidays, a bike or car. You need to make sure that the money coming in covers the money going out, even if you have to borrow.

Running a business follows the same basic principle:

Cash in (from whatever source) must cover cash out.

We will now look at the various sources of business finance.

money received from sales

A business setting up for the first time must estimate carefully the amount of money it will receive from selling its products. The money can be:

- for a manufacturer – income from the sale of products it manufactures
- for a retailer – income from sale of the goods sold in the shops
- for a service provider – income from the services sold

For a business starting up for the first time it is essential that the prices are set at a suitable level – often at the level the competitors are also charging for the same type of product. The amount of money received from sales is normally estimated for the first year of trading. Money received from sales is often referred to as *sales income* or *turnover*.

money contributed by the owner – capital

A business starting up for the first time will rely heavily on the amount of money – the *capital* – invested by the owner(s).

Capital is the money investment of the owner of a business.

For a sole trader or partnership business the capital is the amount put in by the sole proprietor or the partners. For a limited company the capital is the share capital – the money invested by the shareholders of the company.

Capital is normally paid in when a business starts up for the first time, but it is not uncommon for 'top-up' capital to be invested by the owners when the business has a big expansion plan.

finance from the bank

Many businesses rely on borrowing from the bank when they start up and also when they have a short-term need for money. When businesses borrow they have to pay interest to the bank on the amount that they borrow – this is yet another running cost of the business. Bank borrowing is normally either long-term or short term.

long-term bank loans

Businesses can borrow large sums for periods of five to twenty five years when they buy items they will keep in the business for the long-term, for example premises and machinery. These loans operate in the same way as the ordinary house repayment mortgage – you borrow a lump sum and repay it over a set period of time.

short-term bank loans – overdrafts

Overdrafts are the most common form of business borrowing from the bank.

An overdraft is a arrangement in which a business can borrow from time-to-time up to a certain amount from its normal business bank account.

Overdrafts are convenient and flexible because the business only borrows what it needs from time-to-time. This type of borrowing is used to finance running expenses, eg a shop stocking up before Christmas, a farm waiting to be paid for its milk, a manufacturer buying raw materials before making the product.

grants

Businesses can sometimes obtain grants from the Local Authority, from the Government and European Union to provide money for projects which will benefit society and the economy, for example businesses which create jobs in areas of high unemployment, businesses investing in new technology.

other sources of income

Businesses often increase their income by charging for use of their resources, for example:

- renting spare office or warehouse space to other businesses
- undertaking work for other businesses when the other businesses are running at full capacity
- charging for the skills of their staff, eg a business selling the services of its design department to another business

All these activities will increase the amount of cash coming into the business.

Now study the diagram on the next page.

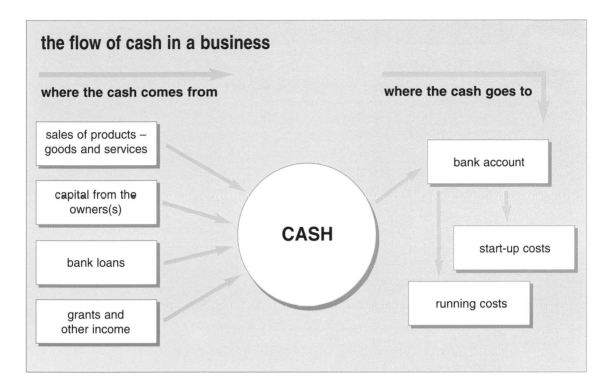

the flow of cash in a business

where the cash comes from

where the cash goes to

sales of products – goods and services

capital from the owners(s)

bank loans

grants and other income

CASH

bank account

start-up costs

running costs

the importance of the bank account

a central record of business transactions

You can see from the diagram shown above that all the money coming in and out of the business passes through the bank account.

The boxes on the left represent the sources of finance. The boxes on the right show that all the money passes through the bank account and is used to pay the costs of the business.

the importance of sales income

Once the business is up and running and the start-up costs have been paid, the most important of the sources of money is the sales income. This money will feed into the bank account and pay the running expenses of the business.

the need for realistic cost and revenue estimates

The estimates of sales revenue and costs must be realistic, as this will enable the business to decide whether or not the product will be profitable. If the revenue is less than forecast and the costs greater than forecast the business may run out of money. This will show in the bank account balance which is likely to become overdrawn (a minus figure).

Case Study

Tariq Inbal
cash flow in a business

situation

Tariq Inbal is starting a fast food business in June of this year. He has worked out his sources of finance and his costs.

sources of finance

• he is putting in £15,000 of capital

• the bank is lending him £10,000

• he has a Local Authority grant of £2,500

• he estimates sales income in June to be £5,000

The total amount of cash coming in in June will therefore be £32,500.

start-up costs

He already owns the premises and estimates his start-up costs to be:

conversion of premises	£15,000
purchase of equipment	£10,000
advertising for the business launch	£500

His start-up costs will therefore be £25,500. These expenses will all be paid for in June.

running costs

Tariq reckons his running costs in June will be:

stocks of food	£1,500
wages	£1,200
insurance	£120
electricity	£150
other expenses	£500

These running costs total £3,470 and will all be paid for in June.

bank account

Tariq has opened up a new bank account, which starts with a zero balance. All the money received and paid out will be passed through this bank account.

questions that will be asked

Tariq Inbal asks a number of questions about the cash flowing in and out of his business.

" How much will I have in the business bank account at the end of June, when all money has been received and all expenses have been paid? "

" How much will I have in the business bank account at the end of July. I estimate that my receipts for July will be £5,000, my running expenses £3,500 and that there will be no other payments into and out of the bank account. "

" How far can I rely on these estimates? My business might be in trouble if they are wrong! "

calculating the bank balance at the end of June and July

The formula is:

bank balance at beginning of month + receipts for the month − payments for the month (including start-up costs and running costs) = bank balance at the end of the month

Using Tariq's figures, the calculation for the month of June is:

	nil	(opening bank balance)
+	£32,500	(cash from sales)
−	£25,500	(start-up costs)
−	£3,470	(running costs)
=	£3,530	(bank balance at end of June)

It then follows that the calculation for the month of July is:

	£3,530	(the opening bank balance for 1 July is the same as the closing bank balance at the end of June)
+	£5,000	(cash from sales in July)
−	£3,500	(the expenses for July)
=	£5,030	(bank balance at end of July)

how reliable are the estimates?

Tariq's figures are only estimates and so cannot be 100% accurate. He might achieve better sales, in which case he will have more money in the bank. He might not do so well, in which case he will finish each month with less money in the bank.

the cash flow forecast

The calculations in the Case Study on the previous pages work out the bank balance at the end of the first two months of trading. This process can be carried out using a table of figures known as a cash flow forecast.

A cash flow forecast is a table which estimates the amounts of money coming into and going out of the bank account each month.

A typical cash flow forecast – which normally estimates figures for a whole year – sets out in a column for each month:

- a totalled up summary of the money coming into the bank account (A)
- a totalled up summary of payments out of the bank account (B)
- the bank balance at the beginning and the end of the month

The cash flow forecast extract below shows only one column of figures; the remaining eleven monthly columns will normally extend off to the right. The figures here relate to J Smithers Limited, a manufacturing company.

J SMITHERS LIMITED CASH FLOW FORECAST 12 months ending 31 December 20-2	January £
Receipts	
Sales	10,000
Capital	100,000
Loans	50,000
Grants	10,000
Other income	1,000
TOTAL RECEIPTS FOR MONTH	171,000
Payments	
Premises	100,000
Equipment	45,000
Raw materials	2,000
Marketing	1,000
Other running expenses	6,000
TOTAL PAYMENTS FOR MONTH	154,000
Bank balance at the beginning of the month	zero
ADD total receipts (A)	171,000
LESS total payments (B)	154,000
BANK BALANCE AT END OF MONTH	17,000

A ⟶ (TOTAL RECEIPTS FOR MONTH)

B ⟶ (TOTAL PAYMENTS FOR MONTH)

A minus B

notes on the cash flow forecast

cash flow forecast – heading

A cash flow forecast must be headed up with the name of the business and the period which the forecast covers, eg '12 months ending 31 December 20-2'. The forecast shown here only shows one month's figures. A twelve month forecast is quite common and is shown on pages 256 and 257.

cash flow forecast – receipts section

Note that in the month of January – the month in which the business will start trading – the receipts section records all the amounts paid into the bank account. This includes £100,000 of capital from the owners, a loan of £50,000, a grant of £10,000. These are one-off *start up* financing items, and do not appear in the columns for the following months. The other two items – sales of £10,000 and other income of £1,000 – are *estimates* which will be entered in each of the following months (see next page).

cash flow forecast – payments section

Just as the Receipts section in January contains a number of one-off payments, so the Payments section for that month records the *estimate* of one-off *start up* costs including premises of £100,000 and equipment of £45,000. Other items such as wages and administration costs are *running costs* and will usually appear each month.

cash flow forecast – bank balance section

The bank balance starts off at zero at the beginning of January and finishes the month at £17,000: this change is the difference between the receipts for the month (A) and payments (B). If the bank balance becomes a minus figure, this is a bank overdraft and is shown in brackets, eg (£25,000).

the importance of timing

It is important to note that the amounts received or paid are entered *in the month in which they are expected to be received or paid*. If payment is to be delayed – eg goods sold on credit (sold in one month, paid for in a later month) this must be allowed for, as it will affect the month-end bank balance.

a note on Value Added Tax (VAT)

The figures shown in a cash flow forecast will include any VAT the business pays or charges. You will not have to worry about VAT when dealing with a cash flow forecast.

the opening and closing bank account balance

The last four lines of the cash flow forecast act as a summary of receipts and payments and calculate the bank account balance. As this business is starting up for the first time the opening bank balance is zero. As we saw in the Case Study the formula is

bank balance at the beginning of the month **add** *receipts for the month* **less** *payments for the month* **equals** *bank balance at the end of the month*

the calculation for January is:

zero + £171,000 − £154,000 = £17,000

What happens next month? If you study the cash flow forecast shown below you will see that columns for the next two months have been added with figures for those months. In each case the bank balance at the end of one month is entered in the next column as the bank balance *at the beginning of the next month*. This is indicated here by the coloured arrows.

J SMITHERS LIMITED

CASH FLOW FORECAST for the .... months ending ....

	January £	February £	March £
Receipts			
Sales	10,000	10,000	10,000
Capital	100,000		
Loans	50,000		
Grants	10,000		
Other income	1,000	1,000	1,000
TOTAL RECEIPTS FOR MONTH (A)	171,000	11,000	11,000
Payments			
Premises	100,000		
Equipment	45,000		
Raw materials	2,000	2,000	3,000
Marketing	1,000		
Other running expenses	6,000	5,000	4,000
TOTAL PAYMENTS FOR MONTH (B)	154,000	7,000	7,000
Bank balance at the beginning of the month	zero	17,000	21,000
ADD total receipts (A)	171,000	11,000	11,000
LESS total payments (B)	154,000	7,000	7,000
BANK BALANCE AT END OF MONTH	17,000	21,000	25,000

Activity 12.1

Calculating the monthly bank balances

You have been given figures for the projected cash receipts and cash payments for a number of businesses for January and February. You have also been given the opening bank balances for January. Remember that a bank balance in brackets is a minus figure – the business is borrowing from the bank on an overdraft.

JANUARY FIGURES	Aztec Ltd	Brown & Co	Celtic Ltd	Dralix Ltd	Everard & Co
	£	£	£	£	£
Total Receipts	10,000	20,000	25,000	34,560	32,000
Total Payments	5,000	12,000	20,000	18,900	30,000
Opening Bank Balance	zero	3,000	5,670	2,100	(3,500)
FEBRUARY FIGURES	Aztec Ltd	Brown & Co	Celtic Ltd	Dralix Ltd	Everard & Co
	£	£	£	£	£
Total Receipts	10,000	20,000	25,000	37,000	32,000
Total Payments	8,000	13,000	18,000	23,000	15,000

1   Draw up a cash flow forecast for each of the five businesses for the two months using the format shown below to calculate the bank balances at the end of January and February.

BUSINESS .... CASH FLOW FORECAST FOR..	January £	February £
Total Receipts for Month		
Total Payments for Month		
Opening Bank Balance ADD Total Receipts for Month LESS Total Payments for Month		
Bank Balance at end of Month		

2   Write down in a few sentences an explanation of what has happened to the bank balance of Everard & Co over the two months.

Bella Jones
cash flow forecast

Bella Jones is starting a mail order company in January to sell specialist CDs.

She will work from a rented office and will employ two part-time staff to help her. She will buy a computer and other essential mailing equipment.

She has £15,000 of capital to invest herself and her father is lending her £2,000 to be repaid at the end of five years. She has also been given an enterprise grant of £1,000.

As far as sales are concerned she reckons she will sell £20,000 of CDs a month; these will cost her £12,000 a month. She will pay for the stock in the month in which she receives it. She will also have to pay monthly office running costs.

She has been asked by her accountant to draw up projected figures for the first twelve months of trading so that he can prepare a cash flow forecast. The accountant stresses that these figures, particularly the sales and running expenses will only be estimates. They will, however help her to see if she will need a bank overdraft in the first year. She has opened up a business bank account which has a zero balance.

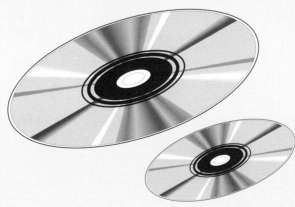

The figures she writes down are shown on the next page

BELLA JONES: ESTIMATED CASH FLOW FIGURES

Receipts	**£**
Capital provided by Bella Jones in January	15,000
Loan from father given in January	2,000
Enterprise Grant received in January	1,000
Forecast monthly sales from January	20,000

Start-up costs	
Computer equipment paid for in January	8,000
Mailing equipment paid for in January	3,000
Other office set-up costs paid for in January	3,500
Marketing campaign paid for in January	2,500

Running costs – paid monthly from January	
Stocks of CDs	12,000
Wages of part-time staff	1,000
Bella's drawings (her living expenses)	2,000
Mailing costs	1,500
Office running costs	1,500
Advertising	1,500

The cash flow forecast set up by Bella's accountant is shown on the next two pages. Study it carefully and then answer the questions which follow on page 258.

Note: VAT is ignored in these calculations.

business name

period of cash flow forecast

CASH FLOW FORECAST

Business: Bella Jones

Period: January - December 20-2

	Jan	Feb	Mar	Apr	May	Jun	Jul
	£	£	£	£	£	£	£
RECEIPTS							
Sales of CDs	20000	20000	20000	20000	20000	20000	20000
Capital	15000						
Loan	2000						
Grant	1000						
TOTAL RECEIPTS	38000	20000	20000	20000	20000	20000	20000
PAYMENTS							
CD purchases	12000	12000	12000	12000	12000	12000	12000
Computers	8000						
Mailing equipment	3000						
Office equipment	3500						
Marketing	2500						
Wages	1000	1000	1000	1000	1000	1000	1000
Owner's drawings	2000	2000	2000	2000	2000	2000	2000
Mailing costs	1500	1500	1500	1500	1500	1500	1500
Office costs	1500	1500	1500	1500	1500	1500	1500
Advertising	1500	1500	1500	1500	1500	1500	1500
TOTAL PAYMENTS	36500	19500	19500	19500	19500	19500	19500
Opening Bank	0	1500	2000	2500	3000	3500	4000
Add Receipts	38000	20000	20000	20000	20000	20000	20000
Less Payments	36500	19500	19500	19500	19500	19500	19500
Closing Bank	1500	2000	2500	3000	3500	4000	4500

totals column for all receipts and payments for the 12 months from January to December; for example CD sales of £20,000 a month total £240,000 for the year

Aug £	Sep £	Oct £	Nov £	Dec £	TOTAL £
20000	20000	20000	20000	20000	240000
					15000
					2000
					1000
					0
					0
20000	20000	20000	20000	20000	258000
12000	12000	12000	12000	12000	144000
					8000
					3000
					3500
					2500
1000	1000	1000	1000	1000	12000
2000	2000	2000	2000	2000	24000
1500	1500	1500	1500	1500	18000
1500	1500	1500	1500	1500	18000
1500	1500	1500	1500	1500	18000
19500	19500	19500	19500	19500	251000
4500	5000	5500	6000	6500	0
20000	20000	20000	20000	20000	258000
19500	19500	19500	19500	19500	251000
5000	5500	6000	6500	7000	7000

opening bank balance

total receipts

total payments

closing bank balance

Activity 12.2

Bella Jones
questions on the Case Study

Analyse the cash flow forecast by answering these questions:

1   What is the period covered by the cash flow forecast?

2   What does the column on the extreme right-hand side of the cash flow forecast represent?

3   Is the bank account increasing or decreasing each month?

4   By what amount is the bank account increasing or decreasing each month?

5   Does this mean the business is likely to be making a profit or a loss?

6   What would happen to the end-of-month bank balance if Bella's sales projections were wrong and she sold £25,000 worth of CDs each month?

7   What would happen to the end-of-month bank balance if Bella's sales projections were wrong and she sold £15,000 worth of CDs each month?

8   Your answers to 6 and 7 should highlight the main advantage of using a cash flow forecast when planning a new business. What does it tell you about the possible future of the business?

9   If you were Bella and the business started to go badly what steps might you take to improve the situation?

10   The cash flow forecast in this Case Study is drawn up on a computer spreadsheet. From your experience so far of constructing cash flow forecasts, what would be the advantages of using a computer in this way?

Activity 12.3

Cash flow forecasts – calculating the monthly bank balance

You have been asked to help two businesses draw up a cash flow forecast for a six month period.

R & R Opticians is starting up for the first time, H H Sports has been trading for some time. The figures you have been given are as follows:

R & R OPTICIANS

	Jan £	Feb £	March £	April £	May £	June £
Receipts						
Capital	10,000					
Loan	5,000					
Sales	10,000	10,000	10,000	10,000	10,000	10,000
Payments						
Equipment	15,000					
Stock	5,000	5,000	5,000	5,000	5,000	5,000
Other expenses	2,000	2,000	2,500	2,000	2,000	2,000
Opening bank balance	zero					

H H SPORTS

	Jan £	Feb £	March £	April £	May £	June £
Receipts						
Sales	20,000	20,000	20,000	20,000	20,000	20,000
Payments						
Stock	15,000	15,000	15,000	15,000	15,000	15,000
Other expenses	3,000	3,000	3,000	3,000	3,000	3,000
Computer equipment purchase						15,000
Opening bank balance	1,000					

1   Using the format shown on page 252, draw up cash flow forecasts for the two businesses for the six months from January to June. Remember that a negative bank balance is shown in brackets.

2   Write a brief explanation of the bank balance of H H Sports as it stands at the end of June.

using a computer spreadsheet

the benefits of a spreadsheet program

The calculations on a cash flow forecast are not particularly difficult, but they do take a long time if you are tackling the task with only pencil, paper, rubber and calculator. The task is, of course, made simple when you have input the worksheet onto a computer spreadsheet program.

A computer spreadsheet is an automatic calculation table set up as a computer file.

With a computer spreadsheet you will be able to change any figure, and the computer will do all the recalculations according to the formulas input:

- if you want to change the estimated figure for sales income, to see what happens if sales are better than expected, or more importantly, what happens if the sales are worse than expected – is the business still feasible, or will you end up with a long row of bracketed figures on the bottom line – ie a bank overdraft?

- if you want to change the start-up costs, eg if a computer costs more than you expected

- if you want to change the running costs, eg if the monthly wages bill goes up

In each case you will be able to see the effect on the important figure of the closing bank balance which indicates the amount of money the business may have to borrow to keep going.

use of formulas in the spreadsheet – column C

Extensive use is made in cash flow forecasts of the adding together of a range of cells. Each cell is given the reference of the column (the letter) and the row (the number). The formulas for the Bella Jones spreadsheet are illustrated on the next two pages. You will need to check your computer manual to find the formula to use for your own program. The formula used here is =Sum(C8..C14) where all the cells between C8 and C14 are added together. (Note that some of these rows are empty; they are included in the formula in case you need to add extra types of income later on).   The formulas for column C are as follows:

- Rows 15 and 32 – Total Receipts   =Sum(C8..C14)

- Rows 29 and 33 – Total Payments   =Sum(C18..C28)

- Row 31 – Opening Bank   =B34

– ie the closing bank balance of the *previous month*. Note that B31 is a value cell into which is entered the opening bank balance for the period.

- Row 34 – Closing Bank   =C31+C32–C33
- Column N – Total column

Each row is totalled, eg cell N9 is =Sum(B9..M9). Column N is also totalled vertically, in the same way as the other columns, except that cell N31 is =B31 and cell N34 is =M34. N32 is =Sum(B32..BM32) and N33 is =Sum(B33..M33).

Case Study

Bella Jones

formulas used for the cash flow forecast

	A	B	C	D	E
1	CASH FLOW FORECAST				
2	Business: Bella Jones				
3	Period: January - December 20-2				
4					
5		Jan	Feb	Mar	Apr
6		£	£	£	£
7	RECEIPTS				
8					
9	Sales of CDs	20000	20000	20000	20000
10	Capital	15000			
11	Loan	2000			
12	Grant	1000			
13					
14					
15	TOTAL RECEIPTS	=SUM(B8..B14)	=SUM(C8..C14)	=SUM(D8..D14)	=SUM(E8..E14)
16					
17	PAYMENTS				
18	CD purchases	12000	12000	12000	12000
19	Computers	8000			
20	Mailing equipment	3000			
21	Office equipment	3500			
22	Marketing	2500			
23	Wages	1000	1000	1000	1000
24	Owner's drawings	2000	2000	2000	2000
25	Mailing costs	1500	1500	1500	1500
26	Office costs	1500	1500	1500	1500
27	Advertising	1500	1500	1500	1500
28					
29	TOTAL PAYMENTS	=SUM(B18..B28)	=SUM(C18..C28)	=SUM(D18..D28)	=SUM(E18..E28)
30					
31	Opening Bank	0	=B34	=C34	=D34
32	Add Receipts	=SUM(B8..B14)	=SUM(C8..C14)	=SUM(D8..D14)	=SUM(E8..E14)
33	Less Payments	=SUM(B18..B28)	=SUM(C18..C28)	=SUM(D18..D28)	=SUM(E18..E28)
34	Closing Bank	=B31+B32-B33	=C31+C32-C33	=D31+D32-D33	=E31+E32-E33
35					

Bella Jones
formulas used for the cash flow forecast

	K	L	M	N
1				
2				
3				
4				
5	Oct	Nov	Dec	TOTAL
6	£	£	£	£
7				
8				
9	20000	20000	20000	=SUM(B9..M9)
10				=SUM(B10..M10)
11				=SUM(B11..M11)
12				=SUM(B12..M12)
13				=SUM(B13..M13)
14				=SUM(B14..M14)
15	=SUM(K8..K14)	=SUM(L8..L14)	=SUM(M8..M14)	=SUM(N8..N14)
16				
17				
18	12000	12000	12000	=SUM(B18..M18)
19				=SUM(B19..M19)
20				=SUM(B20..M20)
21				=SUM(B21..M21)
22				=SUM(B22..M22)
23	1000	1000	1000	=SUM(B23..M23)
24	2000	2000	2000	=SUM(B24..M24)
25	1500	1500	1500	=SUM(B25..M25)
26	1500	1500	1500	=SUM(B26..M26)
27	1500	1500	1500	=SUM(B27..M27)
28				
29	=SUM(K18..K28)	=SUM(L18..L28)	=SUM(M18..M28)	=SUM(N18..N28)
30				
31	=J34	=K34	=L34	=B31
32	=SUM(K8..K14)	=SUM(L8..L14)	=SUM(M8..M14)	=SUM(B32..M32)
33	=SUM(K18..K28)	=SUM(L18..L28)	=SUM(M18..M28)	=SUM(B33..M33)
34	=K31+K32-K33	=L31+L32-L33	=M31+M32-M33	=M34
35				

Note
This spreadsheet is shown to illustrate the formulas used. The months of May to September are not illustrated here, as space does not permit. The formulas in the columns for these months will mirror those of the other months.

Activity 12.4

Ace Designs: using a computer spreadsheet

Mike Moore is setting up a new fashion clothes shop in the town. The business will be called Ace Designs. Mike is the sole trader proprietor of the shop which will open in January of next year. His accountant has asked him to draw up some estimates of costs and income for the first year of trading. The figures he produces are as follows:

	£
start-up costs (to be paid in January)	
Shop premises	100,000
Shop equipment	40,000
Market research	5,000
running costs (to be paid monthly)	
Stock purchases	7,500
Wages	3,500
Other expenses	3,000
financing of business	
Capital introduced by Mike in January	125,000
Bank loan given in January	15,000
Enterprise grant given in January	5,000
Monthly rent from tenant in office upstairs	900
Monthly sales estimate	15,000

1   Using the format shown on the last two pages (or a similar computer spreadsheet file), draw up a cash flow forecast for Ace Designs for the twelve months from January to December. State whether you think the business will be successful.

2   Mike's accountant says he should produce two more cash flow forecasts showing the effect of:
    (a)   increasing the sales estimate by 20% to £18,000 a month
    (b)   decreasing the sales estimate by 20% to £12,000 a month

   You are to create two additional spreadsheet files showing these changes. What effect do the changes have on the business. In the case of the decreased sales cash flow, what could Mike do to salvage the situation?

3   Suggest reasons why the sales figures might fluctuate from month to month. Remember that it is a fashion shop and people buy at different times of the year, sometimes because the 'Sales' are on or other incentives are offered.

CHAPTER SUMMARY

● A business should plan its finances so that its costs can be covered by the expected income from sales and other sources of income.

● Other sources of income include:
  - money contributed by the owner(s) of the business – capital
  - loans and overdrafts from the banks
  - grants from bodies such as the Local Authority and the Government
  - other income such as rent from property let to other businesses

● Flows of cash in and cash out through the bank account can be set out in a table known as a cash flow forecast; this sets out the expected flows of money on a month-by-month basis and helps the owner to plan ahead to see if a business project will pay for itself.

● The cash flow forecast also shows the business the likely bank balance at the end of each month; this tells the owner whether the business will have to borrow from the bank to make up any shortage in cash needed to keep the business running.

● A cash flow forecast can be set up as computer spreadsheet; this makes it easy to rework the forecast if any of the projected figures change.

● A cash flow forecast is only an estimate – an aid to business planning.

KEY TERMS

Turnover	the total amount received in sales income by a business over a set period of time
Overdraft	an arrangement made for a bank customer to borrow from time-to-time on the day-to-day bank account
Capital	money invested in the business by the owner(s)
Bank loan	a fixed amount loan from the bank repaid over a period of years
Cash flow forecast	a table which sets out estimates of the amounts received into and out of the bank account each month and calculates the likely bank balance at the end of each month
Computer spreadsheet	an automatic calculation table set up as a computer file

MULTIPLE CHOICE QUESTIONS

1   Money invested by the owner of a business is called:

   A   a running cost

   B   capital

   C   an overdraft

   D   an enterprise grant

2   The main sales income received by a manufacturer is money from:

   A   raw materials

   B   machinery

   C   provision of services

   D   sale of manufactured goods

3   A bank overdraft is:

   A   a long term loan used to finance a business

   B   capital introduced to finance the business

   C   borrowing on a business bank account

   D   interest charged on a business bank account

4   A cash flow forecast is used to:

   A   calculate the notes and coins needed for wages paid

   B   calculate the amount of stock needed by a business each month

   C   record at the end of each month cash received and cash paid

   D   estimate in advance cash received and cash paid each month

5   An end-of-month bank balance in brackets on a cash flow forecast means:

   A   the figure is positive - there is money in the bank

   B   the figure is negative - there is an overdraft at the bank

   C   the figure is only provisional – it may change at any time

   D   the figure is incorrect and will need to be changed

6   If you increase the monthly sales income figure on a cash flow forecast and the costs remain the same:

   A   the bank balance on the bottom line will increase

   B   the bank balance on the bottom line will decrease

   C   the business will need to borrow more from the bank

   D   the business start-up costs will increase

13

Calculating break-even

> **Unit 3 Business finance:**
> **calculating the break-even point**

what this chapter is about

When a business is starting up or planning a new project it will want to know whether the income from the project will cover the running costs – in other words it will want to know if it will *break-even* and make a profit. The business will also want to know *how many* items, whether they be manufactured goods or services, it needs to sell to cover its running costs and break-even.

what you will learn from this chapter

- break-even is reached when the income from sales of a product is equal to the running costs of producing that product

- running costs include:

  - *variable costs* – costs such as raw materials and stock that are directly related to the number of items produced

  - *fixed costs* – overheads such as insurance and rates – that have to be paid anyway and do not vary with the number of items produced

- start-up costs such as the purchase of equipment are *not* included in break-even calculations

- the break-even point can be calculated by means of a formula and also by the construction of a break-even chart

- the break-even chart helps the business calculate how much profit it will make at different levels of production

- a computer spreadsheet can be used in calculating break-even

what is break-even?

the concept of break-even

A business planning a new project is only likely to go ahead if it is eventually going to make a profit on that project. It will make a profit after it has broken even – as soon as its sales income covers its running costs.

A comparison on a personal level is a group of students planning a trip out. Suppose a group of you are going to a concert and need to hire a minibus which costs £100 for the evening. Everyone is prepared to pay £10 each for the minibus. How many people do you need to break-even? If there are only nine, you will not manage it: your income is only 9 x £10 = £90. You need at least ten people (10 x £10 = £100) to cover the cost and to *break-even*.

a definition of break-even

Break-even is therefore the point at which running costs are covered by the income received. After that point you are making a profit. A definition is:

break-even is the point at which sales income is equal to running costs.

running costs – not start up costs

Note that the business costs involved in the calculation are *running costs* only, eg wages, materials, and overheads such as insurance and rates. Start-up costs such as buying equipment are not included in the break-even calculation. If you think about it, they will already have been financed by the money (capital) the owner has put in or by loans from the bank.

Activity 13.1

Calculating break-even

Calculate whether the following businesses have broken even or not. State in each case the amount of profit or loss they have made.

	income from sales (£)	running costs (£)
Business 1	45,000	35,000
Business 2	46,000	46,000
Business 3	47,000	48,000
Business 4	1,234,738	1,134,576
Business 5	2,983,472	2,983,524

fixed costs and variable costs

running costs

Break-even is the point at which the sales income of a business over a given period equals its running costs. In other words, at break-even all the *running costs* have been paid off by the money coming in from sales.

As we have already seen, running costs are the day-to-day expenses of a business, for example items such as wages and insurance and, in the case of manufacturers and retailers, the purchase of materials made into goods and stock which are then sold as part of day-to-day trading.

When calculating break-even we need to tell the difference between two types of running costs: *fixed* costs and *variable* costs.

fixed costs

Fixed costs are running costs such as rent and insurance which have to be paid anyway, whatever the number of items sold by the business. Even if the business closes down for two weeks holiday and nothing is sold, the fixed costs still have to be paid. Fixed costs can be shown in the form of a graph which shows the cost (£) and the number of items produced, 'the output.' Remember that an item can be an item made in a factory, an item sold in a shop, or a service provided. As you can see in the graph below, the fixed costs of a business remain at the same level, however many items are produced – the line on the graph is a horizontal straight line.

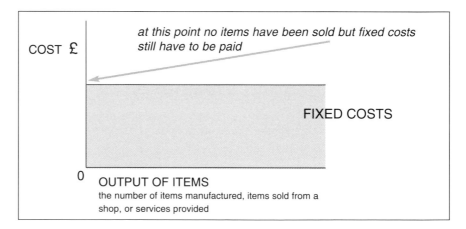

variable costs

Variable costs are running costs which are related to the production of the item itself. Variable costs include expenses such as purchases of materials, stock, and in the case of a manufacturer, the wages paid to production line employees. If the output is nil, variable costs will be zero, if the output increases, so does the total variable cost. As you can see from the straight line on the graph below, total variable costs rise as the number of items produced rises.

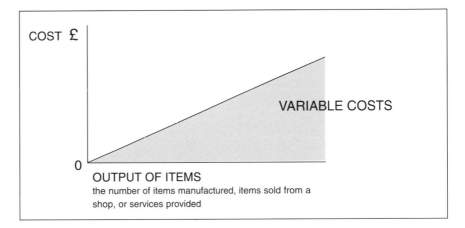

total cost = fixed and variable costs combined

As a business is likely to have to pay both fixed and variable costs, the two costs added together (the total cost) can also be shown in graph form:

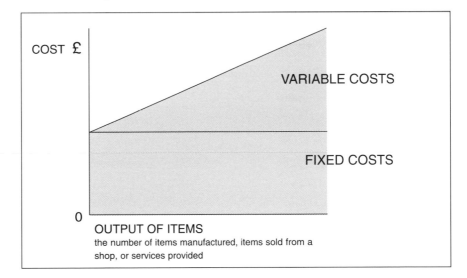

average cost

A business can work out the average cost per item by dividing total cost by the number of units produced at any given level of output. It is, however, the fixed and variable costs added together which we will use in the calculation of break-even.

Case Study

Wurbles Limited
fixed and variable costs

Wurbles LImited has been set up to manufacture the 'Wurble', an electronic cuddly toy which talks and sings.

You have been given the sales income and cost figures for the last month of trading (January 20-2), but they need sorting out. They are:

	£
Sales income	12,000
Office wages	2,000
Rent & rates	2,100
Insurance	150
Advertising	500
Other office expenses	250
Materials	3,500
Production line wages	2,500

You have been asked to sort out the fixed costs and variable costs and to work out the profit or loss for the month. You have been given a form to carry out your calculations. The completed form is shown below.

Business: Wurbles Limited		**Period** January 20-02	
fixed costs		**variable costs**	
description	£	*description*	£
Office wages	2,000	Materials used in production	3,500
Rent & rates	2,100	Production line wages	2,500
Insurance	150		
Advertising	500		
Other office expenses	250		
TOTAL FIXED COSTS	5,000	TOTAL VARIABLE COSTS	6,000
TOTAL RUNNING COSTS (fixed costs + variable costs)			11,000
		Sales	12,000
		less Total Running Costs	11,000
	= PROFIT		1,000

Activity 13.2

Fixed and variable costs

You have been given projected sales income and cost figures for three separate businesses for one month of trading, but the information has not been sorted out.

Business 1 is a manufacturer, Businesses 2 and 3 are shops.

	Business 1 MF Steelware	Business 2 JM Fashions	Business 3 MG Stationers
	£	£	£
Sales income	65,000	50,000	85,000
Raw materials purchased	25,000	-	-
Stock purchased for shop	-	25,000	45,000
Production line wages	12,000	-	-
Sales staff & office wages	2,000	4,500	8,000
Rent and rates	1,200	2,500	2,700
Insurance	500	750	550
Office expenses	1,000	2,460	1,490

1   Draw up three forms set out like the form in the Case Study on the previous page. You could use a computer to draw up the blank form and then print out multiple copies for you to complete.

2   Sort out the fixed costs from the variable costs and enter the descriptions and the amounts in the correct column.

3   Total up the costs columns and calculate the profit (or loss) for the month in the boxes at the bottom of the form.

break-even: calculation by formula

sale of 'units'

When a business sells a product, each item sold is known as a 'unit'. This word is used when the business

- manufactures an item
- buys an item to sell at a profit (a retail shop)
- provides a service

A 'unit' can be a car, a canned drink, a holiday, an insurance policy, a textbook. In all cases it is an item which the business produces or processes and will sell at a price which should enable it to make a profit.

contribution

When a business sells a product – a unit – the income received from each item (unit) sold will be used to pay off the costs of the business. We have seen that costs can be:

- *variable* costs which are related to the level of production (eg materials used, production wages), or
- *fixed* – overheads that the business has to pay anyway (eg rent, gas bills)

The sales income from each item is used to pay off the variable cost of that item, eg a toy which sells for £20 may have a variable cost of £10. The £20 received will pay off these variable costs of £10 . The £10 income that is 'left over' can then be used to make a 'contribution' towards paying off the fixed costs. Take the example of the £20 toy. The figures are:

selling price per unit	=	£20
variable cost per unit	=	£10
fixed costs per month	=	£1,000

Each unit sold will bring in £20. £10 of this will be used to pay the variable cost of that unit. The remaining £10 will be used to make a 'contribution' towards paying off the fixed costs of £1,000, as shown in the diagram on the next page.

The formula is:

contribution = selling price – variable cost per unit

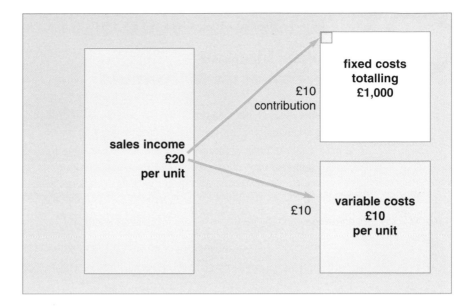

break-even

As you will see from the diagram above, when contributions from the sale of units reaches £1,000, fixed costs have been covered and the break-even point will have been reached. You can work out the number of units you will need to sell to break-even by dividing the fixed costs by the 'contribution', here:

$$\frac{\text{fixed costs (£1,000)}}{\text{contribution (£10)}} \quad = \quad 100 \text{ units}$$

break-even formula

In your external assessment you may be quoted a break-even formula which involves the income and cost figures we have just been discussing. This formula is shown below. Break-even in units equals:

$$\frac{\text{fixed costs (£)}}{\text{selling price per unit (£) less variable cost per unit (£)}}$$

All this formula is doing is quoting contribution as selling price per unit less variable costs per unit. The calculation is exactly the same as shown in the formula higher up this page (ie fixed costs divided by contribution):

$$\frac{\text{fixed costs (£1,000)}}{\text{selling price per unit (£20) less variable cost per unit (£10)}}$$

$$= \text{break-even at 100 units}$$

Case Study

Wurbles Limited
break-even by formula

The 'Wurble' is an electronic cuddly toy which talks and sings. The variable costs (materials and wages) for producing each Wurble are £10 and the selling price is £20 per unit. The fixed costs of running the business are £5,000 per month. How many toys need to be produced and sold each month for the business to cover its costs, ie to break-even?

To obtain an immediate answer the management of Wurbles Limited applies the formula:

$$\text{break-even (units)} = \frac{\text{fixed costs (£)}}{\text{selling price per unit (£) less variable cost per unit (£)}}$$

The calculation is:

$$\frac{£5,000}{£20 - £10} = \frac{£5,000}{£10} = 500 \text{ units}$$

Activity 13.3

Using the break-even formula

1   Using the figures set out in the Case Study above, calculate the number of Wurbles that would need to be made and sold to break-even if the selling price was raised to £30 per unit.

2   Calculate the number of Wurbles that would need to be made and sold to break-even if the selling price was £25, monthly fixed costs £3,000 and the variable cost per unit £10.

3   Calculate the number of Wurbles that would need to be made and sold to break-even if the selling price was £20, monthly fixed costs £6,000 and the variable cost per unit £15.

4   Explain in each case (1 to 3 above) why the break-even quantity has changed from the 500 units calculated in the Case Study. Look at the changes in each case in the figures for price, contribution and fixed costs and see how they affect the number of units needed for break-even.

the break-even graph

The management of Wurbles Limited in the Case Study on the previous page will find the calculation by formula useful, but will point out its limitations. The management might ask questions like:

"How much profit will we make if we sell 200 more Wurbles per month than the break-even amount?"

"How much loss will we make if production is short of the break-even point by 100 units."

The answer is to be found in the construction of a break-even graph. We have already seen a graph (page 269) showing fixed and variable costs. If a sales income line is added to this, a break-even point can be plotted. The Case Study below shows how this is done.

Case Study

Wurbles Limited
drawing a break-even graph

Before a break-even graph can be constructed, a table will be drawn up setting out the income and costs for different numbers of units. A table for Wurbles is shown below. The data used is: selling price per unit £20, variable cost per unit £10, fixed costs per month £5,000. Some of the figures from the table are then used to plot straight lines on the graph. These are:

- the total cost line (Column C)
- the sales income line (Column D)

units of production	fixed costs	variable costs	total cost	sales income	profit/(loss)
	A	B	C	D	E
			A + B		D – C
	£	£	£	£	£
100	5,000	1,000	6,000	2,000	(4,000)
200	5,000	2,000	7,000	4,000	(3,000)
300	5,000	3,000	8,000	6,000	(2 000)
400	5,000	4,000	9,000	8,000	(1,000)
500	5,000	5,000	10,000	10,000	nil
600	5,000	6,000	11,000	12,000	1,000
700	5,000	7,000	12,000	14,000	2,000

notes on the break-even table

- the units of production here are at intervals of 100
- fixed costs (Column A) are fixed at £5,000 for every level of production
- fixed costs (Column A) and variable costs (Column B) are added together to produce the total cost figure (Column C)
- total cost (Column C) is deducted from the sales income figure (Column D) to produce either a positive figure (a profit) or a loss (a negative figure, in brackets) in Column E

As you can see, break-even occurs at 500 units, a result confirmed by the formula calculation (see page 274).

construction of the break-even graph

The graph is constructed as follows:

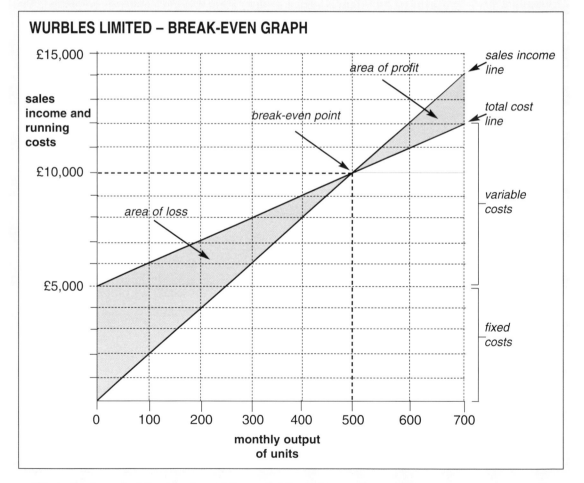

Study the format of the graph and then read the notes on the next page.

notes on the break even graph

- The vertical axis shows money amounts – the total cost and the sales income for different levels of production are plotted on this axis.

- The horizontal axis shows units of output at intervals of 100.

- The fixed costs of £5,000 are the same at all levels of output.

- Total cost is made up of fixed costs and variable costs.

- The total costs line starts, not at zero, but at £5,000. This is because if the output is zero, the business still has to pay the £5,000 fixed costs.

- The point at which the total costs and sales income lines cross is the break-even point.

- From the graph you can read off the break-even point both in terms of units of output (500 units on the horizontal axis) and also in sales income value (£10,000 on the vertical axis).

working out profit and loss from the graph

If you look at the graph on the previous page you will see two shaded areas. On the left of the break-even point is an 'area of loss' and on the right of the break-even point is an 'area of profit'. This means that for levels of output to the left of the break-even point (ie fewer than 500 units) the business will make a loss and for levels of output to the right of the break-even point, the business will make a profit.

If you read off the vertical distance (in £) between the sales income line and the total cost line (ie down the shaded area) you will find the exact amount of profit and loss for any level of output on the graph. Note that each dotted 'box' on the graph represents £1,000 from top to bottom. For example, at an output level of zero you will make a loss of £5,000 (this is the fixed costs figure) and at an output level of 700 units you will make a profit of £2,000.

If you refer back to the table of figures from which the graph was plotted (page 275) you will be able to check these figures taken from the graph against the expected profit and loss totals in the far right-hand column.

how the graph helps Wurbles Limited

The questions asked by the management (see page 275) were:

"How much profit will we make if we sell 200 more Wurbles per month than the break-even amount?"

"How much loss will we make if production is short of the break-even point by 100 units."

By reading the difference between the total cost line and the total income line, the answer to the first question is £2,000 (two dotted 'boxes') and the answer to the second is a loss of £1,000 (one dotted 'box').

Activity 13.4

Reading a break-even graph

You have been given a break-even graph for Insight Limited. Study the graph and answer the questions at the bottom of the page.

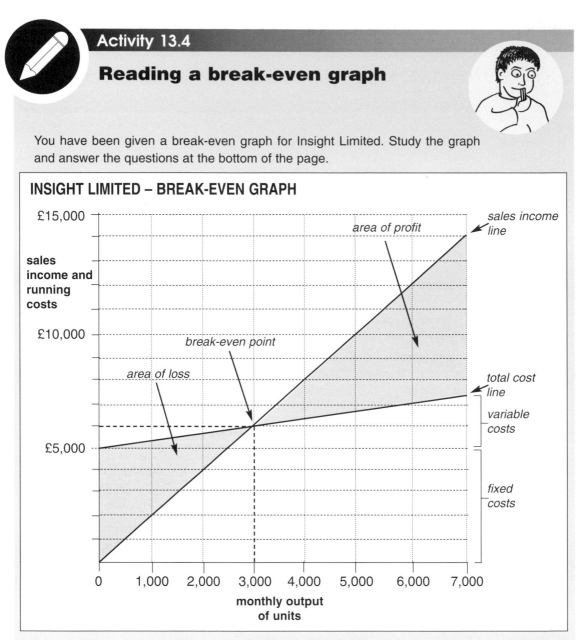

INSIGHT LIMITED – BREAK-EVEN GRAPH

1   How many units does Insight Limited have to produce to break even?

2   What are the fixed costs at the break-even point?

3   What are the variable costs at the break-even point?

4   What loss does Insight Limited make when output is zero units?

5   Why is this loss made?

6   What profit is made by Insight Limited when the output is 6,000 units?

Activity 13.5

Drawing a break-even graph

You have been given the projected monthly figures for two businesses and have been asked to construct break-even graphs for both of them. You have also been given a sheet of paper with hints for drawing break-even graphs.

---

hints for drawing break-even graphs

1   Use graph paper and a sharp pencil.

2.   You only need to plot two points for each line, one at zero output and one at maximum output. The lines will always be straight.

3.   Allow enough space on the vertical axis for the highest of the sales income figures.

4.   Allow enough space on the horizontal axis for the highest of the units of production figures.

5.   Make sure that your graph is correctly labelled.

---

business 1: Framers Limited

Framers Limited makes and sells framed Pop Art Posters. The selling price is £20 per framed poster, the variable cost is £10 per poster and the monthly fixed costs total £3,000.

units of production	fixed costs	variable costs	total cost	sales income	profit/(loss)
	A	B	C	D	E
			A + B		D – C
	£	£	£	£	£
0	3,000	0	3,000	0	(3,000)
100	3,000	1,000	4,000	2,000	(2,000)
200	3,000	2,000	5,000	4,000	(1,000)
300	3,000	3,000	6,000	6,000	nil
400	3,000	4,000	7,000	8,000	1,000
500	3,000	5,000	8,000	10,000	2,000
600	3,000	6,000	9,000	12,000	3,000
700	3,000	7,000	10,000	14,000	4,000
800	3,000	8,000	11,000	16,000	5,000

tasks

1   Calculate the break-even point using the formula method to check the accuracy of the table on the previous page. The formula for the break-even quantity of output is:

$$\frac{\text{fixed costs (£)}}{\text{selling price per unit (£) less variable cost per unit (£)}}$$

2   Draw up a break-even graph, using the hints set out on the previous page.

3   Read off the graph the profit or loss if 100 posters are produced and sold each month.

4   Read off the graph the profit or loss if 600 posters are produced and sold each month.

5   Check the answers to 3 & 4 against the figures in the table on the previous page.

business 2: Winthrop Furniture

Winthrop Furniture makes and sells a wooden garden seat known as the 'Eden'. The figures for this business have not yet been set out in the form of a table. All you have been given are the following monthly figures:

Cost of timber and labour for making seat	£20 per seat
Selling price	£45 per seat
Monthly fixed costs	£15,000

tasks

1   Draw up a table showing fixed costs, variable costs, total costs, sales income, and profit or loss for production of seats in multiples of 100 from zero up to 1,000.

2   Calculate the break-even point using the formula method to check your workings. The formula for the break-even quantity of output is:

$$\frac{\text{fixed costs (£)}}{\text{selling price per unit (£) less variable cost per unit (£)}}$$

3   Draw up a break-even graph, using the hints set out on the previous page.

4   Read off the graph the profit or loss if 200 seats are produced and sold each month.

5   Read off the graph the profit or loss if 1,000 seats are produced and sold each month.

6   Check the answers to 4 & 5 against the figures in the table produced in question 1.

break-even on a computer spreadsheet

The break-even table used in this chapter (see page 279 for an example) can easily be set up on a computer spreadsheet. The illustrations on this and the next page show a suggested layout, using the figures from the Case Study on pages 275 to 277 and a printout of the formulas used. As you will see from the illustrations, all you have to do is to head up the table, and input:

- the units of production in Column A
- the fixed and variable costs and sales income in the box at the top

The spreadsheet does the rest. If your spreadsheet program has a charting facility, you may be able to use the data to produce a break-even graph. The break-even graph produced from the Case Study is shown on the next page.

using the spreadsheet to change data

The spreadsheet has the advantage of allowing you to change the data and calculating the figures for you. You might, for example, want to see the effect on the break-even point of:

- changing the selling price of the unit
- increasing or decreasing the fixed and variable costs

This would be useful in a business situation where you wanted to bring the break-even point down and so increase profitability by, for example, increasing the selling price of the product.

	A	B	C	D	E	F
1	BREAK-EVEN CHART					
2	Name:					
3	Period:					
4						
5	fixed costs (£)	5000				
6	variable cost per item (£)	10				
7	sales income per item (£)	20				
8						
9	units of production	variable costs	fixed costs	total cost	sales income	profit/loss
10	0	0	5000	5000	0	-5000
11	100	1000	5000	6000	2000	-4000
12	200	2000	5000	7000	4000	-3000
13	300	3000	5000	8000	6000	-2000
14	400	4000	5000	9000	8000	-1000
15	500	5000	5000	10000	10000	0
16	600	6000	5000	11000	12000	1000
17	700	7000	5000	12000	14000	2000
18	800	8000	5000	13000	16000	3000
19	900	9000	5000	14000	18000	4000
20	1000	10000	5000	15000	20000	5000
21						

example of a break-even table on a computer spreadsheet

	A	B	C	D	E	F	
1	BREAK-EVEN CHART						
2	Name:						
3	Period:						
4							
5	fixed costs (£)	5000					
6	variable cost per item (£)	10					
7	sales income per item (£)	20					
8							
9	units of production	variable costs	fixed costs	total cost	sales income	profit/loss	
10	0	=B6*A10	=B5	=B10+C10	=B7*A10	=E10-D10	
11	100	=B6*A11	=B5	=B11+C11	=B7*A11	=E11-D11	
12	200	=B6*A12	=B5	=B12+C12	=B7*A12	=E12-D12	
13	300	=B6*A13	=B5	=B13+C13	=B7*A13	=E13-D13	
14	400	=B6*A14	=B5	=B14+C14	=B7*A14	=E14-D14	
15	500	=B6*A15	=B5	=B15+C15	=B7*A15	=E15-D15	
16	600	=B6*A16	=B5	=B16+C16	=B7*A16	=E16-D16	
17	700	=B6*A17	=B5	=B17+C17	=B7*A17	=E17-D17	
18	800	=B6*A18	=B5	=B18+C18	=B7*A18	=E18-D18	
19	900	=B6*A19	=B5	=B19+C19	=B7*A19	=E19-D19	
20	1000	=B6*A20	=B5	=B20+C20	=B7*A20	=E20-D20	
21							

the formulas used on the computer spreadsheet break-even table

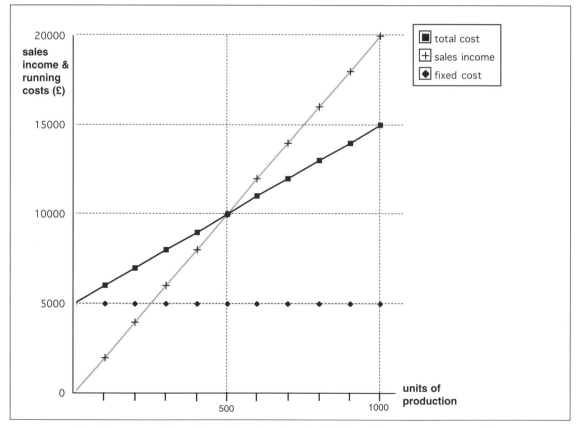

a break-even graph produced from the charting facility of the computer spreadsheet

Activity 13.6

Break-even using a spreadsheet

Jim Nevinson has a business which imports leather handbags from Italy and sells them to retail stores in the UK.

His current monthly income and expense figures are:

Fixed costs per month	£10,000
Variable costs per item	£10
Sales income per item	£30

1   Draw up a break-even chart on a computer spreadsheet. Input units sold in multiples of 100 from zero up to 1,000 per month. How many handbags does Jim have to sell to break-even? What profit will he make if he sells 1,000 handbags a month?

2   If your spreadsheet program has a charting facility, extract a break-even graph and check the break-even and profit figures produced in Task 1.

3   Six months have passed and trading conditions have worsened for Jim and he is having to change the way he operates. He is forced to make a decision between:

(a)   importing bags that are better quality – and so increasing his variable costs to £20 per item, or

(b)   keeping his variable costs at £10 but setting up another office – this will increase his fixed costs by £8,000 to £18,000 per month

Which option should he choose? You are to produce spreadsheet files and break-even graphs for both options and recommend to Jim the choice which provides an earlier break-even point and greater profit.

4   *Note: it is advisable to have your answer to Task 3 checked before carrying out this Task.* Jim is not happy with the profitability projected in Task 3. He suggests putting his selling price up to £40 per item.

Produce a new spreadsheet file and break-even graph based on the recommended choice from Task 3 and a new selling price of £40 per unit. How many handbags does Jim now have to sell to break-even? What profit will he make if he sells 1,000 handbags a month?

5   Suggest to Jim any problems he might encounter in raising his selling price to £40 per item. What is the percentage price increase involved?

CHAPTER SUMMARY

- Break-even is the point at which the income from the sales of a product is equal to the running costs of producing that product. Running costs are made up of fixed costs and variable costs.

- Variable costs are directly related to the number of units produced and sold; examples include the purchase of raw materials and stock.

- Fixed costs are costs that have to be paid anyway and do not vary with the number of items produced and sold; examples include overheads such as rent and insurance.

- The break-even point can be calculated by dividing fixed costs by the selling price per item less the variable cost per item (also known as the 'contribution').

- The break-even chart, which is plotted from figures on a break-even table, helps the business calculate how much profit it will make at different levels of production.

- A computer spreadsheet is useful in handling break-even tables and in constructing break-even charts for different combinations of income and costs.

KEY TERMS

break-even	the point at which sales income is equal to running costs
fixed costs	costs that have to be paid anyway and are not related to the number of units produced and sold
variable costs	costs that vary as the number of units produced and sold varies
contribution	the income from the sale of a unit that helps to pay off the fixed costs; it is calculated by deducting the variable cost per unit from the selling price per unit
break-even formula	$$\frac{\text{fixed costs}}{\text{selling price per unit less variable cost per unit}}$$
break-even table	a table setting out the figures necessary for the plotting of a break-even graph: units of production, fixed costs, variable costs, total cost, sales income, profit/(loss)
break-even graph	a graph which plots lines for sales income and total costs, showing the break-even point and profit/(loss)
area of profit/loss	the areas on a break-even graph which indicate the amount of profit or loss made by the business

MULTIPLE CHOICE QUESTIONS

1 Break-even is the point at which:
A sales income is greater than running costs
B sales income is greater than running costs and start-up costs
C sales income is equal to running costs
D sales income is equal to running costs and start-up costs

2 Variable costs are costs which:
A vary according to the time of year
B vary in the same proportion as fixed costs
C vary according to the number of units produced
D vary in line with the profit of the business

3 Fixed costs are:
A fixed at certain times of the year
B fixed and not dependent on the level of production
C the costs on which the business tax bill is fixed
D the costs which are equal to the running costs

4 'Contribution' is:
A selling price per unit less variable cost per unit
B start-up costs less variable cost per unit
C the amount of profit paid out to the owner
D the sales income received per unit of production

5 Business A has fixed monthly costs of £15,000, a selling price per unit of £10 and a variable cost per unit of £5. Break-even will be achieved when production and sales reach:
A 1,000 units per month
B 1,500 units per month
C 3,000 units per month
D 5,000 units per month

6 On a break-even graph the total cost line when production is zero units will start at:
A zero
B the level of fixed costs
C the break-even point
D the area of profit

14

Business profit and loss

Unit 3 Business finance:
estimating the profit or loss of a business

what this chapter is about

The last chapter explained that break-even shows a business whether a new product will be profitable or not and whether it should go ahead with it. The business will also want to know how much profit it will make from the product after the running costs have been paid. This chapter looks at the way profit – or loss – is calculated by means of a profit and loss statement.

what you will learn from this chapter

- business profit or loss is calculated by deducting running costs from the income received from sales of products and services

- business profit or loss does not take into account start-up costs such as premises or sources of finance such as capital and loans

- a business draws up a profit and loss statement at the end of a trading period such as a year

- a profit and loss statement looks back at the trading period and measures accurately the success of the business; this is different from a cash flow statement which is based on estimates and looks forward from the beginning of the trading period

- a profit and loss statement has a set format which deducts from the sales income the cost of any items that have been sold (if the business sells a product) and the running expenses to produce a net profit (or loss) figure for the period

- a computer spreadsheet is a useful aid in setting up a profit and loss statement

a definition of profit

profit or loss?

A business that sells a product or provides a service receives money from sales; it also incurs running costs. If the sales income is *greater* than the running costs, the difference between these two figures is the *profit* made by the business:

sales income less running costs = profit

For example:

sales income of £10,000 less running costs of £5,000 = £5,000 profit

What if the sales income is *less* than the running costs? The difference between these two figures is the *loss* made by the business. For example:

sales income of £10,000 less running costs of £11,000 = £1,000 loss.

It is common practice to show a loss in brackets, like this . . . (£1,000)

Activity 14.1

Calculating profit

Calculate the profit (or loss) made by the following businesses. If a loss has been made, show the figure in your answer in brackets.

	Sales income	Running costs
	£	£
Business 1	10,000	6,000
Business 2	12,000	8,000
Business 3	10,000	12,000
Business 4	15,600	7,800
Business 5	13,900	15,100
Business 6	145,000	89,000
Business 7	1,200,000	987,650
Business 8	235,000	270,000
Business 9	78,000	45,000
Business 10	12,560	9,654

what costs are included in the calculation?

You will see that the profit calculation does *not* include:

- *financing items* such as capital from the owner or grants or loans
- *start-up costs* such as the purchase of premises or equipment

The profit calculation involves only:

- income from day-to-day trading, for example sales of products and services
- running costs – these include the purchase of materials and stock which a business can then sell, and *overheads* – day-to-day expenses such as wages, telephone bills, rates and insurance

Activity 14.2

Items that make up profit

Calculate the profit (or loss) made by the businesses whose income and costs are shown below. If a loss has been made, show the figure in your answer in brackets. Before working out the profit (or loss) you will need to decide which items are start-up costs or financing items because you will not be able to include these in your calculation.

Business	Receipts	£	Payments	£
1 Travel Agent	Sales of services	45,000	Running costs	35,000
	Loan from bank	5,000	Computer	4,000
2 Manufacturer	Sales of product	62,000	Raw materials	30,000
	Loan from bank	150,000	Insurance	1,000
			Other running costs	20,000
			Premises purchase	100,000
			Machinery purchase	50,000
3 Shop	Sales of stock	100,000	Purchases of stock	50,000
	Capital	50,000	Wages	34,000
			Rates	4,500
			Other running costs	30,000

measuring profit

profit as a percentage

So far in this chapter we have seen how to calculate profit. It is also useful to see how good that profit figure is. This is done by comparing the profit figure and the sales income figure and measuring the profit as a *percentage* of the sales income. For example if a business has a sales income of £100,000 and makes a profit of £10,000, the profit percentage is 10%. In other words, for every £10 of sales, there is a profit of £1.

The profit percentage is calculated as follows:

$$\frac{Profit \ x \ 100}{sales \ income} \quad = \quad profit \ percentage$$

In the example above,

$$\frac{£10,000 \ x \ 100}{£100,000} \quad = \quad 10\%$$

This percentage figure – which is also known as the *profit margin* – is useful in comparing profits made by different businesses and also by the same business from year-to-year.

who is interested in profit?

A number of people will be interested in the profit of a business:

- the owner, who will receive some of the profit
- employees who may receive some of the profit in bonuses and will share in the satisfaction of working for a successful business
- an investor who might want to buy the business
- a lender of money who will want to get the money back in due course
- the Inland Revenue – because business profits are taxed!

Activity 14.3

How profitable is the business?

When you have had the answers to Activity 14.2 checked, work out the profit percentages of the profitable businesses (to the nearest whole number). What does this tell you about the performance of the businesses?

the profit and loss statement

At the end of a financial period – normally at the end of a year – a business will draw up a table of figures known as a *profit and loss statement*. This financial statement sets out in a formal way the calculations you have been practising in this chapter:

SALES INCOME – RUNNING COSTS = PROFIT (OR LOSS)

Notice that the profit and loss statement looks *back* over the year and is very different from the cash flow forecast which, as you saw in the last chapter, looks *forward*. The profit and loss statement is an accurate record of the profit or loss that has been made, the cash flow forecast is only an estimate of the money that will come in and out of the bank account in the future.

The owner of the business should compare the actual results in the profit and loss statement with profit projections made earlier in the year. He or she can then assess the success of the business and the accuracy of the forecasting.

A typical profit and loss statement is shown on the next page. The arrows have been added for illustrative purposes. Note the following points . . .

heading
The statement is headed up with the words 'Profit and Loss Statement' followed by the name of the business and the financial period covered.

format
The statement is presented in two money columns: the expense items are shown on the left and their total is carried over to the right-hand column, as shown by the arrow.

some terminology

cost of sales
The statement shown here is that of a business which makes or sells a product, ie a manufacturer or a shop. The item below the sales for the year is the *cost of sales*.

Cost of sales is the cost to the business of producing the goods that have actually been sold during the financial period of the profit and loss statement

Cost of sales is normally more or less the same as the figure for *purchases* of stock made by the business; it is usually adjusted for stock held at the beginning and the end of the year. In your studies you will not need to worry about these adjustments; as far as you are concerned:

COST OF SALES = PURCHASES OF STOCK AND GOODS

gross profit

Calculating cost of sales – the cost of what has actually been sold – enables the business to calculate profit accurately. *Gross profit* is the profit to the business before the other running expenses (overheads) are deducted. The calculation is:

SALES – COST OF SALES = GROSS PROFIT

The gross profit figure is useful because it shows how much profit is made from the manufacturing or selling process.

net profit

This is the profit after the deduction of overheads such as wages, rates, telephone and so on – the normal running expenses of a business. If the figure is negative, it will be a *loss* and it will be shown in brackets. The formula is:

GROSS PROFIT – OVERHEADS = NET PROFIT

PROFIT AND LOSS STATEMENT

of Henry Ford for the year ended 31 December 2002

	£	£
Sales		200,000
Less Cost of Sales		100,000
Gross profit		100,000
Less overheads		
Wages	40,000	
Rates	3,000	
Telephone	2,000	
Insurance	3,000	
Office expenses	15,000	
		63,000
Net Profit		37,000

what happens to profit?

The net profit is the amount that the business has earned for the owner during the year. Some of this profit can be taken out by the owner during the course of the year as *drawings*. The owner will also want to keep some money in the business as savings or to buy more resources to help the business expand.

Profit is *not* equal to money in the bank. Profit may have been earned during the year, but it may also have been spent.

Case Study

Bella Jones
profit and loss statement

In Chapter 12 we looked at the twelve month Cash Flow Forecast of Bella Jones who set up a CD mailing business (see pages 256 and 257). This forecast suggested that she would end up with £7,000 in the bank at the end of December. But a Cash Flow Forecast is only an estimate. What was her actual profit for the year?

Her accounting records show that her sales did better than expected, but her costs were also higher. These are the actual figures which she took from her accounting records and will use in her profit and loss statement:

	£
Sales	264,000
Purchases (cost of sales)	144,000
Wages	23,500
Mailing costs	15,000
Office costs	24,600
Advertising	19,400

Notice the items that she does **not** include in these figures:

• sources of money such as capital she has put in, loans or grants

• start-up costs such as computers and other equipment

A profit and loss statement only uses **sales figures** and **running costs.**

Her profit and loss statement will look like this:

PROFIT AND LOSS STATEMENT
of Bella Jones for the year ended 31 December 20-2

	£	£
Sales		264,000
Less Cost of Sales		144,000
Gross profit		120,000
Less overheads		
Wages	23,500	
Mailing costs	15,000	
Office costs	24,600	
Advertising	19,400	
		82,500
Net Profit		37,500

---

some questions from Bella – and answers

Bella then asks some questions :

1   "The net profit of £37,500 is far more than the amount I have got in the bank. Why is this?"

2   "What about the money I took out of the business to live on – the drawings of £24,000?"

The answers to these questions are:

1   Net profit is not the same as the money that you have left at the end of the financial period. You may have invested some of this and will have taken some out as living expenses.

2   Your living expenses – 'drawings' – never appear in the profit and loss statement. The net profit is the money that is available to you and the drawings will be deducted from it. You will know that profit needs to work for a business – you cannot take it all out as drawings. You have sensibly kept some money in the business.

Activity 14.4

Jon Gilbert – Hermes Sports
profit and loss statement

Jon Gilbert runs a sports shop 'Hermes Sports' in the town. His financial year ends on December 31. You are his book-keeper and have been going through his financial records with him. You have calculated his income and expenses figures for the year:

	£
Sales for the year	180,000
Cost of sales	85,000
Wages of shop staff	30,000
Rent	12,000
Rates	2,500
Insurance	3,500
Other shop running costs	5,000

1   You are to draw up Jon Gilbert's Profit and Loss statement for the year ending 31 December (use the current year for the year date). Use the format shown on the previous page. The heading should include the words 'Jon Gilbert trading as Hermes Sports'.

2   How much profit has he made on his sales before the overhead costs are deducted. What is this profit called?

3   How much profit has he made on his sales after all the overhead costs are deducted? What is this profit called? What percentage is it of the sales for the year? Calculate to the nearest percentage.

4   How much money is available from the business for Jon's living expenses during the year? Should he take all this money out?

5   A friend of Jon's keeps a similar shop in a nearby town. His sales for the year were £200,000 and his net profit was £40,000. Which business do you think is the more profitable? Compare the percentages of net profit to sales of the two businesses to help you with your decision.

profit and loss statement on a spreadsheet

You will see from the format of the profit and loss statement on page 293 that it can easily be set up on a computer spreadsheet.

Illustrated below is a sample spreadsheet file. You will see that there are only two columns needed for numerical data. It is a good idea to leave some extra rows clear in the overheads section in case you need to input extra items of expense.

On the next page is a copy of this spreadsheet showing the formulas used. You may need to consult your computer manual to check the format of the formulas used on your program; they may differ from those used here.

	A	B	C
1	PROFIT AND LOSS STATEMENT		
2	Name:		
3	Period:		
4			
5		£	£
6			
7	Sales		150000
8	Cost of sales (Purchases)		55000
9			
10	Gross profit		95000
11	Less overheads:		
12			
13			
14	Wages	40000	
15	Rent	12000	
16	Rates	2500	
17	Insurance	3500	
18	Advertising	1500	
19	Other expenses	5000	
20			64500
21	Net profit		30500
22			

a profit and loss statement on a computer spreadsheet

	A	B	C
1	PROFIT AND LOSS STATEMENT		
2	Name:		
3	Period:		
4			
5		£	£
6			
7	Sales		150000
8	Cost of sales (Purchases)		55000
9			
10	Gross profit		=C7-C8
11	Less overheads:		
12			
13			
14	Wages	40000	
15	Rent	12000	
16	Rates	2500	
17	Insurance	3500	
18	Advertising	1500	
19	Other expenses	5000	
20			=SUM(B14..B19)
21	Net profit		=C10-C20
22			

a profit and loss statement on a computer spreadsheet –
showing the formulas used

Activity 14.5

Profit and loss statements on a computer spreadsheet

You have been given the figures for three separate businesses as at 31 December of this year.

You are to:

1   Draw up profit and loss statements for each of the businesses on paper.

2   Set up a suitable spreadsheet file and input the figures from your paper-based originals, using the spreadsheet to check your totals for accuracy.

Fairburn Foods

	£
Sales	175,000
Purchases	95,000
Wages	45,600
Rent	5,000
Rates	3,450
Insurance	2,300
Advertising	2,000
Other expenses	200

Grantley Garden Supplies

	£
Sales	250,900
Purchases	102,984
Wages	67,800
Rent	5,690
Rates	4,010
Insurance	4,560
Advertising	13,450
Other expenses	2,057

Hardy Hi-Fi

	£
Sales	65,000
Purchases	45,000
Wages	15,600
Rent	2,000
Rates	2,100
Insurance	1,950
Advertising	560
Other expenses	500

CHAPTER SUMMARY

- Profit or loss is calculated by deducting running costs from the income received from sales of products and services.

- Profit or loss calculations exclude start-up costs and income from financing (such as capital and loans).

- Business profit – which can be expressed as a percentage – is of interest not only to the owners but also to employees, lenders and the Inland Revenue.

- The profit and loss statement looks back at a trading period such as a year and calculates profit or loss for that period.

- The profit and loss statement of a manufacturer or retailer (who deals in stock) first calculates gross profit – the difference between sales and the cost of sales (the cost of the stock purchased during the trading period).

- The profit and loss statement of any business calculates the net profit (or loss) figure – the profit after deduction of all running costs.

- A computer spreadsheet is a useful aid in setting up a profit and loss statement.

KEY TERMS

profit	sales income minus running costs, where sales income is greater than running costs
loss	sales income minus running costs, where sales income is less than running costs
profit percentage	a method of measuring profit: $\dfrac{\text{profit} \ \times \ 100}{\text{sales income}}$
profit and loss statement	a statement setting out sales income, running costs and the profit figure for a fixed period, normally a year
cost of sales	the cost to the business of buying in the raw materials and stock that has been sold during the financial period
overheads	the day-to-day running expenses, excluding the cost of sales, ie the purchases of raw materials and stock
gross profit	the profit made by a business (that makes or sells a product) before the overheads are deducted: sales *less* cost of sales = gross profit
net profit	the profit made by a business after the overheads have been deducted: gross profit *less* overheads = net profit

MULTIPLE CHOICE QUESTIONS

1   Business profit is calculated as follows:
     A   sales income and capital less running costs
     B   sales income less running costs and start-up costs
     C   sales income less running costs
     D   capital and loans less running costs

2   Cost of sales is:
     A   the cost of the stock plus overheads for the financial period
     B   sales less overheads and stock for the financial period
     C   sales less overheads for the financial period
     D   the cost of the stock sold during the financial period

3   If sales income is £100,000 and profit is £40,000, the profit percentage will be:
     A   4%
     B   40%
     C   2.5%
     D   25%

4   The overheads of a business are:
     A   purchases of raw materials and stocks
     B   start-up costs such as premises and machinery
     C   the total sales income for the year
     D   day-to-day running expenses

5   Gross profit is:
     A   the profit of a business that does not buy and sell stock
     B   net profit less the overheads of a business
     C   sales income less cost of sales
     D   business profit on which tax is payable

6   Net profit is:
     A   sales income less cost of sales
     B   gross profit less overheads
     C   start-up costs less capital from the owner
     D   overheads less the tax payable on profits

15 Financial documents for making purchases

> **Unit 3 Business finance:**
> investigating the flow of financial documents used to make a business purchase

what this chapter is about

When a business buys or sells goods and services it will deal with a variety of financial documents which are completed in a set sequence by the buyer and the seller. The documents used will depend on the type of transaction, but they basically cover the processes of ordering the product, working out how much it costs, requesting payment and then making payment. It is important that the documents are completed accurately – nobody wants the wrong product ordered, the wrong price charged or the wrong amount paid.

what you will learn from this chapter

- a cash purchase is when someone buys something and payment is made straightaway, a credit purchase is when payment is made later

- receipts are normally issued when you make a cash purchase

- a purchase of a product on credit – when payment is made later – can be divided into three stages, each involving a 'flow' of documents (which will be explained in the text):
  - an order is completed by the buyer to order the product
  - the product is supplied and the seller tells the buyer how much is owed
  - payment is made by the buyer

- financial documents must be completed accurately to avoid expensive mistakes and loss of business

- an increasing number of businesses now use computer accounting programs to process and print out financial documents

cash transactions, VAT and receipts

When a business sells goods or services it will either ask for payment to be made straightaway or at a later date:

- a *cash sale* is when payment is made straightaway
- a *credit sale* is when payment is made at a later date

The words 'cash sale' used in this way do not mean that just cash (in the form of notes and coins) is used – a 'cash sale' can be made using cash or a cheque. 'Cash' here means immediate payment and no credit terms.

cash payments and petty cash

Although more and more people are using plastic cards, cash is still the most common method of paying for goods and services – newspapers, magazines, sandwiches, cans of drink, bus fares, stationery – the list is very long. Businesses often keep in a locked box a cash float known as the *petty cash* which is used to buy low-value items used for the business.

receipts

When someone makes a cash purchase for a business – for example going out to buy some stationery – it is important that they obtain a receipt:

- if they have used their own money they will need to get it back from the petty cash tin!
- the business needs to record the fact that money has been spent on stationery – it is a running expense of the business

When the purchase is made most cash tills show on the screen the money amount of the purchase and also the change to be given. The till will also issue a receipt for all purchases when cash, a cheque, a debit card or a credit card is used. In the example below a customer has bought a pack of coloured paper and some disks from Everest Stationery. A till receipt has been issued.

Everest Stationery		retailer
15 High St Mereford		address
08 10 00 15.07		date and time of transaction
Salesperson Tina		salesperson
A4 paper (blue) 5.99		goods purchased
Disks 8.99		goods purchased
TOTAL 14.98		total due
CASH 20.00		£20 (probably a £20 note) given by the customer
CHANGE 5.02		change given
Thank you for your custom		personal message to help public relations
Please retain this receipt in case of any query		advice to retain receipt in case of a problem with the goods
VAT REG 373 2888 11		VAT Registration number

a till receipt

some notes on Value Added Tax (VAT)

You will see that the till receipt shown on the previous page quotes a VAT (Value Added Tax) number but no VAT amount. VAT is quoted on a number of the financial documents you will be investigating and you will need to know what it is and how it works:

• VAT (Value Added Tax) is a government tax on the selling price charged for most goods and services.

• There are some exceptions – eg VAT is not charged on books or food.

• In Britain most businesses must register for VAT.

charging Value Added Tax (VAT)

A business which is registered for VAT charges VAT at the standard rate (currently 17.5 per cent) on the money value of the goods or services it sells. The formula for working out the VAT charged on a sale is:

$$\text{VAT charged } = \text{ Sales amount } \times \frac{17.5}{100}$$

For example, if the business sells goods or services for £200 it has to add on 17.5% of the £200 to the amount charged, ie

$$\text{VAT } = \text{£200 } \times \frac{17.5}{100} = \text{£35.00}$$

The total amount the business receives will be:

$$\text{£200 plus £35.00 (VAT) } = \text{£235.00}$$

The business will keep the £200 but will have to pay the £35 to HM Customs & Excise, the government department which administers VAT.

Please note, however, that receipts and invoices for purchases under £100 (see the receipt on the previous page) do not have to show the VAT amount separately – it is included in the final amount. If you think about it, most till receipts you get from shops do not show the VAT amount, but you still pay it!

the handwritten receipt

When a business buys goods or services, the person doing the purchasing will sometimes need a more formal document than a till receipt to provide evidence that money has been spent on those particular goods or services. It may be a travelling salesman buying petrol, or an office manager buying stationery from a shop. If there is no detailed evidence, the business (or the tax inspectors) may wonder where the money has gone – has the salesman used the money to take his wife out? Has the office manager bought himself a new briefcase? If the seller issues a formal handwritten receipt, there is no doubt about the transaction.

Look at the example shown below. Note that it includes the VAT as a separate item, a type of layout you will see on the documents explained later in the chapter.

Enigma Stationery		**RECEIPT**	No. 765	← receipt number
14 High Street, Broadfield BR1 5FT				
VAT Reg 343 7645 23				customer name and date
Customer...... *B Okojubu*		date...... *1 April 2000*		
50 reams lasercopy paper (white) @ £4.00 each			*200.00*	description and price of goods
50 reams lasercopy paper (blue) @ £4.00 each			*200.00*	
			400.00	
		VAT	*70.00*	← VAT charged
		TOTAL	*470.00*	← total paid

Activity 15.1

Completing receipts

1 Collect a variety of receipts – either blank ones or copies of completed receipts. Sources include local businesses (eg petrol stations) and stationers (who sell blank receipts in pads). Examine and compare them in class.

Design and draw up your own receipt. Use a computer package if you can. Invent your own business name and address for a lighting supplies firm. Remember to include a VAT registration number – you should assume that the business charges VAT. When calculating VAT, round it down to the nearest p.

2 Make (or print out) three copies of your receipt and enter the following sales transactions:

(a) 2 flexilamps @ £13.99, plus 2 candlelight bulbs @85p each sold to George Meredith

(b) 1 standard lamp @ £149.95, plus one 100 watt bulb @ 99p, sold to Alex Bell

(c) 2 Georgian lamps @ £35.99 sold to Miss S Fox

Use today's date and add VAT at the current rate to the prices given.

making a purchase on credit

financial documents for transactions 'on credit'

When a business buys goods or services *on credit* it orders the goods first and then pays later. During this process a number of different financial documents will be issued by the seller and the buyer. We will look in this chapter at a whole range of financial documents by means of a Case Study involving the purchase of fashion clothes.

You must bear in mind that not all purchases involve all the documents listed below. Many purchases are for services, eg office cleaning, and do not involve goods being sent. It is important for your studies, however, that

- you can recognise each of the documents
- you know what they are for
- you can complete a number of them

The financial documents shown here include:

- the *purchase order*, which the buyer sends to the seller
- the *delivery note* which goes with the goods from the seller to the buyer
- the *goods received note* which is sometimes completed by the buyer to record the actual amount of goods received
- the *invoice,* which lists the goods and tells the buyer what is owed
- the *credit note*, which is sent to the buyer if any refund is due
- the *statement,* sent by the seller to remind the buyer what is owed
- the *remittance advice*, sent by the buyer when the goods are paid for
- the *cheque* which is completed by the buyer to pay for the goods

the flow of documents

Before you read the Case Study, examine the diagram set out on the next page. Down the columns representing the buyer and the seller are various activities which lead to transactions, which in turn generate documents.

As we have just seen, you should appreciate that not all the activities happen all the time – the order may be for services, the order may be placed by telephone, you may not get a delivery note, and a credit note is only used when an adjustment is needed.

Most of the time, however, things run smoothly and the invoice is paid following receipt of a statement.

the flow of documents

BUYER   **SELLER**

the order is placed → *purchase order* → the order is received and processed

the receipt of goods is recorded (the buyer may complete a goods received note) ← *delivery note with goods* ← the goods or services are supplied

← *invoice* ← payment is requested

a refund may be requested if there is a problem ← *credit note (if needed)* ← a refund may be agreed if there is a problem

← *statement of account* ← payment is requested again

payment is made → *remittance advice and cheque* → the money is received

Case Study

Cool Socks
buying on credit

Cool Socks Limited manufactures fashion socks in a variety of colours. It supplies a number of different customers, including Trends, a fashion store in Broadfield.

In this Case Study we see an order for 100 pairs of socks placed by Trends with Cool Socks. The socks are delivered, but some are found to be faulty, so a refund has to be made. Finally, payment has to be made for the socks.

The Case Study looks in detail at the purchase and sales documents involved. Now read on.

PURCHASE ORDER – *the buyer orders the goods*

purpose of the document	to order goods or services
who completes it?	the buyer of the goods or services
what happens to it?	it is sent by the buyer to the seller
why must it be accurate?	if it is not completed accurately the wrong products may be ordered

what happens in this case?

Trends orders some socks from Cool Socks. The buyer at Trends will post or fax the authorised purchase order shown below. The order will have been typed out in the office, or produced on a computer accounting program. The details of the socks will have been obtained from Cool Socks' catalogue, or possibly by means of a written or telephoned enquiry.

points to note:

- each purchase order has a specific reference number – this is useful for filing and quoting on later documents such as invoices and statements
- the product code of the goods required is stated in the product code column – this is like the number you write on the slip when ordering something from an Argos store
- the quantity of the goods required is stated in the quantity column – socks are obviously supplied in pairs!
- the purchase order is signed and dated by the person in charge of purchasing – without this authorisation the supplier is unlikely to supply the goods (the order will probably be returned!)

Trends   **PURCHASE ORDER**

4 Friar Street
Broadfield
BR1 3RF
Tel 01908 761234 Fax 01908 761987
VAT REG GB 0745 8383 56

Cool Socks Limited, Unit 45 Elgar Estate, Broadfield, BR7 4ER	purchase order no 47609
	date 25 09 00

product code	quantity	description
45B	100 pairs	Blue Toebar socks

AUTHORISED   signature......*D Signer*......................................date......*25/09/00*

DELIVERY NOTE – *the goods are delivered*

purpose of the document	it states what goods are being delivered
who completes it?	the seller of the goods
what happens to it?	it is sent by the seller to the buyer
why must it be accurate?	if the goods delivered do not tally with the description on the delivery note, the goods may be refused

what happens in this case?

The delivery note is despatched with the goods when the order is ready. It is normally typed in the office or printed out by a computer accounting program. In this case, the delivery note travels with the socks, and a copy will be signed by Trends on receipt.

points to note:

• the delivery note has a numerical reference, useful for filing and later reference if there is a query

• the delivery note quotes the purchase order number – this enables the buyer to 'tie up' the delivery with the original order

• the details of the goods supplied – the quantity and the description – will be checked against the goods themselves

• the delivery note will be signed and dated by the person receiving the goods

---

———————— DELIVERY NOTE ————————

COOL SOCKS LIMITED

Unit 45 Elgar Estate, Broadfield, BR7 4ER
Tel 01908 765314 Fax 01908 765951
VAT REG GB 0745 4672 76

Trends 4 Friar Street Broadfield BR1 3RF	delivery note no delivery method your order date	68873 Lynx Parcels 47609 02 10 00

product code	quantity	description
45B	100 pairs	Blue Toebar socks

Received

signature............*V Williams*............name (capitals)...*V WILLIAMS*............date..*5/10/00*....

Practical exercises featuring the documents in this Case Study are to be found in the next chapter.

GOODS RECEIVED NOTE – *the buyer records receipt of the goods*

purpose of the document	it records what goods have been delivered
who completes it?	the buyer of the goods
what happens to it?	it is kept by the buyer
why must it be accurate?	a mistake may result in a problem with the delivery not being picked up

what happens in this case?

The goods received note (GRN) will be completed by the person in Trends who looks after the stock. In the case of this delivery, ten pairs of the socks have been received damaged – Trends will want a refund.

points to note:

• details of the goods are noted on the form
• the condition of the goods – the damage to the socks – is recorded and this fact will be notified on separate copies to the buyer, to Accounts and to the stockroom
• a goods received note is not used by all businesses

Trends   GOODS RECEIVED NOTE

Supplier

Cool Socks Limited, Unit 45 Elgar Estate, Broadfield, BR7 4ER	GRN no date	1871 05 10 00

quantity	description	order number
100 pairs	Blue Toebar socks	47609

carrier   Lynx Parcels   consignment no   8479347

received by   *V Williams*   checked by   *R Patel*

condition of goods (please tick and comment)	good condition damaged ✓ (10 pairs) shortages	**copies to** Buyer ✓ Accounts

---

Practical exercises featuring the documents in this Case Study are to be found in the next chapter.

INVOICE – *payment is requested by the seller (see next page)*

purpose of the document   it tells the buyer how much is owed and when it has to be paid

who completes it?   the seller of the goods

what happens to it?   it is sent by the seller to the buyer, who checks it carefully and keeps it on file for reference

why must it be accurate?   a mistake could result in the wrong amount being paid; a wrong address could delay payment

what happens in this case?

The invoice, like the delivery note, is prepared in the seller's office, and is either typed or produced on a computer printer using a computer accounting program. Invoices produced by different organisations will vary to some extent in terms of detail, but their basic layout will always be the same.

The invoice prepared by Cool Socks Ltd – illustrated on the next page – is typical of a modern typed or computer-printed document.

points to note:

addresses

The invoice shows the address:

• of the seller/supplier of the goods – Cool Socks Limited
• the place where the invoice should be sent – to Trends
• where the goods are to be sent – it may not always be the same as the invoice address; for example a supermarket ordering a container load of bananas will ask them to be delivered to a distribution warehouse, not to the Accounts Department!

references

There are a number of important references on the invoice:

• the numerical reference of the invoice itself – 787923
• the account number allocated to Trends by the seller – 3993 – for use in the seller's computer accounting program
• the original reference number on the purchase order sent by Trends – 47609 – which will enable the shop to 'tie up' the invoice with the original order

terms

The 'terms' are very important – they state when the invoice has to be paid.

Now look at the document and the explanations on the next two pages to find out what you have to check when you receive an invoice.

INVOICE – *payment is requested by the seller*

──────────────── INVOICE ────────────────

COOL SOCKS LIMITED

Unit 45 Elgar Estate, Broadfield, BR7 4ER
Tel 01908 765314 Fax 01908 765951
VAT REG GB 0745 4672 76

invoice to

Trends
4 Friar Street
Broadfield
BR1 3RF

invoice no   787923
account   3993
your reference   47609

date/tax point   02 10 00

product code	description	quantity	price	unit	total	discount %	net
45B	Blue Toebar socks	100	2.36	pair	236.00	0.00	236.00

GOODS TOTAL	236.00
VAT	41.30
TOTAL	277.30

terms
30 days

Practical exercises featuring the documents in this Case Study are to be found in the next chapter.

points to note and check on the invoice

You will need to check that the reference number quoted here ties up with your purchase order number.

The date here is normally the date on which the goods have been sent to you. It is known as the 'invoice date'. The date is important for calculating when the Invoice is due to be paid. In this case the 'terms' (see the bottom left-hand corner of the invoice) are 30 days. This means the invoice is due to be paid within 30 days after the invoice date. The invoice date is 2 October, so it is due to be paid by 31 October.

The arithmetic and details in this line must be checked very carefully to make sure that you pay the correct amount for what you have ordered:

- *product code* – this is the catalogue number which appeared on the original purchase order and on the delivery note
- *description* – this must agree with the description on the purchase order
- *quantity* – this should agree with the quantity ordered
- *price* – this is the price of each unit shown in the next column
- *unit* is the way in which the unit is counted up and charged for, eg units (single items), pairs (as here), or 10s,100s and so on
- *total* is the unit price multiplied by the number of units
- *discount %* is the percentage allowance (known as trade discount) given to customers who regularly deal with the supplier, ie they receive a certain percentage (eg 10%) deducted from their bill
- *net* is the amount due to the seller after deduction of trade discount, and before VAT is added on

The Goods Total is the total of the column above it. It is the final amount due to the seller before VAT is added on.

Value Added Tax (VAT) is calculated and added on – here it is 17.5% of the Goods Total, ie $£236.00 \times \dfrac{17.5}{100} = £41.30$

The VAT is then added to the Goods Total to produce the actual amount owing:
$£236.00 + £41.30 = £277.30$

The 'terms; explain the conditions on which the goods are supplied. Here '30 days' mean that payment has to be made within 30 days of the invoice date.

CREDIT NOTE – *the seller gives a refund*

purpose of the document   A credit note is a 'refund' document which reduces the amount owed by the buyer. The format of a credit note is very similar to that of an invoice.

who completes it?   the seller of the goods

what happens to it?   it is sent by the seller to the buyer, who checks it carefully and keeps it on file with the invoice

why must it be accurate?   a mistake could result in the wrong amount eventually being paid

what happens in this case?

Trends has received 10 damaged pairs of socks. These will be sent back to Cool Socks with a 'returns note' and a request for *credit* – ie a reduction in the bill for the 10 faulty pairs. Cool Socks will have to issue the credit note for £27.73 shown below.

points to note:
- a credit note can be issued for faulty goods, missing goods, or goods which are not needed
- the credit note quotes the invoice number and states why the credit (refund) is being given

---

———— CREDIT NOTE ————
COOL SOCKS LIMITED
Unit 45 Elgar Estate, Broadfield, BR7 4ER
Tel 01908 765314 Fax 01908 765951
VAT REG GB 0745 4672 76

to

Trends
4 Friar Street
Broadfield
BR1 3RF

credit note no	12157
account	3993
your reference	47609
our invoice	787923
date/tax point	10 10 00

product code	description	quantity	price	unit	total	discount %	net
45B	Blue Toebar socks	10	2.36	pair	23.60	0.00	23.60

Reason for credit
10 pairs of socks received damaged
(Your returns note no. R/N 2384)

GOODS TOTAL	23.60
VAT	4.13
TOTAL	27.73

STATEMENT – *the seller requests payment*

purpose of the document

a statement – which is normally issued at the end of every month – tells the buyer how much is owed

who completes it?

the seller of the goods

what happens to it?

it is sent by the seller to the buyer who checks it against the invoices and credit notes on file

why must it be accurate?

a mistake could result in the wrong amount being paid

what happens in this case?

A seller will not normally expect a buyer to pay each individual invoice as soon as it is received. Instead, a statement of account showing what is owed is sent by the seller to the buyer *at the end of the month.* It shows:

- invoices issued for goods supplied – the full amount due, including VAT
- refunds made on credit notes – including VAT
- payments received from the buyer (if any)

The statement issued by Cool Socks to Trends for the period covering the sale (the invoice) and refund (the credit note) is shown below. Trends now has to pay the £249.57 owing.

——— STATEMENT OF ACCOUNT ———

COOL SOCKS LIMITED

Unit 45 Elgar Estate, Broadfield, BR7 4ER
Tel 01908 765314 Fax 01908 765951
VAT REG GB 0745 4672 76

TO

Trends
4 Friar Street
Broadfield
BR1 3RF

account   3993

date   31 10 00

date	details	debit £	credit £	balance £
02 10 00	Invoice 787923	277.30		277.30
10 10 00	Credit note 12157		27.73	249.57
			AMOUNT NOW DUE	249.57

Practical exercises featuring the documents in this Case Study are to be found in the next chapter.

314 intermediate business

REMITTANCE ADVICE – *the buyer sends a payment advice*

purpose of the document	a remittance advice is a document sent by the buyer to the seller stating that payment is being made
who completes it?	the buyer
what happens to it?	it is sent by the buyer to the seller
why must it be accurate?	a mistake could result in the wrong amount being paid

what happens in this case?

Trends have completed a remittance advice listing the invoice that is being paid and the credit note which is being deducted from the amount owing. Trends will make out a cheque for the total amount of the remittance advice. This is shown on the next page. It will be attached to the remittance advice and will be posted to Cool Socks in November.

points to note:

- the remittance advice quotes the account number (3993) allocated to Trends by Cool Socks – this will help Cool Socks to update their records when the payment is received
- the documents are listed in the columns provided: 'your reference' describes the documents issued by Cool Socks and quotes their numbers; 'our reference' quotes the number of the Purchase Order originally issued by Trends
- the amounts of the invoice and the credit note are entered in the right-hand column – note that the credit note amount is negative, so it is shown in brackets; the total payment amount is shown in the box at the bottom of the form – this will be the amount of the cheque issued
- payment can alternatively be made by computer transfer between bank accounts (BACS); in this case a remittance advice is still sent, but no cheque
- a 'tear-off' printed remittance advice listing all the items is sometimes attached to the statement sent by the seller; all the buyer has to do is to tick the items being paid, and pay!

TO   **REMITTANCE ADVICE** FROM

Cool Socks Limited
Unit 45 Elgar Estate,
Broadfield, BR7 4ER

Trends

4 Friar Street
Broadfield
BR1 3RF

Tel 01908 761234 Fax 01908 761987
VAT REG GB 0745 8383 56

Account 3993   5 November 2000

date	your reference	our reference	payment amount
02 10 00	INVOICE 787923	47609	277.30
10 10 00	CREDIT NOTE 12157	47609	(27.73)
		CHEQUE TOTAL	249.57

CHEQUE – *the buyer sends a payment*

purpose of the document	a payment document which, when completed, can be paid into a bank account; it enables people to settle debts, for example a buyer paying money to a seller
who completes it?	the person who owes the money signs the cheque and writes the amount in words and figures, the name of the person who is to receive the money (the payee) and the date
what happens to it?	it is passed or posted by the buyer to the seller
why must it be accurate?	if the amount is wrong the seller could end up being underpaid or overpaid; also, any mistake on the cheque could result in the banks refusing to let it through the clearing system

what happens in this case?

Trends complete the details on the cheque – including the date, amount and signature – and send it to Cool Socks with the remittance advice.

points to note:

- If a cheque is not completed correctly, it could be refused by the banks. Particular points to note are:
  - the cheque should be signed – it is completely invalid without a signature
  - the amount in words and figures must be the same
  - lines should be drawn after the name of the payee and the amount to prevent fraud
  - the current date should be written in – cheques become invalid after six months

- The lines across the cheque are known as the 'crossing'. The words 'a/c payee only' are an important security measure because they mean that the cheque can only be paid into the account of the person named on the 'pay' line of the cheque.

Albion Bank PLC
7 The Avenue
Broadfield BR1 2AJ
Date _____ 90 47 17

A/c payee only

£

TRENDS

V Williams

072628   90 47 17   11719512

Practical exercises featuring the documents in this Case Study are to be found in the next chapter.

what to do with incorrect cheques

As we saw on the previous page, if you receive a cheque with a mistake, it may not be accepted by the bank you are paying it into. Alternatively it might be returned by the bank of the person paying the money because of a mistake, or because the person has not got any money in the account – it might 'bounce' (be returned by the bank), in which case you will not get your money. How do you avoid this situation?

correcting mistakes

If you receive a cheque with a mistake on it, you will need to get the mistake corrected and any correction initialled by the person writing out the cheque. If the person has posted the cheque to you this means in most cases posting the cheque back again with a covering letter asking for the mistake to be corrected. The most common mistakes that occur are:

mistake	what you do to correct it
there is no signature	send it back asking for a signature
the amount in words and figures differs	send it back asking for it to be corrected and the correction initialled
the name on the 'pay' line is wrong	send it back asking for it to be corrected and the correction initialled
the date is more than six months ago	send it back and ask for the date to be changed and the correction initialled
the date is missing	you can write it in! – this is the one situation where you do not have to send it back

Activity 15.2

Checking cheques

You work in the accounts department of Morton Components Limited. The cheques on the opposite page have been received in this morning's post. The date is 10 November 2000.

1   Examine the cheques and write down what is wrong with them.

2   State in each case what you would do to put matters right.

3   Optional task:
     Word process the text of a letter to be sent to the business which has written out <u>one</u> of the cheques.

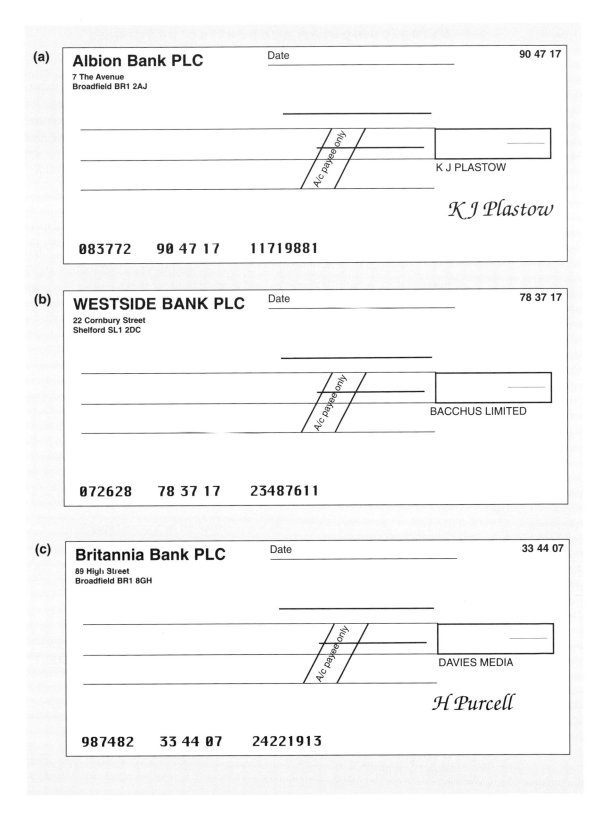

(a)

Albion Bank PLC

7 The Avenue
Broadfield BR1 2AJ

Date

90 47 17

A/c payee only

K J PLASTOW

K J Plastow

083772   90 47 17   11719881

(b)

WESTSIDE BANK PLC

22 Cornbury Street
Shelford SL1 2DC

Date

78 37 17

A/c payee only

BACCHUS LIMITED

072628   78 37 17   23487611

(c)

Britannia Bank PLC

89 High Street
Broadfield BR1 8GH

Date

33 44 07

A/c payee only

DAVIES MEDIA

H Purcell

987482   33 44 07   24221913

---

using computer accounting programs

Although many organisations, particularly small businesses, still use paper-based accounting systems, an increasing number are now operating computerised accounting systems. They are easy to use and can automate operations such as invoicing which take so much time and effort in a manual system. In this chapter we will look at the system developed by Sage plc for PCs which run on Windows. It is commonly used by small and medium-sized businesses and you may find it installed in your school or college.

structure of a Sage computer accounting program

The illustration below is the opening screen of a typical Sage program. It has icons (pictures) of the main functions of the program set out along a horizontal 'toolbar'. The arrows and explanations of these icons have been added here to provide an overview of what the program can do.

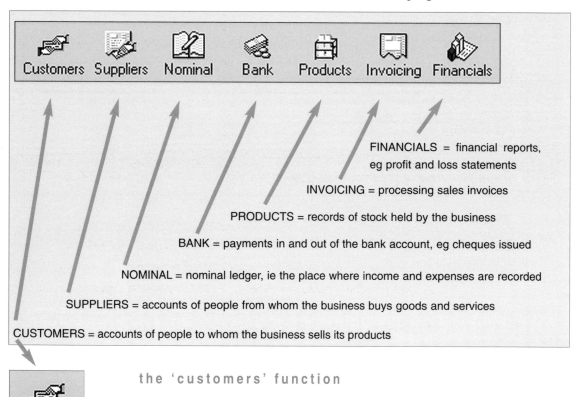

FINANCIALS = financial reports, eg profit and loss statements

INVOICING = processing sales invoices

PRODUCTS = records of stock held by the business

BANK = payments in and out of the bank account, eg cheques issued

NOMINAL = nominal ledger, ie the place where income and expenses are recorded

SUPPLIERS = accounts of people from whom the business buys goods and services

CUSTOMERS = accounts of people to whom the business sells its products

the 'customers' function

The 'Customers' icon on the opening screen enables you to call up the details of the accounts of customers to whom the business sells its products.

If you click on this icon the 'Customers' toolbar (shown at the top of the next page) will appear.

Enigma Limited

34 Packhorse Road
Mereford MR2 7YH
Tel 01908 433927 Fax 01908 433812 email edgar@goblin.co.uk
VAT Reg 727 7262 01

INVOICE

R Patel & Co
Phoenix Business Park
Southampton Road
Salisbury
Wilts
SN1 9LX

invoice no.	27398
invoice date	17/12/1998
order no.	SA234
account ref.	997

quantity	description	discount %	net amount	VAT amount
20	Enigma 35 (black)	0.00	119.00	20.83

Payment 30 days net

Total net	119.00
Total tax	20.83
Carriage	00.00
Invoice total	139.83

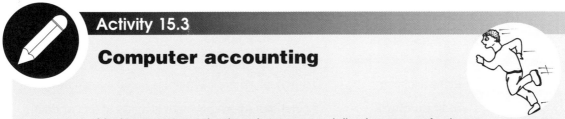

Activity 15.3

Computer accounting

List in two paragraphs the advantages and disadvantages of using a computer accounting package.

If you have the opportunity, ask one of the businesses you are investigating to find out its views.

CHAPTER SUMMARY

- A cash purchase is when someone buys something and payment is made straightaway; a receipt is normally issued for a cash purchase

- A credit purchase is when payment for a purchase is made at a later date; a credit purchase normally involves the issue of a number of different financial documents which 'flow' in a set order

- the 'flow' of documents involves:
  - the buyer issuing a purchase order and a goods received note
  - the seller sending an invoice and a delivery note with the goods, a credit note if any refund is due and a statement to advise the amount owing
  - the buyer sending a cheque and a remittance advice to pay for the goods

- financial documents must be completed accurately and checked on receipt to avoid the wrong goods being supplied or the wrong amount being charged

- an increasing number of businesses now use computer accounting programs to process and print out financial documents

KEY TERMS

documents	make sure that you can define each of the following documents described in this chapter: • receipt • purchase order • delivery note • goods received note • invoice • credit note • statement of account • remittance advice • cheque
cash purchase	a purchase where payment is made straightaway
credit purchase	a purchase where payment is made at a later date
Value Added Tax (VAT)	a tax charged by businesses on the sale of goods and services
discount	a percentage amount deducted from the sale price of an item – often known as 'trade discount'

MULTIPLE CHOICE QUESTIONS

1   A purchase order is used to

   A   tell the purchaser how much the goods cost

   B   place an order with the seller

   C   pay the seller for the goods

   D   fix the price on a purchase of goods

2   A remittance advice is

   A   an advice note telling the buyer what goods were sent

   B   an advice note telling the seller that the wrong goods were sent

   C   a document advising the seller of payment

   D   a document advising the buyer of payment

Questions 3 – 5 relate to the following information:

   An invoice with a number of errors has resulted in the following problems:

   A   the wrong goods sent

   B   a query on the total amount payable

   C   the goods sent to the wrong person

   D   an order sent twice

   Which of these problems is likely to have been caused by the following?

3   The wrong unit price used

4   The wrong product code used

5   The wrong customer account number used

6   Decide whether each of these statements is True (T) or False (F)

   (i)   the goods received note is sent with the goods

   (ii)   the delivery note is sent to the buyer

   A   (i)   T   (ii)   T

   B   (i)   T   (ii)   F

   C   (i)   F   (ii)   T

   D   (i)   F   (ii)   F

16

Financial documents – practical exercises

Unit 3 Business finance:
investigating the flow of financial documents used to make a business purchase

in-tray exercise

In this chapter you will practise completing and checking the financial documents explained in the last chapter. The documents used here are those used in a credit purchase and when paying money into the bank. If you need blank documents they are available in the Appendix (page 373) and also in downloadable form on the Osborne Books website: www.osbornebooks.co.uk in the Resources section.

To remind you of the 'flow' of documents that normally takes place, study the diagram shown below.

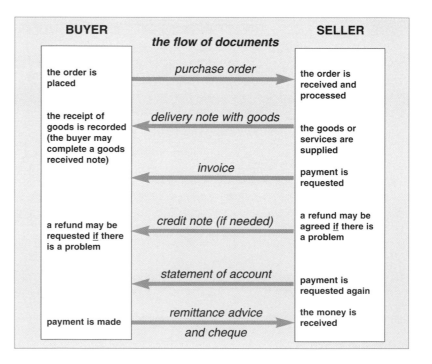

BUYER	the flow of documents	SELLER
the order is placed	purchase order →	the order is received and processed
the receipt of goods is recorded (the buyer may complete a goods received note)	← delivery note with goods	the goods or services are supplied
	← invoice	payment is requested
a refund may be requested if there is a problem	← credit note (if needed)	a refund may be agreed if there is a problem
	← statement of account	payment is requested again
payment is made	remittance advice → and cheque	the money is received

Activity 16.1

Making the purchase

Blank financial documents are available from the Resources section of the Osborne Books website: www.osbornebooks.co.uk

task 1

Work in pairs and play the roles of buyer and seller. The buyer is a clothes shop Oasis, 5 High Street, Mereford MR1 3GF and the seller a clothes importer, Fashions Imports Limited, Unit 4 Beech Industrial Estate, Salebury, Manchester, M62 5FG. You will need copies of blank purchase orders and invoices (see note above). You should use today's date and the current VAT rate, but will need to make up the following details:

* catalogue numbers
* order numbers and invoice numbers

The buyer is to complete two separate purchase orders and the seller is to complete an invoice for each order. The orders are as follows:

(a)   100 pairs of tights (black) at £1.50 each
        25 sweatshirts (green) at £8 each
        50 T shirts (black) at £3.50 each

(b)   25 fleeces (red) at £15 each
        30 pairs of jeans (black) at £17.50 each
        50 pairs of tights (black) at £1.50 each

There is no trade discount available to the buyer. Add VAT at the current rate and round it down to the nearest pence.

task 2

You work for Deansway Trading Company, a wholesaler of office stationery, which trades from The Modern Office, 79 Deansway, Stourminster WR1 2EJ. A customer, The Card Shop of 126 The Crescent, Marshall Green, WR4 5TX, orders the following on order number 9516:

(a)   50 boxes of assorted rubbers at 50p per box, catalogue no 26537

(b)   100 shorthand notebooks at £4 for a pack of 10, catalogue no 72625

(c)   250 ring binders (red) at £2.50p each, catalogue no 72698

VAT is to be charged at the current rate on all items, and a 5% trade discount is given to The Card Shop. Prepare invoice number 8234, under today's date, to be sent to the customer.

Activity 16.2

Checking invoices

task 1

A colleague in the Accounts Department of Cool Socks has prepared this sales invoice. You are to check it and state what is wrong with it. You are then to draw up a new invoice with the same reference number and today's date. Assume the price quoted is correct.

INVOICE ———

COOL SOCKS LIMITED

Unit 45 Elgar Estate, Broadfield, BR7 4ER
Tel 01908 765314 Fax 01908 765951
VAT REG GB 0745 4672 76

invoice to		
Oasis 5 High Street Mereford MR1 3GF		

invoice no		876512
account		3461
your reference		87541

date/tax point

product code	description	quantity	price	unit	total	discount %	net
45R	Red Toebar socks	100	2.45	pair	254.00	10.00	279.40

GOODS TOTAL	279.40
VAT	48.89
TOTAL	230.51

terms: 30 days

task 2

You work in the Oasis clothes shop and have received this invoice in the post. You check it against the Purchase Order, the details of which are:

Order No 98372 for 50 pairs of dark blue Country trousers @ £12.45 a pair (code 234DB). You are normally given 10% trade discount.

The jeans were received, as ordered, on the same day as the invoice.

Check the invoice against the purchase order and if there are any problems contact the Sales Ledger Department of The Jeans Company by e-mail, fax or letter. Draft out the text of your e-mail, fax or letter on a word processing file.

INVOICE

The Jeans Company

Unit 6 Parry Trading Estate, Southfield, SF1 5LR
Tel 01901 333391 Fax 01901 333462 email Jeansco@goblin.com
VAT REG GB 8762 54 27

invoice to

Oasis	
5 High Street	
Mereford	
MR1 3GF	

invoice no	942394
account	2141
your reference	98372
date/tax point	01 12 00

product code	description	quantity	price	unit	total	discount %	net
234B	Country trousers (black)	50	12.45	pair	622.50	5.00	591.38

GOODS TOTAL	591.38
VAT	103.49
TOTAL	694.87

terms: 30 days

Activity 16.3

A goods received note is completed

You work in an insurance broker's office and have just received a consignment of 50 reams of photocopy paper from Wintergreen Stationers. A ream is a packet of 500 sheets. The reams are packed in boxes of five. One of the boxes is badly dented at one end. The 5 reams of paper in this box are unusable as they will jam any photocopier or printer. The delivery note for the paper is shown below.

DELIVERY NOTE

WINTERGREEN STATIONERS

75 Holmes Street, Broadfield, BR2 6TF
Tel 01908 342281 Fax 01908 342538 Email WGreen@newserve.com
VAT REG GB 0822 2422 75

Uplands Insurance Brokers	delivery note no	68673
8 Friar Street	delivery method	Parcelexpress
Broadfield	your order	23423
BR1 3RF	date	01 10 00

product code	quantity	description
A4PPW	50 reams	A4 photocopy paper, white, 80gsm

Received

signature...............*J Rutter*.....................name (capitals)......*J RUTTER*..................date *5/10/00*

---

1   You are to complete a Goods Received Note. See the Appendix and the Osborne website: www.osbornebooks.co.uk for copies of blank documents.

   The goods arrived by Parcelexpress, consignment number 7429472

2   The damaged paper will be sent back to the supplier within the next few days. Write the text of a fax or an email to the supplier on a wordprocessor file, explaining the situation. Include all the references and details which you think will be needed. You should not at this stage ask for a credit note.

The following day the invoice for the goods arrives by post. This will be dealt with in the next Activity.

Activity 16.4

A credit note is requested

The invoice for the photocopy paper delivered in the last Activity is shown below. It should be checked carefully for errors. Uplands Insurance Brokers normally receives a 10% discount on goods supplied.

You are to write a letter to the Accounts Department requesting a credit note for the returned paper. The letter should include the money amount (including VAT) of the credit that is due.

INVOICE
WINTERGREEN STATIONERS
75 Holmes Street, Broadfield, BR2 6TF
Tel 01908 342281 Fax 01908 342538 Email WGreen@newserve.com
VAT REG GB 0822 2422 75

invoice to

Uplands Insurance Brokers
8 Friar Street
Broadfield
BR1 3RF

invoice no	9384
account	3455
your reference	23423
date/tax point	01 10 00

product code	description	quantity	price	unit	total	discount %	net
A4PPW	A4 photocopy paper white, 80gsm	50	1.70	ream	85.00	10.00	76.50

GOODS TOTAL	76.50
VAT	13.38
TOTAL	89.88

terms: 30 days

Activity 16.5

A credit note is issued

When you have had your answer to Activity 16.4 checked you should complete the credit note issued by Wintergreen Stationers, the suppliers of the damaged paper. Do not forget the discount!

You will find a blank credit note in the Appendix and in the Resources section of the Osborne Books website: www.osbornebooks.co.uk

Activity 16.6

Sending statements

It is the end of the month of October in the Accounts Department of Wintergreen Stationers. You have been asked to prepare the statements for two of your customers. Their statements for last month (issued on 29 September) are illustrated on the next page – they will be needed for the starting balance for October. You will see how the starting balance (Balance b/f) is shown on the September statements.

The transactions on the two accounts for October are shown below.

Tiny Toys Limited

Date	Transaction	Amount (£)
10 10 00	Payment received	105.00
13 10 00	Invoice 9410	560.00
20 10 00	Invoice 9488	3450.50
26 10 00	Credit note 12180	230.50

R Patel Associates

Date	Transaction	Amount (£)
10 10 00	Payment received	4999.83
16 10 00	Invoice 9433	1098.50
22 10 00	Invoice 9501	678.35
26 10 00	Credit note 12183	670.00

You will find a blank credit note in the Appendix and in the Resources section of the Osborne Books website: www.osbornebooks.co.uk

STATEMENT OF ACCOUNT

WINTERGREEN STATIONERS

75 Holmes Street, Broadfield, BR2 6TF
Tel 01908 342281 Fax 01908 342538 Email WGreen@newserve.com
VAT REG GB 0822 2422 75

TO

Tiny Toys Limited
56 Broad Avenue
Brocknell
BK7 6CV

account   3001

date   29 09 00

date	details	debit £	credit £	balance £
01 09 00	Balance b/f			139.67
05 09 00	Payment received		139.67	nil
19 09 00	Invoice 9276	150.00		150.00
25 09 00	Credit note 12157		45.00	105.00

AMOUNT NOW DUE   105.00

STATEMENT OF ACCOUNT

WINTERGREEN STATIONERS

75 Holmes Street, Broadfield, BR2 6TF
Tel 01908 342281 Fax 01908 342538 Email WGreen@newserve.com
VAT REG GB 0822 2422 75

TO

R Patel Associates
78 Greenford Mansions
Mereford
MR3 8KJ

account   3067

date   29 09 00

date	details	debit £	credit £	balance £
01 09 00	Balance b/f			679.05
06 09 00	Payment received		679.05	nil
21 09 00	Invoice 9303	5345.50		5345.50
25 09 00	Credit note 12162		345.67	4999.83

AMOUNT NOW DUE   4999.83

Activity 16.7

Remittance advices and cheques

It is now the first week of November in the Accounts Department of Wintergreen Stationers. The October statements from suppliers are arriving in the post. Two are shown on the next two pages.

You are asked to make out a remittance advice and a cheque (ready for signing) to settle both accounts. Make up purchase order numbers.

A sample cheque is shown on the next page. Blank remittance advices and cheques can be found in the Appendix and on the Osborne website: www.osbornebooks.co.uk

You find the following note attached to the paperwork relating to the Hilliard & Brown Account.

NOTE TO FILE
19 October 2000

Hilliard & Brown - disputed invoice

Please note that we should not pay their invoice 3213 for £1,256.90 because the goods on the invoice have not been delivered. Please check each month when paying against their statement.

R Otter

Accounts Supervisor, Purchase Ledger

You check to see if the goods have arrived and find that they have not.

Albion Bank PLC

7 The Avenue
Broadfield BR1 2AJ

Date _____

90 47 17

A/c payee only

£

WINTERGREEN STATIONERY

123238   90 47 17   45195234

STATEMENT OF ACCOUNT

PRONTO SUPPLIES

Unit 17, Blakefield Estate, Broadfield, BR4 9TG
Tel 01908 482111 Fax 01908 482471 Email Pronto@imp.com
VAT REG GB4452 2411 21

TO

| Wintergreen Stationers |
| 75 Holmes Street |
| Broadfield |
| BK2 6TF |

account   2343

date   31 10 00

date	details	debit £	credit £	balance £
02 10 00	Balance b/f			234.75
05 10 00	Payment received		234.75	nil
19 10 00	Invoice 8717	290.75		290.75
22 10 00	Invoice 8734	654.10		944.85
25 10 00	Invoice 8766	125.00		1069.85

AMOUNT NOW DUE   1069.85

STATEMENT

HILLIARD & BROWN

99 Caxton Street, Norwich, NR2 7VB
Tel 01603 342281 Fax 01603 342538 Email Hillibrown@newserve.com
VAT REG GB 4532 1121 06

TO

Wintergreen Stationers
75 Holmes Street
Broadfield
BK2 6TF

account   2234

date   31 10 00

date	details	debit £	credit £	balance £
02 10 00	Balance b/f			560.00
05 10 00	Payment received		560.00	nil
19 10 00	Invoice 3213	1256.90		1256.90
22 10 00	Invoice 3244	987.60		2244.50
25 10 00	Credit note 4501		135.00	2109.50

AMOUNT NOW DUE   2109.50

Individuals and the organisation

a study text for Human Resources optional units offered by the awarding bodies

unit coverage

The text in this section provides study material and Activities for the externally assessed Human Resources optional unit offered by the Awarding Bodies under various different titles.

This section should be studied in conjunction with a reading of Chapter 10 'Businesses and employees'. The material in this section expands on and provides the extra material required for a study of the optional unit.

The unit requirements of the Awarding Bodies have been mapped and common areas subdivided into topic sections as shown below.

unit topics

Individuals and the organisation

what this unit is about

This unit builds on the material in Unit 1 'Investigating how businesses work'. The success of any organisation depends a great deal upon how its employees are treated by the employer. This Unit looks at the main elements of this relationship.

what you will learn from this unit

- There are a number of important roles in any organisation which have to be performed effectively for that organisation to be effective and profitable.

- Human resource managers use person specifications and job descriptions to ensure that they recruit the best people to fill job vacancies.

- In all organisations the employer has a number of important responsibilities to their employees. Equally, the employees have important responsibilities to the employer.

- One of the most effective ways to work is in teams. As a team member the employee can be far more valuable to the organisation and get more satisfaction from his or her job.

- Employees need to be trained properly in order to do their jobs effectively.

- Employees must be motivated to work hard and make a full contribution to the success of their organisation. Motivated employees are more likely to stay in an organisation where they feel they are valued and well paid. There are many ways by which an organisation can motivate and retain its employees.

TOPIC 1	**job roles in organisations**

This section will look at the main roles held by people in a typical business organisation – a limited company – and examine their responsibilities and powers. Other organisations, such as public sector bodies and charities, have similar job roles. The limited company is chosen here as it is a common form of business and is likely to the type you are investigating for your Portfolio.

The main job roles we will examine are:

- directors (including the role of chairman and managing director)
- managers
- supervisors
- operatives
- assistants

The diagram below shows how these jobs are structured in a business.

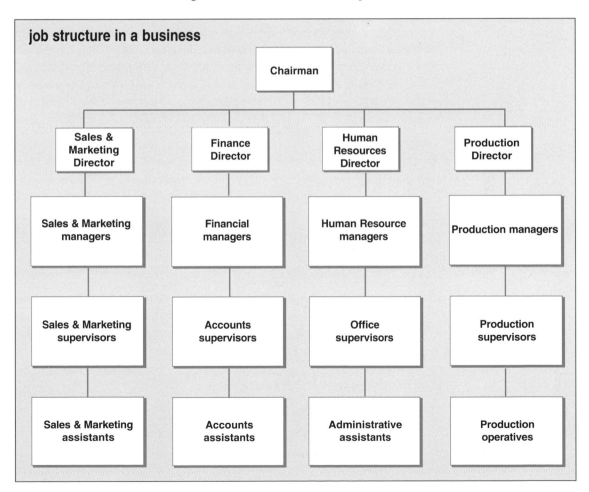

job structure in a business

Chairman

Sales & Marketing Director	Finance Director	Human Resources Director	Production Director
Sales & Marketing managers	Financial managers	Human Resource managers	Production managers
Sales & Marketing supervisors	Accounts supervisors	Office supervisors	Production supervisors
Sales & Marketing assistants	Accounts assistants	Administrative assistants	Production operatives

the directors

The Companies Act 1985 requires that private and public limited companies must have at least two directors to decide on the policy of the organisation and to look after the interests of the shareholders who actually own the business. In the case of small companies the directors may themselves be the only shareholders. In most businesses there will be two types of director – executive directors and non-executive directors.

executive directors

Executive directors are those who actually work in the organisation. The Production Director or the Finance Director are examples. Executive Directors are usually highly paid and will probably own large numbers of shares in the organisation. The most important will be the Managing Director.

non-executive directors

Non-executive directors are appointed on a part time basis to attend the board meetings and give perhaps one or two days a month of their time to the organisation. They are often appointed for their influence. For example, retired politicians are sometimes appointed to the boards of large companies because they have useful contacts and influence which can be very helpful to these businesses.

Another type of non-executive director, becoming increasingly common, is the employee representative or worker director. 'Worker directors' are elected by fellow employees to represent the interests of the workforce.

The Chairman of the Board

The directors of a company will elect a chairman. It will be the chairman's job to:

- Chair the meetings of the board of directors.
- Represent the company. Big companies deal with television and newspapers all the time and they value a well-spoken and influential person to act as chairman because they can create a good image for the company. Sometimes former politicians become company chairmen.

the main roles of directors

The key duties of directors in a company include:

- To plan the long term strategy of the organisation.
- To appoint the right management team to ensure that this strategy is put into effect.

- To oversee all major financial decisions.
- To ensure that shareholders interests are always protected.
- To ensure that the company always operates within the law.

managing director

The Managing Director is the link between the management and the board of directors. The Managing Director will be entrusted with a number of roles by the board of directors:

- Obtaining for the shareholders of the company the best return on their investment. If you buy shares in a company you expect two benefits.

  Firstly, a yearly or half yearly share of the company profits. This is called a 'dividend'. Secondly you would expect the shares to go up in value if the business is doing well.

  It is increasingly common for managing directors who do not achieve good results to be dismissed in the same way as unsuccessful football managers.

- Having a plan for the longer term growth of the business.
  Managing directors need plans to cope with changes in the economy and with the changing demand for their products.

- Making sure that the business has the right mixture and the right quality of human, financial and physical resources available.

- Making sure they have enough money to acquire the right mix and quality of resources.

- Motivating staff to work hard.

- Ensuring that the company takes advantage of all the new opportunities which may occur. For example, the investment into high profit mobile phone technology.

- Bringing in the right team of managers to help achieve these goals.

Activity 1

Types of directors

1   If you are investigating a limited company as part of your studies, find out from one of the directors (or their PA or secretary) what their job role in the company is and write notes about it.

2   Think of two advantages and two disadvantages to employees of being able to elect one or more of their fellow employees to the board of the company in which they are employed.

the managers

In each department there will be a team of managers. The main roles of the department manager will be as follows – these roles will be similar whatever kind of business it is . . .

- To ensure that their staff are motivated to work effectively.
- To ensure they reach their targets eg sales figures.
- To carry out the administration of the department – this will include the appointment and dismissal of staff.
- To allocate work between the members of their department. This will call for some sensitivity and tact to keep everyone as happy as possible.
- Ensuring all staff know what is going on. This is not as easy as it sounds!
- Making sure that their staff use methods such as suggestion schemes to encourage them to say what they think and to contribute their own ideas on how to run the department.

Activity 2

The role of managers

1 In your investigation of a business as part of your studies, find out from one of the managers what his or her job role in the business is and write down a description of what that job involves.

2 Look again at the list of the roles of managers above and at the description you have written. What personal skills do you think managers need to carry out their job successfully.

other employees

Each manager is responsible for a team of staff. Obviously the size of this team will vary considerably. In a factory the team under a Human Resources manager will be very much smaller that the team under the Production manager. The members of this team will include . . .

supervisors

Supervisors are now more commonly called 'First line managers'. The job has changed in recent years and this has meant that the characteristics of the modern line manager are very different to the old style supervisor.

The traditional supervisor . . . "The old style"	The first line manager . . . "The new style"
Older	Younger
Paid wages	Paid a salary
Is not clear whether he sees himself as a manager or an employee ('one of the lads'...)	Definitely part of 'the management'
Poor education means he is unsure of his real capabilities	Educated and confident of his capabilities
Poorly trained	Well trained – often with diplomas or management qualifications
Finds IT, computers etc a bit frightening	Well trained in the use of computers
Just follows his managers orders, without question	Will plan his workload with his manager and asks lots of questions
Backward looking	Forward looking
A Trade Union member	Not in a Trade Union
No career plans	Keenly ambitious
Uninterested in the views/ideas of his staff	Very interested in staff ideas

The main reasons why this change is occurring include:

- The decline in trade unionism in the UK.
- Changing technologies used in industry.
- The shift away from manufacturing jobs to service jobs.
- The ownership of key firms by multinationals (especially by Japanese companies).

A 'first line' manager or supervisor will take responsibility for a number of 'operatives' and will be expected to ensure that:

- Operatives are reaching their production targets.
- Operatives are identified who are not reaching their targets so that they can be helped to reach them.
- They introduce changes in the way of working to improve efficiency and profitability.

operatives

Operatives is a broad term which will mean anybody who carries out the day to day work assigned to them by supervisors or first line managers. The term is often taken to mean someone who carries out a physical operation (such as working on a production line) rather than a 'desk job' such as an accounts assistant.

Operatives are expected to reach target output levels and to produce that output to very high quality standards. Today there is increasing emphasis on 'employee involvement' activities in which all employees are encouraged to take part. These include suggestion schemes and 'quality groups' where all employees work out new ways of improving the quality of their work. These can be motivating to the employees.

Most operatives have limited career prospects and, for younger staff in particular, this can be very demotivating. More and more operatives are employed today on short contracts so that they can be got rid of easily if levels of business fall sharply. In cleaning, catering and security services this is particularly common. Obviously an atmosphere like this is very demotivating and employees will constantly look for better jobs where there is more job security.

assistants or support staff

These terms usually refer to staff at a similar level to operatives but in a more clerical/administrative environment.

Like operatives they have targets to achieve, in terms of quality and quantity. They are increasingly affected by big changes in working conditions often linked with large-scale redundancies. New technology has destroyed many of the lower-grade clerical jobs and the Internet will undoubtedly destroy large numbers of service industry jobs in areas that offered secure, promising, 'career jobs' only a few years ago – travel agencies, recruitment consultancies and insurance offices being three examples. Having said all that, unlike many 'operatives' they are more likely to feel that they have a career within the organisation and this may motivate them to work hard.

Activity 3

Operatives and assistants

If you do a part-time job or know someone who works as an operative or assistant, write down a description of what that job involves, whether it involves 'team discussions' and what prospects it has for promotion and career progression.

| TOPIC 2 | **the special role of the manager** |

We have seen how managers fit into the structure of a business; we will now examine what managers actually do in their day-to-day work. Whatever job they choose the key features of the job will be the same. There will be routine tasks such as planning and decision making, problem solving, setting and achieving targets. There will also be non-routine tasks such as dealing with emergencies or accidents.

routine tasks: planning and decision making

All management is basically concerned with making decisions. Bad managers are often people who may have many other very good qualities but their one big weakness is they either make the wrong decisions most of the time or they 'dither' around and cannot make a decision at all.

It is important at this stage to distinguish between several levels of decision making: low risk decisions, medium risk decisions and high risk decisions. At a personal level, rather than a business one, a low level risk might be making a decision where to go for a holiday; a medium one could be a decision to move house and a high one could be a decision to change one's job. The higher risk levels involve higher costs if they go wrong and they are also much harder to put right.

Activity 4

Decision making

Fred Thomson owns 'Imperial Coaches', a small bus and coach company. He employs a supervisor, seven full time and one part time drivers, an office clerk, two mechanics and a cleaner. Set out below is a series of decisions which relate to his business. Identify which decisions only he can make and which decisions other staff could make. Then classify each decision into one of the three risk levels outlined earlier.

1   When to order spare parts for coach maintenance work?

2   Whether to give a refund to a day trip passenger who complained about the driver's rudeness?

3   Whether to ask a mother to control her unruly child on one of the company's bus services?

4   Whether to apply to the Department of Transport for permission to run a new bus service?

5   Whether to buy a new coach costing £126,000?

problem solving

Making decisions is often a simple choice between a number of alternatives. Problem solving involves analysing. a situation and then coming to a decision. A good manager will be able to work through a problem in an analytical way. Once he or she has sorted it out by weighing everything up he or she should then be able to make a sensible decision.

This is one approach to problem solving – it is in nine stages:

1 Define the situation – what is the problem? Be specific.

2 What caused the problem? Are there several causes?

3 Collect all the facts – some problems will not involve many facts but others may be very complicated (for example a dispute with the workforce).

4 Analyse the facts – pick out the relevant ones and discard the rest.

5 Identify the true cause of the problem, not just some of the obvious symptoms. For example, if workforce morale is bad is it really an unpopular supervisor who is to blame? Could that be disguising the real problem? (bad working conditions, low esteem, low pay, poor career prospects?)

6 Consider what to do about the problem – sometimes there will only be one option but usually there are several possible options. Which is best? An evaluation of the pros and cons of all the possibilities will be needed.

7 Make a decision – after weighing up all the possibilities the manager must make the final decision. Even if the options all look equally bad (or equally good) a manager has to choose one of them.

8 Present that decision to the workforce – once the decision is made it has to be outlined to everyone so they can see how it will affect them.

9 Check that the decision made is being put into effect as quickly as possible, and with the minimum of inconvenience to everyone.

setting and achieving targets

Setting and achieving targets only used to be associated with production or sales departments but today they are associated with all departments in an organisation. Obviously, the size and kind of target will vary widely but every manager will have responsibility for achieving targets and motivating the employees to achieve them. There are two types of target:

- A *positive* target is where the employee has to aim to *increase* something – eg increased sales.

- A *negative* target is where the employee has to aim to *reduce* something – eg the number of faulty products made.

how do managers make targeting effective ?

- The individual target must support the achievement of a higher level target. For example, each sales rep will have an individual target but the sales department as a whole will also have a well-publicised target, which is the responsibility of the manager. This motivates staff because they then feel they are working together to a common goal and that their personal performance is vital to the overall target.

- Achieving a target should make the employee work hard but on the other hand it should not make them suffer stress or illness. Employers can now be sued for compensation if they place employees under too much stress. Managers must be aware of this problem.

- Managers must give positive rewards for the achievement of targets.

- Managers must help staff who fail to achieve their targets by providing them with extra training so that they can achieve the targets later on.

non-routine managerial tasks

A non-routine task could be virtually anything which a manager could have to deal with on a 'once in a lifetime' basis. Here are some examples . . .

- The supervisor in the production department begins work one Monday morning and is told that the Production manager has been taken seriously ill and will not be at work for at least 2 months. He must therefore take over during that period.

- The supply of parts which are used to make the organisation's products has stopped because of a sudden strike at the parts supplier. The organisation has only got 4 weeks stock of parts.

- A college orders 20,000 prospectuses to send to households in its catchment area. A fire at the printers means they will be at least four weeks late.

- Food poisoning in the company canteen means that 45 out of 97 production staff are away sick for at least two weeks.

Activity 5

Dealing with non-routine situations

Work in groups of three or four for this activity.

Choose one of the problems listed in the 'non-routine managerial tasks' section above. Discuss how you would deal with the problem and write down notes listing the actions you would take. Nominate someone from the group to explain your decision to the class, and then discuss in class.

job descriptions and person specifications

For effective recruitment and selection of new employees most organisations now use both job descriptions and person specifications.

Note – you need to refer to Chapter 10, page 202 before reading any further.

job descriptions

A job description describes what a job involves.

More and more organisations have job descriptions for every job they have – from the caretaker to the managing director.

In drawing up a job description the Human Resources department has a number of alternatives. These are:

(a)   the department itself can draw up a description of what the job entails

(b)   the department can get the existing job holder to do it instead

(c)   the department can interview the job holder to find out what he or she does

In most cases it is probably best to combine approaches. Clearly approach (b) and (c) may produce a biased view of what the job involves. After all, most people are likely to exaggerate the importance of what they do and the effort and ability that is required to do it. On the other hand, approach (a) will probably miss out many little but important tasks which are not obvious unless you actually do the job yourself.

The aim of drawing up a job description is to itemise all the tasks involved in a job and to try to allocate a proportion of the working week to each task. The list of tasks, and the relative importance of each one, is vitally important for several reasons:

- In carrying out appraisals (see page 359) a manager cannot appraise his/her employees if he/she does not know what the job comprises.

- When analysing the job for training needs (see page 355) the manager must be able to see what tasks a job involves so that he/she can determine what training may be required.

- In planning the size of the workforce for the future, it will be necessary to know exactly what tasks each job involves in case the re-allocation of tasks between jobs is required, eg three people may be required to share the work of a fourth post which is being made redundant – this cannot be done fairly without a detailed knowledge of the tasks involved in the fourth post.

- For pay determination – many employers now rely upon sophisticated job-evaluation exercises to determine what work and responsibilities are involved in every job in the organisation. Having done this, the jobs can then be ranked and allocated a salary or wage level. A simple and common example is to give clerical jobs which include the responsibility of handling money a higher ranking than clerical jobs which do not. Clearly, none of this is possible without good quality detailed job descriptions.

writing the job description

From all the information collected, by whichever method is chosen, it will then be necessary to draw up the document itself. Most people applying for jobs will get a job description along with the application form and a person specification (see the next page).

The main features of a job description are (see page 350 for an example):

1   the job title

2   the location of the job

3   a brief outline of what the employing organisation does

4   the main purpose of the job

5   a detailed list of the main tasks required in the job

6   the standards that the job holder will be required to achieve

7   pay and other benefits

8   promotion prospects

9   the person to whom the job holder reports

10   the person(s) who report(s) to the job holder

Note the following points:

- Employees are nowadays expected to be more flexible and to be able to do a wider range of work. This means that job titles (point 1) tend to be broader than they used to be.

- It is important to be precise about the location of the job (point 2) because it can otherwise cause problems after someone has been offered the job

- Point 3 is important in that a go-ahead, successful, organisation will find it easier to attract applicants of an above average quality. Points 4, 5 and 6 are the essentials of the job description, so that anyone interested in applying will know what they would be required to do if offered the job.

- Points 7 and 8 are needed as attractions to draw in good quality applicants.

- Finally, points 9 and 10 give the applicant a clear idea of the position of the job within the organisation.

In summary, the job description has a number of roles, not least of which is to turn enquiries from capable people into real job applications. Therefore, presentation of the job description is very important, although, regrettably, often forgotten by many employers.

person specifications

The difference between a person specification and a job description is that a person specification sets out the qualities of an ideal candidate, the job description defines the duties and responsibilities of the job.

A person specification will be drawn up after the job description has been prepared (see page 351 for an example). It identifies the kind of person who is needed to carry out that particular job, and will be invaluable in the recruitment process. The best-known method of drawing up person specifications is called the 'seven-point plan' originally devised by Alec Rodger. This bases the person specification upon seven separate groups of characteristics:

1 Physique, health and appearance – this includes grooming, looks, dress sense, voice, hearing and eyesight as well as general health matters.
2 Attainments – this includes educational qualifications such as GCSEs, A levels and degrees and vocational qualifications such as NVQs and job experience.
3 General intelligence – this is estimated by IQ tests and by assessment of general reasoning ability.
4 Special aptitudes – what special skills does a person have? These include skills with words, with numbers, with musical instruments, with artistic technique and with mechanical equipment.
5 Interests – are they intellectual or practical or social or a mixture of them all?
6 Disposition – this is an assessment of the person's acceptability by other people, leadership qualities, the person's emotional stability and self-reliance.
7 Circumstances – factors such as age, whether single or married, whether mobile or not.

The Rodgers Seven Point plan usually requires managers to distinguish between essential and desirable qualities under each of the seven headings. For example, five GCSEs at grade C or above might be an essential 'Attainment' to do a particular job whereas two GCE 'A' levels might be desirable but not essential.

The Activity on the next three pages includes a job description for an Administrative Assistant in an engineering firm, a person specification related to this and the CV of Mary Thompson, who is applying for the post.

Activity 6

CURRICULUM VITAE

Name	Mary Elizabeth Thompson
Address	14 Goodwood Drive, Chellaston, Derby, DE6 8TG
Tel Number	07781-554590 (Mobile)
Date of birth	13.8.78
Marital status	Single

Employment history

Organisation:	Fairey Whitworth Cycles Limited, Nottingham Road, Derby
Job role:	Clerical officer
Dates:	1995 to present day
Duties in role:	Clerical work of a wide variety
	Dealing with personal callers in absence of my manager.
	I set up several new office systems to improve office efficiency and installed new software packages where appropriate.

Education	Derby Comprehensive School (1989 – 1995)
	Five GCSEs in Maths, English Language, German, History and Biology
	GNVQ Intermediate Business

Post-school training	Word processing course 1995
	Interviewing skills 1996
	Report writing 1997
	Certificate in Personnel Practice (IPD) 2000

JOB DESCRIPTION

Job title	Administrative Assistant
Organisation	Acme Tool Company, Victoria Street, Derby, Derbyshire DE7 5RW
Responsible to	Office Manager
Purpose of job	To handle the administrative function of the commercial department, ensuring the smooth running of data systems and general office functions
Duties	Opening the post and distribution of mail within the organisation
	Answering telephone enquiries
	Inputting orders and purchases on the computer
	Maintaining a customer and supplier database
	Dealing with internal and external correspondence
	Preparation of monthly commercial statistics for the department
	Taking minutes at the departmental meetings each month
	Maintaining computer and manually based filing systems
Job location	Head office, Victoria Street, Derby
Physical conditions	Our head office is a modern purpose-built block of offices with a high quality staff restaurant and a social club. Apart from the social club, smoking is not permitted in any part of the building.
Appraisals	All employees are appraised by their immediate supervisor each year. Satisfactory appraisal is required in order to qualify for pay increments.
Salary	£14,000 rising by three yearly increments to £15,500.
Enquiries	Write to Arthur Summers, Personnel Officer, at the above address or ring 01332 567845. You are very welcome to ring Sarah Phillips, Administration Manager for an informal chat about this post on 01332 567856

PERSON SPECIFICATION

Physical make up — Fit and healthy

Attainments — Five GCSEs at grade C or above or a GNVQ Intermediate in Business

General intelligence — Able to use own initiative and good at mental arithmetic

Aptitudes — Ability to use a computer including basic software packages

Willingness to work as part of a small team

Disposition — Friendly and helpful. Preparedness to work largely unsupervised

Interests — A mixture of social and intellectual interests would be looked for in the successful candidate

Previous experience — Some work experience in an office environment is highly desirable although training will be given

Circumstances — A driving licence would be an advantage

questions

1   Do you think Mary is suitable for the job?

Write down a list of Mary's qualifications, achievements and skills which you can match up with the requirements of the job.

2   Write down five questions that you think you should ask Mary in the interview.

TOPIC 4 **responsibilities of the employer**

contract of employment

A business contract is an agreement in which one person or business agrees to do something for another person or business for payment of some kind. A contract is recognised in law – if one of the two people or businesses does not carry out their side of the bargain, it could end up in the courts.

The contract of employment is the same as any other business contract. If you are an employer, you offer work to someone and then pay them to do the job. You must pay them to do the work – although what you pay is entirely a matter between you and the employee, so long as you pay at least the Minimum Wage. If you are offering a job to Leonardo de Caprio or Demi Moore you will have to pay far more for their efforts and ability than you would to somebody in an 'ordinary' job.

A business contract does not have to be in writing – for example if you agree to buy something, but the law states that in the case of employment where terms are very important, certain details must be in writing (see next page).

Activity 7

Rates of pay

Assume that you are an employer.

1   Find out the minimum hourly rate (the 'Minimum Wage') you are allowed by law to pay an employee. Why would you want to pay them this rate?

2   What reasons might you have for paying an employee 20% above the average wage for the job for your district or town ?

When making an employment contract the employer must take note of other conditions too.

*   Both parties to the contract (you and your employee) must be old enough to work and be in good mental health. In the UK you cannot employ anybody to do anything until they are over 13 years old (except for acting contracts where strict rules apply).

*   You cannot have an employment contract which involves paying someone to do something illegal eg you cannot employ anyone to serve drinks in a pub if they are under 18.

As an employer you must provide an employee with a 'Written Statement of Terms and Conditions of Employment'.

written terms and conditions of employment

What does this statement include?

- The employer's name (this could be a company name rather than the name of a person) and the employee's name.

- The date when the employment begins – this must be precise because the entitlement to certain legal rights only applies after specific lengths of service, eg protection against unfair dismissal by the employer only applies after exactly one year's service whereas protection against racial discrimination begins from the first day of your job.

- The job title – this can be a very broad title which may enable an employer to exploit employees. A new employee needs to be aware of this to ensure that he is not being taken advantage of. For example, a job as 'Secretary to the Managing Director' is not the same as an ordinary secretary's job and this should mean higher pay.

- Details of how the grievance and disciplinary procedures operate must be provided.

- The stated terms on which the employment contract is based –

The pay rate – this must be at least the Minimum Wage which applies at the time (see the last Activity). The Equal Pay Act requires that men and women doing the same job should receive the same rate of pay.

How it is paid – weekly, monthly, direct to the bank, by cheque

Special arrangements – for example the statement should also give details of whether paid overtime is available from time to time. Where overtime is available the employer should state what the rate of payment will be eg it might be 'time and a half' or even 'double time'.

Hours of work – the number of hours required, for example 37 hours per week and the times of starting and finishing work each day eg 9 am till 5 pm. The Working Time Directive requires that employees in most jobs should work no more than 48 hours per week, averaged over 17 weeks. Employees can opt out if they wish – eg if they want to work a lot of overtime.

Holiday pay entitlement – since 1999 all employees have been entitled to four weeks paid holiday.

Sick pay entitlement – eg 3 months full pay and 3 months half pay.

Pension entitlement – many employers will provide employees with an occupational pension although no employer is legally required to.

The length of notice required if you decide to leave or if the employer decides to get rid of you. This must by law be at least one week.

An example of written terms of employment drawn up as a formal contract of employment follows on the next page.

CONTRACT OF EMPLOYMENT
Particulars of Terms and Conditions of Employment pursuant to the Employment
Protection (Consolidation) Act 1978

Employer............ Osborne Electronics Limited ....

Employee........... Helen Cassidy ....

1. **Continuous Employment**
   You are on a fixed term contract of ....2...................years
   Your continuous service dates from......20 January 1998..................

2. **Job Title**
   You are employed as.......Computer operator..........................

3. **Salary**
   The rate of your salary is......£12,400...........per annum, paid monthly

4. **Hours of Work**
   Your normal hours of work are ..35...... hours a week, worked over a five day period
   (Mondays to Fridays inclusive)

5. **Leave**
   You are entitled to.....22..........days paid holiday per annum in addition to statutory
   holidays. The leave is to be taken at a time convenient to the employer.

6. **Sickness**
   Notification of absence should be made on the first day of sickness, in writing or by
   telephone.
   If you are absent for a period in excess of five working days, a doctor's certificate
   must be submitted to the employer.
   Regulations for payment during periods of sickness or injury may be inspected on
   request in the Administration Manager's Office.

7. **Notice**
   The length of notice for termination of employment required from employer or
   employee is.....4.........weeks, subject to statutory requirements.

8. **Grievance Procedure**
   In cases of dissatisfaction with disciplinary procedure you are to apply in the first
   instance to the Manager of the Sales Department. Details of the rules of the
   Company and disciplinary procedures may be obtained from the Administration
   Manager's Office.

9. **Pension Scheme**
   Details of the contributory Company Pension Scheme, for which you are eligible,
   may be obtained from the Administration Manager's Office.

   Signed this.....20th......day of....January..19...98....

   C Osborne

   C J Osborne, Managing Director and Company Secretary

why do employers provide training?

the need for training

All jobs require some basic skills and an employee is expected to be skilled up to the level required to do the job they have been given. If training is not provided a number of problems can, and probably will, arise.

legal implications

Some training is necessary for legal reasons, for example some health and safety training is required for all employees. New employees must be trained on the equipment thcy arc to use before they are allowed to use it unsupervised.

financial implications

A poorly trained workforce is not going to be as effective as a well trained one. This means that there will be lower output per employee and more output will be poorly made, and therefore wasted. Poor training will also make better employees leave and so recruitment costs will rise.

ethical implications

It is a mark of a good 'ethical' organisation that all employees receive proper training so that they can work safely and efficiently. They should also be encouraged to develop themselves with further training so they are better motivated and feel they have a more secure future.

training programmes

These are the main reasons for running training programmes:

new employees require initial training

This is to ensure that the job is done competently and safely. All new employees must be given training immediately after the induction procedures have been carried out.

updating training is essential

This is so that an employee can do a new job efficiently or be more effective in their existing job.

Increasingly employees are required to learn new skills in place of skills that are becoming redundant. Nowadays there are many organisations in which employees are expected to update knowledge and skills as part of their job.

multi-skilling training

Multi-skilling means that employees are trained to do several jobs rather than just one. Employers gain because:

- an employee can do the work of somebody who is absent through illness or holidays

- employees are more motivated because doing several jobs is usually more interesting than doing just one; where an employee is able to do several jobs it increases his or her value to the organisation and makes him/her feel more appreciated and more secure; better motivation in the workforce reduces staff turnover which in turn saves money.

Government training schemes

There is money available from the Government to encourage employers to train people. The government runs a training scheme, known as 'New Deal', in which organisations receive financial help to recruit young people. During that period the employer provides a proper training programme which increases the young persons chances of finding a secure job.

training courses

We will now examine the main types of training course that organisations may run. Such courses develop employees in their existing roles and provide an opportunity to acquire higher grade jobs.

'in-house' training courses

This is where employers run courses inside their own organisation. Courses run 'in-house' will be ones where it is impractical and unrealistic to offer any other alternative – an obvious example would be the organisation's induction programme. The main benefits of using in-house courses are:

- they are fairly cheap
- the course content is tailor-made for the organisation
- references and examples to highlight points can be related to that organisation
- people know each another, so there is no time wasted in having to get to know people

external courses

Sometimes it is necessary to send staff to do courses elsewhere. This may be with another employer or at a specialist training centre or at the factory of an equipment supplier.

The benefits of using external courses are:

- they bring together specialist trainers and tutors who would never be available to an in-house course because of their high cost
- course members are from several organisations which means they learn more about each other and how their organisations operate

External courses are generally quite expensive and this means employers have to think very seriously about the value of such courses to the organisation.

vocational and professional courses

Internal and external courses often have to be reinforced by courses provided by local colleges and universities. These courses provide the essential knowledge to support what is learnt in the workplace and on internal courses. College courses include vocational courses and professional courses:

- vocational courses provide training in job-related skills, eg IT skills
- professional courses – all the professions operate professional training schemes which enable people to acquire qualifications for their career development.

developing the role of employees

Employees are encouraged to develop themselves because it motivates them to work harder and they are of greater value to the organisation if they have extra skills and knowledge.

To enable employees to develop themselves organisations use a range of techniques. Ways of developing employees include . . .

job rotation

Giving people a range of jobs in rotation widens their experiences and increases their skills.

job enlargement

Giving people extra tasks to do gives management a better idea of the employees true capacity, ability and stamina.

job enrichment

Adding more interesting and more difficult tasks to the job. This might be done with a person who appears very able to see just how capable he or she really is.

Activity 8

Investigating training

Talk to people who have jobs – friends, family or employees of a business you are investigating.

1   Write notes on internal and external training courses for employees.

2   List the advantages to the employer of training employees.

2   List the advantages to the employee of being trained by the employer.

providing an induction programme

Employers should provide some form of induction for all new staff. It is fair to say that the quality of induction varies tremendously from excellent to downright poor. In the latter cases it can be little surprise if many of their employees do not stay very long.

what should a good induction programme include?

Immediately after accepting a job offer the new employee should be sent all the details relating to it. This should include:

- joining instructions – the date of starting work, where to go and who to ask for on arrival

- details of the social facilities such as canteens, sports clubs, medical care and pension provisions

- a 'Written Statement' of the terms of their employment

On the first day at work an employee should expect:

- a tour of the buildings to show the newcomer all the important areas – the sick room, the canteen, the pay office, toilets, car parking etc – and to introduce them to the important staff such as the pay and personnel clerks and the nurse

- an introduction to their new workplace and their fellow employees

- some background detail about the organisation – the easiest and best way to do this is to show them a video

Wherever possible somebody fairly senior should at least meet them and introduce them to the organisation. This creates a good impression. It shows that the employee will be valued by the organisation.

Activity 9

Induction programmes

Divide into groups of three or four students and discuss how you would provide an induction programme for a new member of the class starting in the middle of term time.

Write down a suggested day's programme for the new member of the class.

TOPIC 6	**providing an appraisal scheme**

performance appraisal

Regular assessment of an employee's work performance is commonplace. It is now welcomed both by managers and by employees so long as it is done fairly and the process is fully explained to the employees.

The assessment of work performance is called Performance Appraisal and it is normally carried out by the job holder's boss. This means that at the top end the Managing Director appraises the most senior level of managers. At the bottom end the supervisors appraise the lowest grades of staff.

how often does an employee get appraised?

Appraisals take up much management time, so having them just once every year is quite common. However, this is unsatisfactory – once every six months is much more beneficial because it gives employees more regular feedback on performance, and managers can assess how far objectives laid down at the last appraisal have actually been achieved.

What kind of documentation is used by an appraiser – ie the person doing the appraisal?

*   a blank sheet of paper

    – this gives the appraiser freedom to write what he or she likes but there is the danger that key issues may be missed out

*   a form with questions and spaces for the appraiser to complete

*   a rating form – for each heading the appraiser simply gives a mark out of, say, 10 or a grade (A to E)

The best choice is probably a mixture of all three. This means having a form with spaces to make brief comments in but with a larger space at the end for more detail. The spaces may also have boxes for grades or marks out of 10.

how are appraisals carried out?

At the appraisal interview the appraiser will set some objectives for the appraisee to achieve over the next six to twelve months. This will be discussed with the 'appraisee' (the person being appraised) who has to agree in writing that the objectives are reasonable ones. An example could be that the appraisee has to achieve a qualification in that period. After the period ends the two people get together and assess the progress (or lack of it) made.

In many organisations reaching these objectives means that the employee gets a pay rise. This may be on top of a standard pay rise or instead of any other kind of pay rise. This makes a successful appraisal very important, especially in the second case.

Most organisations do not use appraisals for deciding on pay rises. They are seen purely as a way of developing employees so that they are more effective in their jobs.

the main benefits of an appraisal

- It helps to identify training needs – if the appraiser identifies lack of competence in some aspect of a person's work, extra training can be arranged and then checked on at the next appraisal.

- It may reveal other problems – all kinds of things can cause poor quality work and these can be uncovered by an appraisal. For example, the employee may have money problems or family problems.

- It may untap useful new skills – the appraisal process may show that a person has skills or other abilities which they have not used before. They may then be given a new or redesigned job which uses more of their talents. The organisation will now get more value from them, they will benefit from doing a more interesting job and, hopefully, they will get a pay rise!

- It improves communications between employees and management: it gives managers the chance to sit down and talk seriously with their staff about their work and career prospects. A few words of encouragement and praise for doing a good job are often highly motivating.

- It provides disciplinary documentation – if the employer needs to dismiss somebody the existence of thorough appraisal records which identify the person's inabilities or laziness will be very useful. This is especially true if the employee fights against the dismissal in an Employment Tribunal. The employer will need proper records to show the Tribunal that they have acted fairly at all stages. The appraisal records should show that the employee was given several chances to improve their work effort or were offered extra training to help them to become better at the job.

- It helps to fix pay rises – see above.

training to appraise

It is essential to provide managers and supervisors with proper training on how to appraise their staff. This is usually done through a short course including some role playing by the participating managers. They may be given a case study about an imaginary employee and then told to write up an appraisal of that person's work performance.

the appraisal report

The essential features of an appraisal report will be as follows:

- A clear outline of what the employee is supposed to do in his/her job.
- A list of any performance indicators laid down in the job – as noted above the most common method is to set a series of objectives at the last appraisal and then check up, 6 or 12 months later, to see if these objectives have actually been achieved.
- An examination of the strengths of the employee.
- An examination of the weaknesses of the employee.
- The advice given to the employee in relation to future performance. This should include:
  - praise for strengths
  - helpful criticisms of the weaknesses the manager has identified. Not destructive criticism since that helps nobody.
- An action plan for the next few months until the next appraisal. This will list the key objectives which the employee will be expected to have achieved by then. If extra training or experience or qualifications are believed necessary to help achieve these objectives then the organisation should (within reason) provide the opportunities to acquire them.
- Advising the employee that if he/she is unhappy about the appraisal outcome he/she may formally appeal to senior management to have another interview.

Activity 10

Appraisal

Discuss and compare appraisal of employees in the workplace with appraisal of students by tutors on a business course at school or college.

Draw up a list of topics which you would expect to discuss with your tutor.

What differences are there between the role of a student and an employee?

TOPIC 7	**the responsibilities of the employee**

The written terms and conditions described on page 353 state clearly what is required of the employee. These are known as 'explicit' terms.

implied terms in the Employment Contract

Employers have the right to expect employees to understand and abide by 'implicit' terms and conditions as well. These are not written down anywhere because there is an assumption that all employees will understand that these implicit conditions apply to them. In real life many employees do not always understand this and they sometimes lose their jobs as a result. The main implied terms are listed below.

employees must be available, willing and capable to work

For example, if you were in prison you could not work and, therefore, it would be reasonable to dismiss you.

employees must take reasonable care and skill in their job

For example, machinery must be used in line with the instructions given. Employees should not use a VDU for longer than the guidelines set down by the employer.

employees must take proper care of premises and equipment

This means that equipment should be properly maintained, repaired when necessary, and kept as secure as is reasonably possible. For instance, if a computer is stolen because an employee fails to lock up the office at the end of the day, or if a company car is left unlocked and then stolen, this could be a disciplinary offence.

the employee must obey reasonable orders

The employee must act in good faith – 'good faith' means that an employee must always behave in a honest and fair manner to his employer. It definitely is not 'acting in good faith' to . . .

work for a competitor's business in your spare time

or

give confidential details about your employer's business to other people

or

ignore your employer's dress code

or

behave badly in public (eg frequently being found drunk in the street)

compliance with health and safety regulations

Employees are required to observe the rules and regulations laid down in the 1974 Health and Safety at Work Act and in other, related, legislation (for example, the COSHH regulations – see below). The 1974 Act states that the employer is responsible for making sure that the workplace is safe and healthy to work in. Examples of this are safe entrances and exits, safe equipment and machinery and safe systems of work (see page 214)

employees duties under the 1974 Act

The 1974 Health and Safety at Work Act was also important because it placed more responsibility than ever before on the employee to ensure their own safety and the safety of fellow employees. It means that employers can punish employees who get involved in either . . .

- 'horseplay' – fooling about which causes accidents to other employees.
- disregard of safety requirements in the operation of one's job – see above.

As well as the 1974 Act more recent legislation has brought in further protection for employees, for example the COSHH regulations. This stands for 'control of substances hazardous to health' and it lays down very strict rules on how dangerous chemicals are to be handled, stored and recorded.

Regulations on the use of VDUs (visual display units) have been introduced because of the problems they are now known to cause (particularly eyesight problems and repetitive strain injury in the arms) All employers are now legally required to carry out risk assessments of all activities carried out in their organisations.

Activity 11

Employee responsibilities

1   Write down a list of the things that an employee would be expected to do (his or her responsibilities) as set out in a 'written terms and conditions of employment' or contract of employment (see page 354 for an example).

2   The responsibilities set out in the list taken from the contract are 'explicit' – there is no doubt about them. Word process a guide for new employees setting out a list of 'rules' which are not set out in the contract (for example taking care of equipment and premises). These are the 'implicit' terms.

working with others

team membership and job roles

Under each manager or supervisor there will be a 'team' of staff and obviously the size of this team will vary considerably. In a factory the team under a Personnel manager will be very much smaller than the team under the Production manager or the Distribution manager.

Let us look at a typical personnel department. How is it structured?

The structure of the personnel department at Letchurch Garden Furniture Limited (see the Case Study in Chapter 10, pages 197 to 200) is set out below.

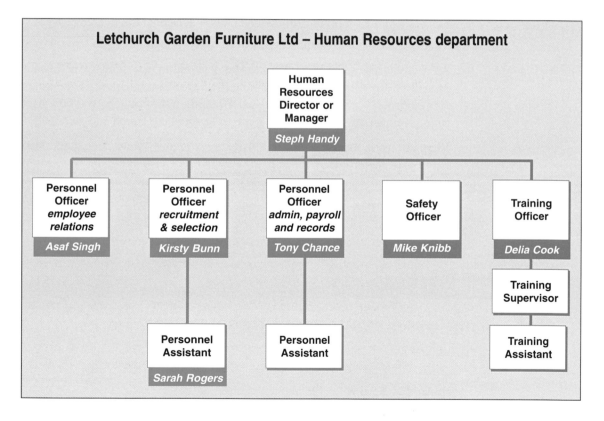

Letchurch Garden Furniture Ltd – Human Resources department

Stephanie Handy, the personnel manager/director, manages a team of 9 staff. How does she make it work effectively ?

Stephanie takes pride in the fact that her department really does work as a team. She says that these are the main benefits of working as a team . . .

If you work in a team there is a better, friendlier, atmosphere which encourages staff to work more effectively.

A team solves problems better than an individual ever could.

A team encourages creativity and new ideas – look at all the designers, architects, advertising agencies – they usually work in teams because they can 'bounce ideas' off each other.

Teams motivate people because they do things together.

The team can discipline its members and make sure they are all pulling their weight. People know they cannot let each other down.

You can get jobs done more quickly with teamwork.

It means that everyone relies upon everyone else and that – if necessary – they are capable enough to do each others work at certain times.

A team also provides a career structure because staff at the bottom can see that there is a career 'ladder' to climb. This is important for staff motivation and it increases their commitment to the organisation.

When an individual team member faces a personal crisis (as most people do at some time) other members will rally round to help them.

Stephanie adds that she thinks her team works well because they

- listen to one another
- criticise constructively (helpfully)
- accept helpful criticism – they must not take it personally
- make suggestions to help each other to work more effectively – they must not selfishly guard ideas as 'their own'
- accept that where a team member has a problem it should be recognised that it is the team's problem for them all to help sort out

Stephanie knows all the team members well, both in work and at a personal level. When she gave the team members their roles she knew

- what they liked to do
- what they were good at
  and
- what they were most useful for

A successful team does improve the commitment of team members because they do not feel isolated and they feel they have some support if they have problems.

Activity 12

Teamwork

Discuss these examples of teamwork . . .

1   a group of students working together gathering evidence as part of a college project.

2   a football/rugby/netball/hockey team

3   a couple in a car, one driving, the other reading the map and giving directions

Give a list of reasons why teams like these may not always work well together. Try to link your answer to Stephanie Handy's comments on page 365.

TOPIC 9   motivating individuals at work

People who write about motivation often ask the question 'what do people get from going to work?'

Just how important is what a person earns when trying to answer this question? How important in a job are non-money rewards – the fact that the employee gets praise for their efforts or they enjoy doing the work?

intrinsic and extrinsic motivation in the work place

All reasons for working are either intrinsic or extrinsic.

intrinsic motivation

This is where the employees are motivated by what the job actually involves. The job itself is interesting and sometimes this can mean it ends up dominating the person's entire life.

extrinsic motivation

This means the employee only sees the job as a means to an end. In other words it just provides money but nothing else. The interesting and challenging parts of life are found outside the job eg through one's hobbies and sporting activities. In no way will the job ever dominate this person's life!

Most employees want at least some of these features from a job. All of these motivate employees in different ways . . .

to be able to use their brains and skills properly

This makes the job more interesting and it means the employee should be properly rewarded for the abilities they have got.

to have job security

This makes the employee feel 'recognised' by their employer. Insecure jobs demotivate people because they have to be constantly looking round for another job.

to get on with work mates and their immediate boss

This is a crucial motivating factor. Isolated employees who do not mix with colleagues well find it hard to work in teams. This reduces their value to the organisation.

to have good pay and good working conditions

Although pay and good conditions are not everything it is very hard to motivate employees in other ways if they are badly paid and have to work in a tumbledown factory or office.

to have non-financial rewards like clubs and a decent restaurant

The same point applies here. Social clubs also motivate employees because they encourage them to mix outside work. This helps in encouraging team work.

to receive promotion, responsibility, praise and recognition

Without promotion and extra responsibility many employees would be very demotivated and would leave. Extra responsibility (eg job enrichment) without promotion is seen as a 'con trick' by most employees and creates bitterness. This also applies to praise without promotion.

to have a decent pension scheme and free private health insurance

These benefits help to make an employee secure and they encourage them to stay with the organisation. Pensions motivate people because it indicates that the employer expects them to work there for a long time and that they are interested in their welfare after they have retired.

In other words, most people want intrinsic job satisfaction and enough money to pursue extrinsic satisfaction as well.

Activity 13

Motivation at work

Talk to friends and family who have a job and draw on any experience you have of temporary work or work experience. Find out about and draw up two lists for . . .

1   features of the work itself – ie the actual tasks that people do – which motivates them and makes them enjoy it and work well

2   perks and working conditions which help make the job more enjoyable

Discuss in class any features about jobs which can cause problems.

TOPIC 10   **retaining employees**

Employee retention – keeping employees from leaving – is a major role of the Human Resources manager. When people leave they usually have to be replaced. This is disruptive and costly. It can influence the effectiveness of the organisation in a number of ways:

- Replacement costs – recruitment, selection and induction costs. Also, if unemployment in the area is low there may be a shortage of suitable recruits.

- Training costs – even if a good quality recruit is appointed they will still need fairly expensive training.

- Output implications – the new recruit will not be making the organisation any money until he or she has been trained for the job. Even after training is completed it may be some time before the new recruit is as efficient as other staff.

Finding ways of keeping staff turnover as low as possible is therefore most important.

how can employers retain staff ?

offer a decent rate of pay

The most common reason for leaving is pay. If pay rates for the particular job are better in another organisation then it is quite likely the job holder will consider moving. The convenience of the existing job and long standing working friendships will put some people off going elsewhere, but the cost of living and the need to provide the best possible lifestyle makes better pay very attractive.

offer promotion opportunities

Where there are few career progression opportunities in an organisation people will leave. On the other hand organisations that promote internally will retain good quality staff.

provide training and development opportunities for all staff

Organisations which offer the chance to gain more qualifications and a wider variety of skills are more likely to keep their staff.

provide a pleasant working environment

Working in unpleasant, dirty and unsafe conditions with poor canteen and social facilities will encourage people to leave if other organisations nearby offer something better. Today legislation such as the Factories Acts, the Health and Safety at Work Act and European Regulations mean that bad working conditions are fairly unusual.

treat everyone fairly

If an employee is treated badly, either by management or by fellow employees, then he or she will be more likely to try to get a job elsewhere. The commonest examples of bad treatment are discrimination against employees on grounds of race, sex, age or disability.

make the job interesting and stimulating

Even with the best will in the world it is far harder to achieve this than any of the other points listed above! It is often very difficult to make a boring job more interesting. Good pay and conditions often make a job very acceptable and pleasant but they do not make it interesting.

Boring work will encourage people to leave if there are more interesting alternatives elsewhere. This is still true even when unemployment is high.

Activity 14

Retaining employees

Suppose you have a job which is really boring. Think of five areas (eg pay) in which your employer could improve your chances of staying in that job. List them in order of importance.

UNIT SUMMARY

- Within any organisation there are a number of key job roles that have to be carried out efficiently.

- Management is all about the performance of routine and non routine tasks in a methodical way. Tasks have to be ranked in order of priority.

- Job descriptions and person specifications are a vital tool to help employers to recruit and select the right people to fill these job roles.

- Employers have a number of important responsibilities to their employees. There are legal, financial and ethical problems if they do not bother to look after employees properly.

- Employees have responsibilities to behave properly whilst working, to take care of their employers property and to obey health and safety rules.

- In most situations employees work more successfully in teams than on their own.

- There are a wide range of factors that motivate people at work. What motivates one employee will not necessarily motivate another. Employers need to know their employees well to find out what motivates them to work hard.

- Employers can easily lose good employees if they are not treated properly. They must understand that recruitment and training costs and output levels are badly affected if staff turnover is too high.

KEY TERMS

Person Specification A outline of the characteristics,qualifications and experience needed by an applicant to fill a job vacancy

Job Description A description of the main elements of a job.

Curriculum Vitae An outline of a person's background, qualifications and experience.

First Line Manager A modern term for a supervisor of other employees.

Employee Involvement A range of employee activities which are used to encourage all employees to take a greater interest in the organisation

Multi Skilling Where employees are trained in a range of job skills so that the employer can use them more efficiently. Types of multi skilling include job enlargement, job rotation and job enrichment.

Induction The programme of activities provided for all new employees so that they can get to know about their new employer, meet their new colleagues, and settle into the organisation quickly.

Appraisal A regular assessment of the employee's performance which may, or may not, be linked to pay rises.

Appendix – Financial documents

This appendix contains photocopiable financial documents for use in student activities.

The documents are:

1   purchase order

2   delivery note

3   goods received note

4   invoice

5   credit note

6   statement of account

7   remittance advice

8   cheque

The documents are also available in A4 format on www.osbornebooks.co.uk

PURCHASE ORDER

from

to

purchase order no

date

product code	quantity	description

AUTHORISED

signature...date...

DELIVERY NOTE

from

to

delivery note no

delivery method

order reference

date

product code	quantity	description

RECEIVED

signature..name (capitals)...

date...

GOODS RECEIVED NOTE

organisation

supplier

GRN no

date

quantity	description	order number

carrier   **consignment number**

received by   **checked by**

condition of goods   **copies to**

good condition   Buyer

damaged   Accounts

shortages   Stockroom

INVOICE

from

to

invoice no

account

your reference

date/tax point

product code	description	quantity	price	unit	total	discount %	net

terms

GOODS TOTAL		
VAT		
TOTAL		

CREDIT NOTE

from

to

credit note no

account

your reference

our invoice

date/tax point

product code	description	quantity	price	unit	total	discount %	net

reasons for credit		GOODS TOTAL	
		VAT	
		TOTAL	

STATEMENT OF ACCOUNT

from

to

account

date

date	details		debit	credit	balance

	AMOUNT NOW DUE	

REMITTANCE ADVICE

to

from

account no

date

date	your reference	our reference	payment amount

CHEQUE TOTAL

Bank:

Date

Branch:

Pay

A/c payee only

index

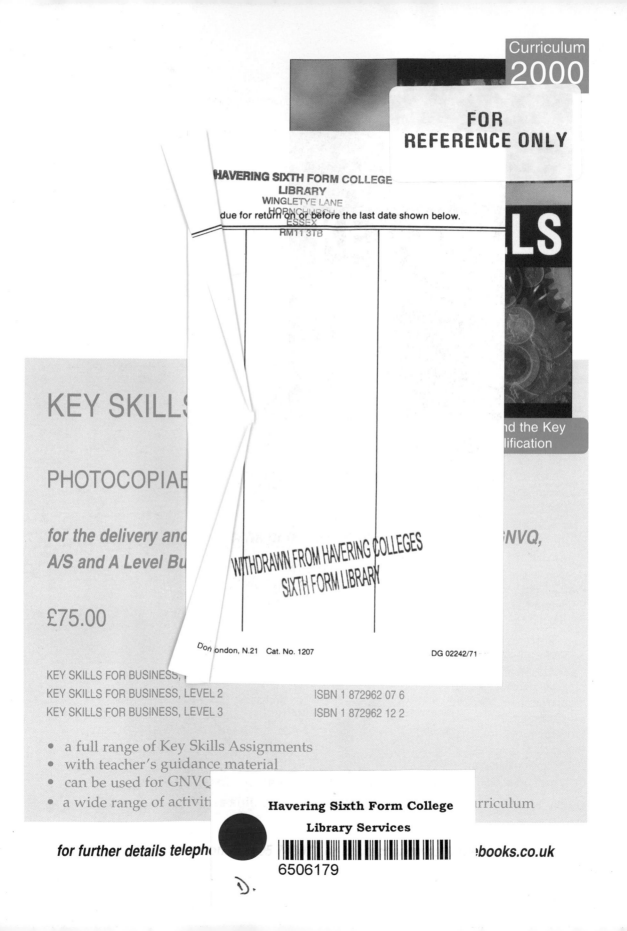

Curriculum
2000

FOR
REFERENCE ONLY

HAVERING SIXTH FORM COLLEGE
LIBRARY
WINGLETYE LANE
HORNCHURCH
ESSEX
RM11 3TB

due for return on or before the last date shown below.

WITHDRAWN FROM HAVERING COLLEGES
SIXTH FORM LIBRARY

Don ondon, N.21   Cat. No. 1207   DG 02242/71

KEY SKILLS

PHOTOCOPIAB

for the delivery and ... GNVQ,
A/S and A Level Bu...

...nd the Key
...lification

£75.00

KEY SKILLS FOR BUSINESS,
KEY SKILLS FOR BUSINESS, LEVEL 2   ISBN 1 872962 07 6
KEY SKILLS FOR BUSINESS, LEVEL 3   ISBN 1 872962 12 2

- a full range of Key Skills Assignments
- with teacher's guidance material
- can be used for GNVQ
- a wide range of activiti... ...urriculum

for further details teleph... ...ebooks.co.uk

Havering Sixth Form College
Library Services

6506179

D.